THE TEENAGE
SURVIVAL GUIDE

Kathy McCoy

THE TEENAGE
SURVIVAL GUIDE

Kathy McCoy

WALLABY
A WALLABY BOOK
PUBLISHED BY SIMON & SCHUSTER
NEW YORK

Copyright © 1981 by Kathy McCoy
All rights reserved
including the right of reproduction
in whole or in part in any form
Published by Wallaby Books
A Simon & Schuster Division of
Gulf & Western Corporation
Simon & Schuster Building
1230 Avenue of the Americas
New York, New York 10020
WALLABY and colophon are trademarks of Simon & Schuster
First Wallaby Books Printing February 1981
10 9 8 7 6 5 4 3 2 1
Manufactured in the United States of America
Library of Congress Cataloging in Publication Data

McCoy, Kathy, date.
  The teenage survival guide.

  SUMMARY: Advice for teenagers on such aspects of
growing up as identity, parents, siblings, school,
friends, dating, love, sex, etiquette, crisis-coping,
and planning the future.
    1. Adolescence—Juvenile literature. 2. Sex
instruction for youth. 3. Dating (Social customs)—
Juvenile literature. 4. Interpersonal relations—
Juvenile literature. [1. Conduct of life.
2. Adolescence. 3. Sex instruction for youth.
4. Dating (Social customs) 5. Interpersonal relations]
I. Title.
HQ796.M2218   305.2'3   80-26963

ISBN 0-671-41162-4

Special thanks to:

• Eugene Brissie, my editor at Wallaby Books, for coming up with the idea for this book; and my agent, Susan Ann Protter, for helping to make the idea a reality—and to both for their warm support and encouragement throughout my work on this project.

• The editors of *Glamour, Bride's, Mademoiselle, TEEN,* and *Woman's Day* for giving us permission to use a number of interview quotes that had already appeared in some of my articles for their magazines.

• All of the teenagers who asked the questions that make up such an important part of this book, and the mental health professionals (quoted throughout the book) who helped answer them. I am particularly grateful to Dr. Charles Wibbelsman, my dear friend and coauthor of *The Teenage Body Book,* for his constant encouragement and advice, as well as his generosity in sharing his research resources with me.

• My husband, Bob Stover, for his invaluable suggestions, warm support, love, and belief in me.

DEDICATION

To my parents, James L. McCoy and Caron Ethel Curtis McCoy. Together we struggled to survive my adolescence, sharing much love and anger, many tears, and a lot of laughter in the process. They taught me many things: how to write, how to work, how to plan, and how to dream. They both died just before this book went to press and *The Teenage Survival Guide* is dedicated to their memory.

CONTENTS

Gearing Up For Survival

I need some survival tips. I'm shy, don't have much confidence, and have trouble with put-downs at school. How can I start to feel better about myself?

Kevin, 15, Columbus, Oh.

Everyone says "Be yourself!" but I don't know who I am yet! And with things changing for women now, I don't know whether to be like my mom or like those career women I read about in magazines. How can I find what's best for me?

Sue, 14, Denver, Co.

My biggest problem is jealousy. I squeeze the life out of my love relationships by being too jealous and possessive. Why do I do this and how can I change?

Phil, 17, St. Paul, Mn.

My parents are getting a divorce and my whole life is falling apart. . . .

Jonelle, 13, Detroit, Mi.

The future scares me. There are too many decisions to make about college or not, a career, and finding someone to love. I wish I were a little kid again. I'm really confused!

Carla, 16, Arcadia, Ca.

Kevin, Sue, Phil, Jonelle, and Carla are just a few of the concerned teenagers that Dr. Charles Wibbelsman and I met while traveling around the country telling young people about our book, *The Teenage Body Book.* We talked with teens in a variety of settings: in TV studios, radio stations, over the phone, in bookstores, and in schools. We also received letters from a number of young people who had read our book and wanted more. A typical letter came from a 15-year-old Miami girl named Joanne:

Now that I know all kinds of interesting and helpful things about my body, health, and sexual self, I'd like to know more about my feelings, my emotions, and how to cope with everyday life situations—like overcoming bad moods. Also, how can I make friendships that last? How can I tell if a guy really likes or loves me? How can I live through another five months with a crabby math teacher who hates me? What about the pros and cons of college, and tips for finding a good part-time job? How can I stop fighting—and start really talking—with my parents? Well, you get the idea. I guess what I need to know basically is how to stay sane and survive the next few years!

The Teenage Survival Guide has been written in response to Joanne's letter, to the hundreds of questions and problems that teens across the nation have shared with us. You may discover *yourself* or some people very much like you on these pages.

Together, we will explore many important areas of your life: identity and self-image; family problems and conflicts; school; friendships, dating, and love relationships; changing sex roles; special situations (like applying for a job and earning extra cash); serious concerns (like coping with fears and phobias, family illness, rape, incest, suicidal feelings, or a substance abuse problem); and advice on planning for your future.

Since this book was inspired by—and its direction determined by—teenagers, it may be able to help you sort through some of your very real concerns and choices. It will try to answer your questions without sermons or judgmental hassles and help you to discover who you are and who you might become. Self-discovery is vital for survival and growth.

Self-discovery, you will find, is a journey without end. This book can't give you instant solutions and guarantees of living happily ever after. Such promises would be unrealistic. But it may give you some valuable ideas about discovering and growing in your uniqueness. It may also give you some helpful suggestions for coping effectively with parents, family, friends, enemies, boyfriends, girlfriends, and other special people in your life. The diversity of this book mirrors the diversity of your life right now: the special joy, pains, pressures, and pleasures you feel as you grow toward independence.

It may be reassuring, as you read these pages, to note that you are not alone in your uncertainty, your pain, your hopes, and your dreams. Many others share your feelings. And many people care. We wish you hope, courage, excitement, and joy as you plan your future and as you live in the present as a unique, growing, loving person!

Best Wishes,
KATHY McCOY

THE TEENAGE
SURVIVAL GUIDE

Kathy McCoy

CHAPTER ONE

"Who Am I Anyway?"

I have this problem: I don't know who I am! How do I find out? Am I my relationships (daughter, sister, friend)? Am I who people say I am (friendly, thoughtful, stubborn)? Am I the way I see myself (which isn't too good sometimes)? There's a difference, too, between the person I'd like to be and the person other people say I should be. Help!

Nancy J.

I hate to mention this because the whole identity crisis thing seems like a cliché, but it's sure real to me! I try to be one of the guys, but I usually feel like I'm kind of on the outside and I also don't like the idea of losing myself in a crowd anyway. I want to be my own person, but right now I don't have a clue about who that person might be!
Steve W.

If you have ever felt like Nancy or Steve—join the club! Confusion and uncertainty about your identity are common, not only in adolescence, but also throughout the various stages of life. For example, many women who have devoted themselves to home and family for years may struggle to discover new facets of their identity when their children begin to grow up, need them less, and finally leave home. Your mother may be experiencing this right now as she seeks to define herself in new ways apart from her role as a mother. Many men and career women, too, begin to reassess their roles, values, and goals as they approach middle age.

But while your identity search is a lifelong process, it is especially intense in adolescence, when your body is changing so rapidly; when you're expected to—and want to—take more responsibility for your life; while at the same time, you still live in your childhood environment, complete with parental rules and restrictions. In a very real sense, you're between two worlds—that of childhood and that of adulthood—and this is a time when you feel a special need to discover who you are as an individual.

When people talk about self-discovery, they often use phrases like *identity* and *self-image*. While the two terms may, in some instances, be quite similar, they are also distinct from each other.

IDENTITY

Identity is who you *are,* and has many components, some of which will remain the same throughout your life and some of which will change. The components of your identity include the following.

Your Roots   Your ethnic, geographic, racial, and religious origins, as well as your birth order in your family and your sex, are all an important part of who you are. While all people are—basically—similar in many ways, growing up as the youngest child in a large Italian Catholic family in Boston is a somewhat different experience from growing up in Malibu as the only child of wealthy, nonreligious parents who have divorced and remarried. Being raised as the eldest child in a close, two-child Jewish family in Skokie, Illinois is not quite like coming from a deeply religious black Baptist family in Mississippi, or like growing up on a small farm in rural Kansas. Also, growing up female, despite our changing society, is still different in a number of ways from growing up male.

While you may grow up with love and with happy, sad, or bittersweet memories whatever your roots, these various factors will influence you deeply throughout your life. They will give you a unique sense of who you are, based on your beginnings—and will be expressed in your sense of family, the ethnic or religious traditions you follow, your hobbies, interests, and food preferences, and your view of the world and your place in it.

The Past You and Your Experiences   The child you once were is still very much a part of you. Dr. W. Hugh Missildine, a Columbus, Ohio psychiatrist, in his best-selling book called *Your Inner Child of the Past*, contends that "We do not live entirely in the present. You are not only a soon-to-be adult, but also the child you once were, complete with the attitudes and reactions—both positive and negative—that you have developed in response to your home situation."

If, for example, you spent much of your childhood in an atmosphere of love and mutual respect, you may find growing up and forming new relationships relatively painless. However, if you were punished excessively, you may be very critical of yourself right now and may have trouble enjoying close relationships with others. If you had a lot of responsibility thrust on you at an early age, the child within you may be unable to relax and have fun now because you never learned to play. If you were pushed into activities and were supervised very closely throughout childhood, you may find yourself having trouble taking responsibility for yourself now. If you spent your childhood suffering through parental fights and family arguments, you might do anything to avoid conflicts and confrontations with others now—even when avoiding conflict is not in your best interest.

You may feel these leftover conflicts from childhood with special intensity right now. "That's because you're probably still living in your childhood home," says Dr. Missildine. "You're living with your external past as well as with your inner child and your present young adult. You're getting directions not only from your parents, but also from yourself."

Your past will not always bring conflict, of course. A relatively happy childhood may give you an extra measure of strength and confidence as you cope with all the changes and challenges of adolescence. And a less-than-ideal past can also help you to develop special resources for coping. Much depends on how you see and utilize your past to help you in the present time. For better or for worse, your past is an important part of who you are now.

Your Attitude and View of the World How you see the world may be closely tied in with your past. Your experiences and what you were taught as a child can greatly influence how you see your world now. And, of course, some people seem to be born with certain personality traits that influence their view of the world.

"My sister Sharon is a born pessimist," says Linda, 15. "She's a year older than I am and always expects the worst no matter what. I feel pretty good about things most of the time. I expect things to go OK. I expect other people to be nice and am surprised if they aren't. Sharon—she's surprised when things go right. She almost seems relieved when things go wrong. 'There, see, I *knew* that would happen,' is what she's always saying. Things go wrong for her more than they do for me. She seems to bring trouble on herself by expecting it!"

Your attitude toward others and the world at large—whether you are warm or suspicious, dread or look forward to new challenges, find the world a friendly or a frightening place—can have a great impact on who you are.

Your Habits, Interests, and Activities What excites you? What do you enjoy? When you have a free choice, how do you choose to spend your time? What is your idea of a perfect day—what would you do and which people would you spend time with?

The interests, activities, and people who endure in your life can offer you some valuable clues about who you are. If you have few interests or things you enjoy doing, that's an important clue, too. If you spend much of your time in passive pursuits—like watching TV—it could mean that you haven't found the motivation to develop more active interests that could add more fun and excitement to your life.

Your Special Qualities No one on earth has exactly the same collection of physical and emotional traits that you have. Even if you're an identical twin, you probably have personality traits and experiences that differ from those of your twin. Your special talents and skills, how you develop and use them, how you choose to be—in big ways and in little ways, what ideas and values you take from your family and friends and which ones you reject—all these elements and more add up to a thoroughly unique you. The combination is, largely, your own choice, and nobody else puts himself or herself together in quite the same way.

Discovering your own unique qualities means developing your own point of view about yourself—*acting* in a way you choose instead of *reacting* in a certain way just to be different from—or just like—your parents or friends. Making observations about yourself—even in little ways—can be a good way to begin to develop this personal point of view.

When asked to complete the sentence, "I am a person who . . . ," a 15-year-old sophomore named Peter made the following observations: "I am a person who . . . likes being active in sports yet who likes being alone sometimes to listen to old jazz records from the thirties (which no one but *me* seems to like!). I am a person who is happy to help my friends, but I get a little embarrassed asking for a favor myself. I'm a person who is grumpy first thing in the morning, but feel better after breakfast. I like working on old cars, camping out at the beach with friends, and pigging out on bacon pizzas. I'm a person who is uncomfortable in a suit and tie and who feels shy at school dances, but great when I have a chance to just talk with a girl in a less formal atmosphere. I'm a person who wants to be a success in a career (I don't know what yet!), but I want to be a *personal* success, too. I want to have good friends and a family eventually and not lose myself in a job."

You, too, might want to try completing the sentence "I am a person who. . . ." It can be fun, interesting, and enlightening to think about the special qualities, feelings, and ideas that make you unique!

Your Values You have developed much of your sense of what you believe is good and right from your childhood training, but as you grow into adolescence, you will be adding some new values and questioning some old ones.

"I used to think that going to church every Sunday made me a good person," says 17-year-old Donna. "Now I also think that how I act the other days of the week is important, too. I believe in being loyal to my friends, not two-faced and sarcastic. I try to be more tolerant of differences than I used to be. I believe in setting a goal and working hard to attain it. Those are my values."

"My family believes in strict etiquette, which involves *not* discussing problems openly," says Scott, 18. "As I get older, I find that I value manners to the extent that I like to make myself and others feel comfortable in any situation, but I don't care about picky little details. I value openness and honesty in talking about feelings of any kind. I believe that, in order to be close, people have to level with each other. In another person—and in myself—I really value honesty and vulnerability."

What qualities do *you* value in yourself and others? What guidelines do you use—or plan to use—in making choices and to improve the quality of your life and the lives of those around you? Ideas, personal philosophies, and valued qualities and ways of being are also a part of who you are.

Your Dreams and Goals Your dreams for the future, both fantasies and clear-cut plans, are an important part of your identity right now. While these dreams can change with the years, having short- and long-term goals can give direction to your life. These can include not only career plans and dreams of marriage and family, but also visions of becoming the person you would like to be. Who would you like to grow to become by this time next year? What strong points in yourself would you like to reinforce? What faults or problems would you like to change by next year? Five years from now? What would you like to be doing ten years from now?

Thirteen-year-old Marilyn sees college, work, independence, travel, and finding someone special to love as goals for her future. She also plans to work on being less critical of herself and others. What about you? You might try listing your goals—personal, educational, and professional. Check them again in a few months to see how they—and you—might be changing.

Some aspects of your identity—such as goals, interests, attitude, values, and personal qualities—can and often do change with the passage of time and/or as the result of your own choices. Others—such as your childhood memories and your roots—remain constant, although your feelings toward them can change.

Although classmates may write in your yearbook, "Stay just the way you are. Don't ever change!" you *will* change in some ways as time goes by, as you grow into independence and experience many new things. But, in some ways, too, you're likely to be the same basic person. When you become an adult, you will carry parts of your adolescence—positive as well as negative impressions, feelings, and experiences—with you much as you carry your childhood with you now. Whether carrying these feelings with you causes learning, growth, and new understanding or whether you are weighed down with fear and uncertainty depends on how you choose to deal with your feelings and experiences, and how you choose to see yourself.

SELF-IMAGE

How you *see* yourself (which may or may not be an accurate perception of who you are) is called *self-image*. Dr. Howard Newburger, a psychologist in Rye, New York, explains that "self-image is the picture we have of ourselves. It is made up of two elements: the things we expect of ourselves which balance out, either constructively or destructively, with what is expected of us by others. How you see yourself is very important."

If you have a positive self-image, you can enjoy your good qualities and live with—or change—what you don't like about yourself. You take mistakes or failures in stride, learning from them instead of putting yourself down. You have a good sense of what goals are right and realistic for you and you thoroughly enjoy any successes—even tiny ones—that come your way.

If you have a negative self-image, however, you may be so busy putting yourself down for your weaknesses that you don't have time to discover your very real strengths. You may expect so much of yourself that you can't possibly live up to your own expectations. You may fail to see and enjoy the successes you do have because you're too busy striving for something more. You may be consumed with feelings of inadequacy, depression, jealousy, and helplessness. You may see yourself as an unchangeable loser.

"And this loser image becomes a self-perpetuating habit," Dr. Newburger points out. "It can be as much of a habit as smoking, drinking, or drug addiction. Someone with a poor self-image will accept put-downs from others and adopt negative attitudes and behavior that reinforce his or her loser image."

A negative self-image is often the cause of many painful feelings such as self-hatred, loneliness, jealousy, boredom, shyness, and depression. In the rest of this chapter, we will be exploring some of these problem feelings and how to cope with such feelings, improve your self-image, and get a clearer picture of who you *really* are.

SELF-HATE AND FEELINGS OF INFERIORITY

I'm a really rotten person. I can't stand my personality or anything about myself. I'd like to change, but nothing I do seems to help. Any suggestions?

Bruce B.

I have this feeling that nothing will ever turn out right for me. I say dumb things and get people mad at me. I eat too much when I'm bored or lonely (which is often) and then the other kids make fun of me because I'm fat. I try to get involved in school activities, but I can't do anything right and everybody hates me because of this. I hate myself, too. What can I do?

Dorie R.

Could you—like Bruce and Dorie—be suffering from self-hate and feelings of inferiority? Maybe your feelings are a bit more subtle and not quite as strong as theirs, but you may experience some pangs of low self-esteem nevertheless.

For example:

• You're walking down the hall at school, and as you pass a large group of girls, they burst into uproarious laughter. Do you immediately assume that they're laughing at you, feel terrible, and walk away as fast as you can?

• If a friend criticizes you, do you immediately assume he or she is right?

• You hear that a classmate doesn't like you. Does it ruin your day and make you feel worthless? Do you need to have *everyone* like you?

• Do you hang around with people who put you down, but stay with them because you figure you're lucky to have any friends at all?

• Do you often fantasize about being someone else and find that, given a choice, you would *never* choose to be you?

• Do you engage in compulsive behavior—overeating, drinking too much, or taking drugs—that can hurt you in some ways?

• Do you really *need* to win all the time? If you get a lower grade than you expected or fail to win a prize in your school's art or poetry contest, for example, do you feel like a complete failure?

• Do you find yourself plagued with a persistent case of the "If only . . ."s ("If only I had a boyfriend/girlfriend, if only my parents were rich, if only I had a car, if only I could be beautiful/handsome, and athletic . . . ," etc.)?

If you do feel inferior at times—or all the time—this could be due to a number of factors.

You Have New Insights Into Your Limitations   As you change and grow in adolescence, your intellectual awareness sharpens. Suddenly, you discover all kinds of personal limitations, faults, and shortcomings in yourself and others that had escaped your notice before.

"Maybe you're 14 and feeling suddenly clumsy," says Dr. Helen De Rosis, a New York psychiatrist and author of several books, including *Women and Anxiety* and *The Book of Hope: How Women Can Overcome Depression* (coauthored with Victoria Pellegrino). "Maybe you were a clumsy child, too, but didn't realize it. Or maybe you find that you speak with an accent you don't like. You've always had this accent, but suddenly it seems undesirable as your senses sharpen and you become more critical of yourself."

Your growing awareness of your limitations can be an asset or a liability. If you become supercritical of yourself (to the extent that you lose sight of your good points) and are prone to criticize everyone around you as well, you're using your new awareness in a negative, hurtful way.

If you use your new insights in a positive way, however, you will become more aware of your strong points and ways to develop them. You may get some ideas for ways to compensate for or change any faults or limitations you have. You will also begin to develop a good sense of which goals are realistic for you and which ones aren't.

For example, if you're clumsy, but interested in physical activities nevertheless, it might be unrealistic to aim for a career as a ballerina or as an NBA superstar. Recreational dance classes, basket shooting for fun, jogging, or race walking, however, might help satisfy your need to be active—and help your coordination too!

In exploring your strong points, you may discover abilities you didn't know you had. Tom, for example, has an intense interest in sports even though he is not a talented athlete himself. He finds a great deal of satisfaction serving as a timekeeper and assistant trainer for various varsity sports at his school. Janice, whose musical skill is average at best, still enjoys being in her school band and has found a unique niche as a champion fundraiser for band activities. Her talent for organization, her winning way with people, her perseverance and energy make Janice a very special person in the eyes of her schoolmates and, most important, in her own eyes as well.

Maybe you're convinced that you're nothing but a collection of limitations. You might find yourself echoing the words of 14-year-old Sally, who insists that "I can't think of any strong points I might have. I'm not pretty or popular or talented in any of the ways that count."

All strong, positive traits you have—even ones you consider to be small and unimportant—*do* count. Everyone has an impressive array of assets. It may simply take some positive thinking and investigation to discover what yours are. Personal traits like patience, compassion, and being conscientious about keeping promises and secrets are important. Working hard and doing the best you can is quite an asset. Maybe you get along well with others, are a good babysitter, a dependable teammate, a kind and treasured friend. Maybe you feel things deeply—pain, yes, but also joy in small things. That extra measure of sensitivity, even though it can mean pain at times, makes you special.

There are so many things that are *right* about you. It's important not to get so preoccupied with your limitations that you lose sight of your very real strengths.

You May Have Unrealistic Expectations for Yourself There are some things you're unlikely to accomplish—no matter how terrific you are.

Being loved and admired by everyone is one unrealistic goal that a lot of people have. While some people have more friends and admirers than others, no one is universally loved. If you're like most people, you will find that a few people may care deeply about you and fewer still will actively hate or dislike you. Some may feel you're okay. Many will simply feel indifferent. This indifference—which you might interpret as dislike—has little to do with you personally. Most people are so concerned about themselves that they have a fairly limited

amount of emotional energy left over to become deeply involved with too many others—and those important others tend to be close friends and relatives. You may feel the same way—when you really stop to think about it.

Always being perfect is another unrealistic expectation. You're always going to make mistakes. You'll be good in some things and terrible in others. It's important to realize this fact and also the fact that it takes time to develop not only certain skills, but also maturity.

"If parts of your personality seem immature, right now, this could be natural for your age and background," says Dr. De Rosis. "Growth and change take time. What may seem like bad qualities to you right now might just be temporary ways of being. You may be impatient to grow up more quickly than is possible."

Skills take not only time but a lot of practice to develop. Mark is down on himself because, after two months of ice-skating lessons, he isn't looking much like Robin Cousins or Charlie Tickner. What he doesn't realize—or chooses not to see—is the fact that these two outstanding skaters have *years* of training and practice behind them. It takes years of falling down, starting over, tedious practice, hard training, and discipline to make a world-class champion skater—and even those who have made it to the top are not immune to mistakes. Charlie Tickner slipped during a crucial moment in his Olympic competition. Eric Heiden lost a speed-skating race only a few weeks after his Lake Placid triumphs. And even though Nadia Comaneci was the first female gymnast to score a perfect "10" in the Montreal Olympics, she doesn't *always* make perfect scores.

No matter how proficient you become at a particular skill, you'll always be human, capable of errors, and a bit short of absolute perfection. It's important to accept your mistakes, learn from them, and be gentle with yourself when your human limitations are apparent.

You May Be Getting Confusing Messages From Parents and Peers If your parents are like most, they love you dearly and want the very best for you. However, even the most well-meaning parent can give you some confusing messages—like criticizing you in a way that sounds hurtful (even though such suggestions may be motivated by loving concern). Or your parents may praise you so lavishly that you begin to question their sincerity and the value of any of their comments.

Dealing with criticism can be especially difficult, since making constructive criticism *sound* loving and constructive is an art. Since most parents themselves grew up being criticized in less than ideal ways, they may not always know how to communicate the love they feel for you along with their suggestions for changes you could make.

"Constructive suggestions have an underlying tone of 'I love and accept you. But I still need to guide you so that you can deal constructively with yourself,' " says Dr. De Rosis. "However, many things are said in a different tone."

Diane's mother, for example, is a beautiful ex-model who was prom queen twice in her high school years. It hurts her to see 16-year-old Diane—who is rather ordinary-looking, with long, flyaway hair and a prominent nose—going through so many self-doubts. She is convinced that improving Diane's appearance would help and is quick with suggestions about how to do this. She is bewildered, though, when Diane invariably reacts with sullen resentment or angry tears. What Diane's mother doesn't realize is that her daughter is hearing some hidden—and hurtful—messages in some of her well-meant advice.

"If you would only fix your hair—anything but the style you have—and get your nose fixed—I'll make an appointment with the doctor—you'd be so much prettier and life would be so different for you . . ." is the beginning of the regular routine that always ends with Diane running off in tears, feeling more worthless than ever.

"Diane's mother means well, but her words carry the implication for her daughter that with her nose and hair fixed, Diane would be a nicer, more lovable and worthwhile person than she is now," says Dr. De Rosis. "It would be more constructive to say 'Let's try some new hairstyles. It might be fun to experiment together. . . .' "

Some parents, too, may overreact to what they see as your imperfections or problems. Dan's father, for example, can't stand to hear Dan singing and playing his guitar. He tells Dan that it's because he has a terrible voice. The fact is, Dan's voice is about average and not at all unpleasant to hear, but Dan's dad, who always felt that he himself couldn't sing, is letting his feelings about his own voice influence his opinion of and reaction to Dan's singing.

Jean's mom, who is more upset than her daughter over Jean's infrequent dates, is letting her own memories of high school—when popularity was her first priority—color her feelings for Jean's situation. While Jean would like to have more dates than she does, she's so busy with her activities, her studies, and her special group of friends—both male and female—that her low-key romantic life isn't a major worry for her—except when she sees her mother getting upset and implying that if she isn't popular now, she'll miss out on all that matters in life.

When some parental reactions and criticisms seem off-the-wall, it may help to understand that your parents may be reacting not only out of concern for you, but also to ghosts from their own past.

Their own insecurities and fears may also cause some of your friends or classmates to be especially critical of you. Some people who like to hurl or trade insults "in fun" may be afraid of getting too close to another person and so build verbal barriers. Others criticize you for actions, traits, or feelings that they most dislike in themselves. Some, too, try to gain some amount of power over others by sitting in constant judgment, tearing others down in a (usually futile) attempt to build themselves up.

If you know this, you will realize that when a classmate or friend criticizes you, his or her motive may not always be to help you. In fact, the criticism itself may not only be nonconstructive, but also inaccurate. So it's a good idea to weigh his or her comments with your own view of reality and of yourself. You might also ask—either out loud or in your mind—"Why are you telling me this?"

Some young people suffer from too much praise rather than excessive criticism.

Carole, for example, is feeling bad about herself because she got a "C" in art and didn't make her school's choral group. Her doting parents have praised her artistic and musical gifts for years, seeing her as a multi-talented wonder child.

Carole is, in fact, a very nice person who has lots of patience and compassion, a lively sense of humor, a good eye for color, and a growing interest in interior design. She's an average artist, however, and is, quite frankly, no threat to either Beverly Sills *or* Olivia Newton-John.

You might think that all the praise that Carole has received from her parents would have built her ego up to the point where she could feel good about herself despite any limitations she might have. Doesn't real despair come from a family that relegates your original artwork to the darkest corner of the garage? Or a family that retreats, howling with derision, to a far corner of the house whenever you try to sing in the shower? Perhaps. But excessive, unrealistic praise can hurt, too. It can bring with it a lot of pressure and confusion.

At the moment, Carole is feeling angry, scared, and confused. How can she be average when her parents always said she was the greatest? Will they still love her, even if she isn't so great at art and music? Is she still a worthwhile person even if she isn't a prodigy? She feels angry at her parents, wondering if they meant to mislead her or if they're simply too out-of-it to see her very human limitations. She is beginning to wonder if anything they've told her is true.

"Praise is better when it's appropriate and modest," says Dr. De Rosis. "When praise is habitually piled on, it's easy to get the idea that if your efforts don't result in something great, its not worth anything. You may begin to view yourself only in terms of extremes—as the best or nothing.

You May Be Getting Some Confusing Messages From Society Many unrealistic expectations and unfair labels we pin on ourselves result from some confusing messages we get from society. For example:

• There are those fairy tales where "beautiful" is synonymous with "good" and only wicked witches aren't pretty.

• There are the erroneous black-and-white "rules" that say "Good people do this; bad people do that," not allowing for the fact that we are *all* combinations of good and bad qualities.

• There is the popular notion of competing, winning, and being Number One. Champions are venerated; runners-up, forgotten.

"This win/lose model, which we see most clearly in competitive sports like tennis, can be very damaging to self-esteem because credit can only go to one person—the best—and everyone else is discredited," says Dr. De Rosis. "The choice, too often, seems to be between being Number One and nothing, even though, in most sports events, the competitors are all good athletes and the difference between the winner and the other contenders is often minute."

This "winner take all" attitude can deeply affect our feelings about ourselves—whether or not we're competitive athletes.

"Many young people have the feeling that they *must* be the best all the time," says Dr. De Rosis. "They may feel that peak performances are the only acceptable ones. This attitude can cause terrible stress and strains."

Adhering to a strict winner/loser philosophy can make you a loser in life, no matter how many times you may win. Putting pressure on yourself to be better than someone else all the time is not only an unrealistic goal, it can also rob you of the opportunity to be close to others. It can also take away much of the joy of striving and the satisfaction of accomplishing some of your goals.

"I would like to see young people do what they like to do and are willing to work at," says Dr. De Rosis. "Doing well, under these conditions, does not result in a contest where someone becomes a loser if you're the winner. In the win/lose situation, someone—sometimes both the winner and loser—ends up feeling bad. However, if you do something because you want to and be-

cause it's fun, that feeling comes across and there is no loser."

When you start to develop realistic expectations for yourself, you will realize that you can't always be the best or even do some things well—and that's OK. Both your strengths and your limitations are part of who you are.

"If you can learn to give yourself credit for your positive points and learn to live with (or change) what you don't like, you'll start feeling good about yourself," says Dr. De Rosis. "You're a person who is good at some things, not so good at others. Sometimes you're kind and brave; sometimes you're neither. Discovering the many ways you can be—and what makes you special—is an exciting experience."

Recognizing your basic right to be—minus the frills of achievement—is another step away from self-hate.

"You don't need any justification for your existence, like prizes or special accomplishments," says Dr. Theodore Isaac Rubin, a New York psychiatrist and author of many books, including *Compassion and Self-Hate: An Alternative to Despair.* "These may give you some satisfaction, but they in no way justify your existence. You would *be* without these and you are infinitely more important than any prizes or accomplishments. This realization may help to free you from the self-hating need to be universally loved or admired, unfailingly sweet, helpful, giving, or wise. You must learn to love and accept the fool in you as well as the wise person."

You are a fascinating combination of feelings, moods, strengths and weaknesses, habits, and dreams. Accepting all of these—and changing only what you choose to and want to change—is the best way to overcome self-hate and can give you new insights into the special person you really are!

LONELINESS

I don't know what's wrong with me, but I'm 15 and always lonely. I have people around me all the time, but I'm still lonely. There's no logical reason, I guess. I just don't seem to connect with people. I don't fit in anywhere. What can I do?

Pat

It may be no surprise to you that recent studies have revealed that young people of high school and college age are the loneliest people in our society today.

Loneliness at this time in your life has many faces, many reasons.

Loneliness is one where once there were two. It can

...ke of a loss in your life. You may have ...dear by death, by a romantic breakup, or ...special someone moved away—geograph- ...tionally. Or maybe *you* have suddenly real- ...ou don't have much to share with a lifelong friend a..ymore and you wonder if life means always being left—or leaving others—behind.

Loneliness can mean losing part of yourself and mourning that loss. Perhaps you've lost a dream, an illusion, a treasured way of being. Perhaps you're feeling suddenly alone as you realize that your parents don't always have all the answers and can't always be there for you the way you once expected. Perhaps you're suddenly feeling the loss of your childhood spontaneity.

Loneliness can be a side effect of growing up. As you feel grown-up hurt, fear, and pressure for the first time, you may feel very much alone and wonder if you're the only person in your world who feels so much pain and uncertainty.

Loneliness means feeling that you're on the outside looking in, having that uncomfortable sense of not belonging, whether you're alone or in a crowd. It can mean being a stranger in a new school or someone who is labeled "different" or someone who can't seem to communicate with others.

Loneliness is an ache, a longing for someone to care and reach out to you. It can be the feeling that every time you reach out, your hand comes back empty because there's no one there for you. Maybe you wonder and worry that life will always be this way.

Loneliness is being alone when you don't want to be. It can be a side effect of shyness and can result in serious problems like severe depression, alcohol or drug abuse, or even suicide.

If you've ever felt—or are feeling—the pain of loneliness, you're *not* alone. Everyone has moments of loneliness, and we all know that often this loneliness has nothing to do with being physically alone. You can feel lonely in a crowd, trapped inside yourself and unable to reach out.

There is a difference between a loner and a lonely person. The loner often chooses to be alone and looks forward to times of solitude. He or she does not feel that life is empty. A feeling of emptiness, however, is common in lonely people, who feel hurt that other people don't reach out to them and seem to care.

What can you do to cope with such painful feelings of isolation? How can you break the pattern of loneliness? Since the problem of loneliness tends to be rooted inside you, changing this pattern must also start from within.

Work on Developing a More Positive Attitude This means working on your self-image, pinpointing your assets, and resolving to change the negative aspects of your life that are changeable.

Barbara, for example, found that she became less self-conscious and more outgoing after losing 20 pounds. Is there something you don't like about yourself, something you could change, that keeps you from being as outgoing as *you* would like?

Ted recently made a decision to try to be more optimistic about social situations. He made a vow to himself to try not to anticipate disaster. So far, his resolution has made him less fearful of getting involved in social situations and nothing recently has been socially disastrous!

It might help to make a list of everything that's *right* with your life, especially if you have trouble thinking of any good things about life as it is right now. Keep a diary for a week and every day write down *anything* that happens that makes you feel good (or even pleasantly neutral!). It might be an unexpected smile from someone or the feeling you got yesterday walking to the bus stop in the crisp morning air. Or it might have been the happy surprise you felt when your kid brother *didn't* bug you during your favorite TV program (or maybe he even did or said something halfway nice for a change!) There are a lot of tiny positive happenings in everyone's daily life, and these can add up to a lot of good feelings if you begin to notice—and remember—them!

Developing a more positive attitude can also mean eliminating negative assumptions—like the old "Everyone hates me!" line we've all used at one time or another. Don't mistake indifference for dislike. And be aware that your attitude might change some of this indifference.

To see what an impact your attitude and assumptions can have, you might like to try a little experiment that 15-year-old Julie tried not long ago. Julie decided to go to school one day assuming that she was generally liked. She held her head higher that day. She smiled at people and said "Hello" more often. She even started a few conversations.

This experiment, of course, was not a one-day miracle cure for Julie's loneliness, but it was a start. Some people began to notice her for the first time. Some smiled back and some talked to her a little. The attention encouraged Julie to keep trying to reach out to others.

Start an Interest Campaign Developing some special interests and abilities—for example, running, bowling, painting, or volunteer work at a hospital or for a political campaign—can bring many benefits. First, just by becoming more active, you tend to become less lonely. (You don't have as much time to dwell on your loneliness!) You may be around more people, including some who will share your new interests. You will find, too, that being active and involved will make you more interesting to others in general.

Cultivate an Appreciation for Moments Alone Do you panic when you face a Saturday afternoon—or night—by yourself? If you can learn to look at such alone times in a positive way, they can be a joy. Time alone can give you unique opportunities—to think, to dream, and to indulge yourself in pursuits like listening to all *your* favorite records, writing to a pen pal, taking a long walk or a soothing hot bath or shower, or maybe reading something just for fun. Or it might feel good to do nothing—to loaf without feeling that you have to give excuses to anybody.

Share Your Vulnerability, Your Feelings, With Others Let people start to know who you are. Sharing what you feel, from your fears and uncertainties to your dreams, can help in many ways. In talking with others, you can work through and better understand some of your own feelings. You may also feel immensely reassured to find that you're not alone, that others share some of the same feelings and can empathize with you. And others—whether they are your peers, adult friends, relatives, or parents—may become more open about their own feelings with you.

Start Showing Interest in Others If you want to be noticed by others, start noticing them! Develop a curiosity about the special things that make those around you interesting and unique. Quietly notice these little things—the ways others express themselves, how they relate to others, their special talents. Let these things matter to you. Start asking questions, expressing your interest. Most people love being asked questions about themselves and their interests. They also love sincere compliments. A question, a compliment, an important small fact remembered (like a birthday, a goal, or a funny comment), a smile—all these can help you begin to connect with another person.

Don't Be so Afraid of Taking a Risk Reaching out to others can be risky. There will be times when you get very little response or, worse still, rejection. Many lonely people are afraid to reach out because of this, but such fears can only perpetuate the cycle of loneliness. If you take a risk, something wonderful may happen. If you don't, nothing will happen. Being rejected or ig-

nored *can* hurt, but you can survive. It doesn't have to be a tragedy.

The real tragedy is the person who is too afraid to open his or her heart to others, who never lets his or her special warmth and vulnerability show. Maybe this person avoids the sting of rejection, but he or she may never know the sweetness of acceptance and the joy of being close to someone.

When you risk making contact with others, you will experience pleasure and pain, acceptance and rejection. There will be times of joyful sharing and times with a bittersweet edge of loneliness. But the emptiness, the hopeless on-the-outside-forever feeling will no longer be there. For you will know what it means to reach out to others. You will know both the pain of rejection and the joy of being close—and you won't be so afraid of either one. You will know that, whatever happens, you will survive and that you have much to share.

SHYNESS

I'm shy and it's ruining my life. No one notices me at school because I'm too shy to talk to anyone and even to ask questions or volunteer answers in class. I've never had a date, but even if a guy asked me out, I don't know what I'd do. I wouldn't know how to talk to someone on a date. I hate being shy, but I don't know how to be any different.

Shy Hermit

I feel dumb even asking this, but I'm sort of shy and I think I'm missing out on stuff because of it. I was going to join the staff of the school paper. I thought I could report sports scores or something, but the editor said they needed someone to do interviews on the Feature page. I didn't pursue it because I don't know how to do an interview. I'm not the type to go around asking people a lot of questions. Even worse, I have trouble asking girls out. I don't very often because I make a fool of myself every time. How can I get over this shyness?

Kevin J.

If you—like "Shy Hermit" or Kevin—feel that shyness is a problem for you, you're probably also painfully aware that shyness can make you feel isolated and different. It can keep you from living the life you would like to live.

What you may *not* be aware of, however, is the fact that you have lots of company. According to a Stanford University study, almost half of all those polled (42 percent) considered themselves shy. Another survey recently revealed that 80 percent of the several thousand people interviewed reported that shyness had been a problem for them at some time in life.

Shyness can afflict people in many different ways. Some people feel scared and awkward in certain situations, but manage to hide these feelings and *appear* to be at ease. Some have trouble conversing with strangers, but are confident in close personal relationships. Others have no trouble with informal occasions—an afternoon with friends, a beach picnic, or a typical day at school—but freeze at a more structured social situation like a party or dance. Some find it difficult to converse with anyone. Some, too, find that shyness is a fleeting problem—it comes and goes in special situations or at certain times in their life.

According to psychologists, shyness is especially common in adolescence. This is because timidity is often a reaction to a new and different situation—and change is a major part of your life as a teen.

"Changing schools—especially making the transition from junior high to high school—can be very difficult because it means meeting new people, facing new pressures, and adjusting to new rules," says Norma Waters, a family counselor in Los Angeles. "It's tough, too, because your peers are so important right now. You probably want to be liked and accepted and are afraid of being different. Yet your shyness makes you *feel* very different. Shy boys who have grown up with the internal message that assertiveness equals masculinity may suffer especially."

What causes people to be shy?

While some counselors feel that shyness *can* mean that you're so preoccupied with yourself that you can't relate easily to others, many feel that the roots of shyness may be found in poor self-image, often prompted from certain childhood experiences—like being ridiculed by classmates for being different in some way (too fat, too skinny, too tall, too short, having freckles, wearing glasses, etc.). A number of therapists believe, too, that many shy teenagers (and adults, too) share similar home backgrounds. They seem to come from homes where their parents had very high expectations of them. Held to impossibly high standards and fearful of failure, a child in such a situation may develop the habit of hanging back, afraid to try anything for fear of making a mistake and/or being rejected.

If this sounds like the story of your life so far, keep in mind that you cannot change the past. However, you can change the present and the future. The following suggestions may give you some ideas for change.

Make a List of Times, Situations, and People With Whom You Feel Shy. Then Ask Yourself "What's the Worst That Could Happen?" Maybe your most terrible fantasy is being at a party with no one to talk to. Or summoning the nerve to tell a story you think is funny, only no one laughs. Or standing up in class and forgetting your answer or giving a wrong one. Or having a conversation with someone you especially like and not knowing what to say next.

When you think about it, most people are *not* the life of any party. Jokes fall flat, people give wrong answers, and silence looms large in some conversations—and most manage to survive nevertheless. People who don't suffer from shyness are not too critical of themselves when something like this happens to them. They may think "Oh, that was embarrassing!" or "Well, you can't win them all!" and then go on without dwelling on the incident. And the people around them usually aren't terribly critical either. They're just relieved that something embarrassing didn't happen to them!

It's helpful to remember this when you're being critical of yourself or expecting others to be that way. You need to give yourself room to make mistakes. A mistake or a less-than-ideal experience can be a valuable learning experience. Viewing possible mistakes as opportunities to learn may help diminish some of your fear of failure—and may enable you to take some risks.

Take Little Steps Away From Your Shy Behavior Don't try to take too many risks all at once. Start small. Try talking to just one person at school today. Say "Hi" to five people this week. Next week, you might add a simple, sincere compliment or observation to your greeting. Taking these small steps can help you get in touch with others and feel good about yourself because you tried something that was difficult—but not impossible—for you.

If others' responses aren't overwhelming, don't despair. It takes many people time to get past indifference and to the point of wanting to know another person. If someone is in a bad mood and isn't friendly, this may have nothing to do with you. You are not responsible for his or her sour mood, and since you are in control of your own behavior, you can still be friendly. One slight doesn't have to spoil your day.

Be Aware of—and Change—Your Body Language Very often, shy people put others off in subtle ways. They lean away from people, fold their arms tightly across their chests, and avoid eye contact. This can make others vaguely uneasy—sometimes giving them the feeling that you don't want to get to know them. Try leaning forward to listen to someone. Make eye contact. Physically open yourself up a little. It seems like a small matter, but changing your body language can make a surprising difference in the way others tend to react to you!

Admit That You Feel Shy or Awkward Such an admission may sound out-of-the-question, but the fact is, sharing your feelings is a vital part of reaching out to others.

"If you can say 'I feel uncomfortable' or 'I feel shy,' others can respond to you in a helpful way and may feel good that you could confide in them," says Norma Waters.

Sharing your vulnerability may enable others to help you and may make it easier for them to share their feelings with you. Making the first move and admitting that you're uneasy may make everyone feel more comfortable and may win you some great new friends!

Mike, nervous during his first date with Penny, finally came out and told her how he felt. "I thought that Penny would think 'Boy, what a creep!' " he says. "But she smiled, laughed a little, and said 'I'm glad I'm not the *only* one who's nervous!' That kind of broke the ice. The rest of the evening was fun. We've gone out several times since and like each other a lot."

Scale Down Your Expectations If you're like most shy people, you have very high expectations of yourself. You're convinced that you can't just do an OK interview for your school newspaper, but must somehow come on like Mike Wallace or Barbara Walters and stun your subject with your sharp-edged questions and insights. You can't just go to a party, you must be the *life* of that party or you feel like a social zero. With such high expectations, your probability of failure is high—and you know it—so you hesitate to take *any* risks.

Keep in mind that very few of us can consistently be the center of attention and that no one is perfect. Even the most successful people make mistakes sometimes. Even the most popular people you know aren't always in the spotlight or universally liked.

So it's important to give yourself realistic goals—and give yourself credit for trying to reach out to others.

It's vital, too, to realize that combating shyness does *not* mean changing your whole personality and becoming very talkative and outgoing. Maybe it's your nature to be quiet. You can be quiet and sensitive and listen a lot and be considered an interesting, fun friend. Accepting your own quiet nature, feeling comfortable with yourself as you are, and using your sensitivity and listening talents to advantage in your relationships with others can make a great difference in your life.

Counselor Norma Waters often tells shy clients the old fable about a contest between the wind and the sun over which was more powerful.

"The wind and the sun debated over which could induce the traveler along the way to remove his coat," she says. "The wind blew furiously, but the traveler only wrapped his coat more tightly around him. Then the sun shone warmly on him. Before long, the traveler removed his coat. The fable points up the fact that pushing too hard to relate to others, being too *on*, may make people wrap themselves more tightly in their shells, so to speak, but genuine warmth seems to get through to most people. Warmth is something you don't always have to express verbally. Other people can generally feel it. As a sensitive person, you may be uniquely able to cultivate this sense of warmth and caring about others."

JEALOUSY

I'm so jealous, it's terrible! I'm jealous of everybody: my best girlfriend, my brother—and I'm really paranoid about my boyfriend maybe liking someone else. It seems like anyone else's good luck or success takes away from me and if something good happens to me, I'm not satisfied because I compare it to what everyone else has and it doesn't seem like much. I'm really making myself and lots of other people miserable with this jealousy thing. How can I get myself to stop?

Mindy M.

Jealousy can have many forms. Maybe you're jealous of a friend's good fortune when she makes the cheerleading squad or wins a special honor. Maybe you're jealous of a stranger or a classmate you don't know too well who seems to have it all. Maybe you're jealous of a sibling whom your parents seem to favor or who seems to be smarter, more attractive, or more popular than you are. Maybe you're part of a love triangle—or dating someone who is also dating others—and you can't help being jealous of the others in your special someone's life. Or maybe, like Mindy, you find yourself jealous much of the time in a variety of circumstances.

Jealousy will be discussed in later chapters, but because it's such a problem for so many young people it merits some attention here as well.

Whether you feel constant jealousy or only occasional pangs, your first reaction may be one of guilt. "I *shouldn't* feel jealous," you may say to yourself. "I'm a terrible person!"

The first thing you need to understand about jealousy, however, is that it is a practically universal feeling. It strikes everyone at times and is *not* bad—but just another human feeling.

Low self-esteem and insecurity are usually at the root

of your jealous feelings. You feel that everyone is better—or has more—than you do. You feel that you have little to give and fear losing a loved one because of this. You fear that because you have so little to offer, a look, a smile, or a brief conversation with someone else might cause your boyfriend or girlfriend to leave you.

What can you do to help yourself if jealousy is a problem for you?

Admit to Yourself That You're Jealous—Without Putting Yourself Down for Feeling the Way You Do   Since you're experiencing a common human feeling, one growing from your own poor self-image, it's vital to be kind and compassionate with yourself. There is no reason to feel guilty about being jealous. Our feelings are neither good nor bad in themselves—they just *are*.

Think About—or Even Write Down—What Sparks Your Jealous Feelings   Be very specific about what you envy in others—and the others that you envy. After you've completed your list, think of things you *don't* envy about each person.

For example, Jim has been feeling jealous of his younger brother Joe because of Joe's athletic ability and close relationship with their father. However, Jim doesn't envy Joe's academic record *(not* impressive) or his friendships (which Jim considers shallow and completely activity-oriented).

Linda has been secretly jealous of her friend Sue because Sue is popular and a cheerleader. However, after thinking about Sue's total life situation, Linda has decided that she wouldn't want to trade places with Sue and inherit her alcoholic mother or bratty little brother.

Emily, who finds herself jealous of Cheryl Ladd's looks, money, fame, and success, finds that she does *not* envy the actress her broken marriage, lack of privacy, hours of work, and the stresses involved in maintaining a growing career.

What this exercise can do is make you look at others' lives in total and stop idealizing their situations. No one has an easy, carefree life. No one has it all. This exercise can also pinpoint the qualities that you envy in others, which could tell you something about what you feel you lack.

Think About Your Own Special Qualities   Maybe you don't have athletic prowess. Maybe you're not as witty or outgoing as someone else. But you're definitely not a have-not. You're very special in your own way. What are the qualities you especially like about yourself? What people, circumstances, activities, and other things in your life bring you pleasure?

Growing to appreciate your own uniqueness can help alleviate your jealousy for others.

Share Your Feelings With Someone   Admitting your jealous feelings to someone who cares, someone you can trust, can help you in several ways. That person may reassure you that your feelings are not at all unusual and may also point out to you that you have a lot going for you, too.

Analyze Your Feelings as Clues for Possible Changes in Your Life   The fact that you are jealous can be a valuable clue that your self-esteem isn't as high as it could be and that you need to start appreciating *you* more. Looking closely at your feelings can also give you clues about what you feel you lack. Ask yourself if this is something you can change. If so, you might want to make some changes—like losing weight, combating shyness, or studying harder and procrastinating less, for example. If it's something you can't really change—if, for example, you envy someone else's height, family wealth, and the like—learn to be accepting of these differences. Maybe you're not as tall as you'd like to be and your family is far from rich, but when you really think about it, you and your family have some special assets and advantages, too! Carol, who was on a scholarship at a private school, had been envying some of her rich classmates for some time before one of them confided that she was jealous of Carol "because you have a nice mom and there's lots of love in your family." Carol began to see that she was rich in ways she had never imagined. You might make similar discoveries!

DAYREAMING

I'm a daydreamer. In my dreams, I see myself being a successful lawyer or an airline pilot, wildly popular with women, and driving a Porsche or Mercedes 450SL or maybe a Corvette. I also dream about having confidence and clear skin! Do you think such daydreaming is helpful or harmful to me? I sure enjoy it even though I'm 15 and a long way off from accomplishing any of those goals—if I ever do!

Paul K.

I'm 16 and live in a dream world. I don't have any friends and spend most of my time dreaming about being someone else. Help me.

Janet U.

Paul and Janet represent two different sides of daydreaming. Janet, whose life is taken over by her dreams, has such a poor self-image that she can't face the reality of being herself. Because her dreams are always focused on the impossible—being someone else—and because they keep her from having friends and activities and from finding ways to improve her real life, Janet's daydreams are potentially harmful.

If you have a problem like Janet's—if you *constantly* feel cut off from reality or have trouble living in your real world—ask yourself what you might be trying to escape in your own life? What changes would you like to make—*possible* changes—to improve the quality of your life? How can you go about making such changes? Because your self-esteem is so low right now, you might find it helpful to get some encouragement and advice in this regard from someone close to you—a parent, teacher, or special friend—or from a Family Service counselor.

If you're like most people, however, your daydreams are more likely to resemble Paul's. You might dream of the future and goals you would like to achieve. You might fantasize about being loved and/or having sex. You may find yourself—especially in hectic, painful, or boring moments—daydreaming about being someplace peaceful and far away.

In the past, daydreams were viewed in a negative way. Sigmund Freud insisted that "happy people never make fantasies; only unsatisfied ones do."

Recent research by psychologists is proving Freud wrong. While daydreams can certainly help ease pain and boredom, they can also bring extra happiness into lives that are already quite satisfactory. Today, many psychologists believe that daydreaming—especially for adolescents—is not only normal, but a vital part of growing up.

Daydreams can help you develop a sense of yourself as a separate person.

Daydreams can be risk-free rehearsals for situations you may encounter in the future.

Daydreams can also help you to cope temporarily with unsettling changes and events.

"A daydream can cushion pain, alleviate feelings of inadequacy, and give you a glimpse of your potential," says psychologist Howard Newburger. "It's important to pay attention to your dreams. You may catch a glimpse of what—or who—you could be. Very often, your major interests and career objectives are determined in your childhood and adolescent daydreams. It is within our daydreams, many times, that our expectations evolve."

At times, the pull between your daydreams and emerging reality can be painful. Dr. Jerome L. Singer, a professor of psychology at Yale University who has written a book called *The Inner World of Daydreaming,* contends that in adolescence, your fantasies are constantly being tested against reality and a number of these dreams must be given up within a relatively short time. In a few years, some options will be closed to you forever. Choices you make—like whether or not to go to college, which career you pursue, the decision to marry young, having a child while still in your teens—will greatly influence the direction your life takes and may preclude some other possibilities.

However, if you feel successful in fulfilling *some* of your dreams, you will be able to let others go with a minimum of pain. You may find satisfaction also in translating some dreams into lifelong hobbies rather than careers. For example, if you love acting, singing, or playing tennis, you may be happy participating in community theatre, singing in your church choir, or enjoying active sports in your spare time.

You can use daydreams to try on certain behaviors and choices. "You can try on certain actions mentally first," says Dr. Newburger. "That way, you're better able to visualize the outcome of your contemplated actions."

The ability to do this is crucial, researchers have found. In a study by Dr. George Spivack and Dr. Murray Levine of the Devereaux Foundation, it was discovered that middle-class teenagers with a history of delinquency showed a limited ability to look ahead and see the consequences of their actions. They were also less able to envision intermediate steps in attaining their goals. They showed a lack of creative thoughts and ideas.

Creative daydreaming is often a source of inspiration—not only for the attainment of goals, but also for all kinds of creative endeavors. Artists, writers, and many scientists, too, find inspiration in their daydreams. It is said that Einstein, while daydreaming about what would happen if a man could fly into space at the speed of light, developed some important features of his theory of relativity.

You may not make an earthshaking discovery in your daydreams, but you can make some important discoveries about yourself.

"Daydreams can help you understand yourself better," says Dr. Newburger. "You can become more aware of positive and negative habits this way. One patient of mine, for example, found that he was daydreaming about saying to a pretty girl 'If you ever break up with your boyfriend, let me know!' When he really thought about this daydream, he saw that he was always putting himself in a secondary position. When you're aware of such trends in your daydreams, you can look for behavior that may be keeping you from realizing your true potential."

Dr. Marvin Schiff, a physician and weight-control specialist in Los Angeles, asks his patients to use daydreaming and meditation techniques to discover the elements of their poor self-image.

"I ask them to look back on their lives and to think about their crutches, their rationalizations, their fears, and their hopes," he says. "Then, when they've thought about their problems, I ask them to imagine themselves solving these problems successfully—and to savor that feeling of success."

Of course, dreaming isn't enough. Daydreams aren't meant to replace your activities and they can't become reality without any effort on your part. But they can be a barometer of your feelings and your growth.

Dr. Newburger suggests keeping a diary of your daydreams. Maybe, at first, your daydreams have a vindictive tone ("I'll show them! I'll be so famous and successful that they'll be sorry they were mean to me!") or are often compensations for hurt and rejection.

"As time goes by, you may find your dreams becoming less compensatory and more positive," says Dr. Newburger. "By keeping a diary of these, you can see how much you are growing and changing."

It is important, of course, to find a balance between dreaming and *doing*. "Dreams show you possibilities," Dr. Newburger points out. "*Actions* make them reality."

Many psychologists believe that, while there is danger in dreaming too much and doing too little, the greatest danger, perhaps, is in not dreaming at all—getting so immersed in what *is* that you refuse to imagine what might be. If you lose your dreams, you lose a vital part of yourself.

STRESS AND ANXIETY

I don't know exactly what's wrong, but I don't seem to be in control of my life. My activities are controlling me. I'm always on the go and never have time to myself, but then when I do have a moment to relax, I can't because I think of a million things I should be doing. The problem is, I'm not enjoying anything anymore. What can I do?
Maureen Z.

Sometimes I find myself crying for no reason at all. In the last year or so, I've been getting so nervous about everything. I'm 14 and have been going through a lot of changes with my body and with school, plus we moved eight months ago and my folks are having money problems and aren't getting along too good. I worry a lot. Am I crazy or going crazy, do you think?
Kim Y.

Stress is a fact of life for all of us. Stress can be a valuable part of our lives, helping us to accomplish goals. There is no such thing as a stress-free existence.

However, physicians and psychologists often try, in their research projects, to distinguish between helpful stress—which keeps our lives productive and interesting—and harmful stress, which overloads us physically, mentally, and emotionally.

All of us have differing tolerance levels for stress. Some can handle a lot of different projects and responsibilities without feeling distressed. Others have a very low tolerance for stressful pressures and changes.

Change is a major element of stress. Even happy changes—like graduating or getting married or getting a first job—are stressful. Drs. Thomas A. Holmes and Richard H. Rohe have devised a Social Readjustment Rating Scale to measure significant stress caused by life changes over a one-year period. A score of 150 points can signal high stress due to change—and the possibilities of stress-related illnesses and problems such as headaches, ulcers, eating disorders, and catching a lot of colds. In some cases, stress seems to increase the body's vulnerability to disease.

It doesn't really take too much in the way of change to chalk up those points. If, for example, you graduate (26 points), get married right away (50), go on a honeymoon (13), move to a new apartment (20), go into debt to buy home furnishings (17), and start a new job (26), you will have over 150 points. If you add in-law problems (29) and a pregnancy that first year (40), you would have well over 200 stress points and would be vulnerable to stress-related problems like anxiety, depression, and the like.

However, you don't have to wait for milestones like graduation or marriage to feel real stress. In a recent survey, stress and nervousness emerged as the number-one problem reported by teens.

You face many pressures as an adolescent. You may feel pressure from your peers and from your parents to measure up to their varying expectations of you. You may find, however, that your greatest pressures come from within. There are the pressures that come with conflicting feelings—the fact that you feel both love and hate for your parents; that you love yet compete with some friends; that you're trying to become your own person and define your own values while being part of the crowd as well.

There is stress, too, in waiting for the things you want. You're eager to be independent, yet still must depend on your parents in many ways. There are demands made on you from all sides. You may feel that you're in a strange transition phase of life—a time when you have increasing responsibility for yourself without some of the compensations of total freedom.

Then there are the pressures of discovering who you are and making important decisions about your future and the direction your life will take.

Having a high tolerance for stress as well as having a loving and supportive family, and fairly clear-cut goals and interests may keep adolescent stress manageable for some teens. For some others, however, pressures from within and from others, uncertainty about the future, and inability to deal with stress in a positive way can cause problems.

When you're under a lot of stress, you may start to feel a lack of control over your life. You may laugh or cry at seemingly inappropriate times. You may feel nervous and upset about everything. You may feel angry, confused, and continually harassed. You may become more and more impatient—with yourself, with others, and with all the little delays of daily life (like waiting in the cafeteria line). You may find yourself getting involved in so many projects you have little time to yourself and you may find yourself unable to relax when you do have a few moments free.

People deal with stress overload in a number of ways. Some, of course, live a lifetime racing the clock, working too hard and accomplishing too little. Some use overeating, drinking, or drug use to calm their feelings. Some give up and refuse to face any stressful situations—which can mean, in effect, dropping out of life, refusing to live up to one's potential, refusing to take any risks (which keep life interesting!)

None of these are constructive ways of dealing with the stresses you'll always face.

The following may help you begin to see and deal with the stresses you feel in a more positive way.

Know Your Stress Limit Know what the stresses are in your life and how much you can take before you start feeling exhausted, trapped, and overwhelmed.

Kelly finds that her stress-overload signal is a feeling that everything is an obligation and nothing is fun. She has a full academic load, a part-time job, and lots of activities and friends, and says, "When I start to dread things I usually enjoy, I know it's time to slow down!"

John has found that his stress signal is his tendency to pick fights with his younger brother. He is discovering that, many times, his angry feelings toward Josh have little to do with Josh and a lot to do with stress. Now he's trying to find more direct and helpful ways to deal with his feelings.

"I know I've had it when I feel tired all the time and oversleep in the morning," says Jennifer, a 15-year-old

who is active in school, church, and community theatre work. "I also find myself getting colds or headaches a lot. I'm trying to learn to slow down before getting sick, though, to listen to my body when it says 'Enough already!' "

Peter says that his cue for slowing down is a feeling of "the weight of the world on my shoulders—like I have to take responsibility for and solve everything *right now!*"

Knowing your stress limits can help you to make wiser choices for *you.*

Jennifer recently decided to pursue most of her community theatre work in the summer, giving herself more free time when school is in session.

Peter made a list for himself of things he can do now and things that will have to wait. "And I'm trying not to worry—too much—about the things on my 'wait' list," he says with a smile.

Mark and Renee, who are getting married soon, have decided to work, follow a conservative budget, and put off having a family for at least a few years. "We want to become a family in stages," Renee explains. "First, we'll work on being a happy family of two, working out our relationship and building up a bank account before having a baby. If I had to become a new wife, a new adult, and a new mother all in one year, I don't think I'd manage very well!"

Taking your life stresses in moderate doses can cut down a lot on your anxieties and banish that helpless, out-of-control feeling.

Start Small Don't try to change your life—or lifestyle—around all at once. Take one problem or change at a time without worrying about the others at the same time. Taking on twenty things at once will almost always guarantee you a stress overload. Taken one at a time, however, challenges can be met and problems solved.

Get a Fresh Perspective If you're a stress-prone person, you feel everything intensely and see every pressure in your life as a life-and-death matter.

While feeling intensely about your endeavors can be energizing, seeing everything as an emergency can cut *down* on your effectiveness. Some people, for example, get so anxious during tests—feeling that if they don't do well, that's *it*—that their anxiety breaks their concentration and they *don't* do well!

"Young people often see everything as irrevocable," says Sheri Kesselman, a family counselor in California. "Life isn't like that. If you don't get what you want one time, you'll get it another time. Learn to ask yourself 'Is this really worth all the anxiety? What is my r ness accomplishing?' Put things in proper persp you see one thing—a test, a date, or whatever—as the turning point in your life, of course you'll be nervous! But life goes on, whatever the outcome of the situation you're nervous about. It *isn't* the end of the world."

Try to Separate Who You Are From What You Do
"Feeling that you *are* your work can be so stressful that it can immobilize you," says Dr. Barry Schwartz, a psychiatrist who coauthored a study of stress among medical students at the Medical College of Pennsylvania. "You may feel, for example, that when a paper is graded, you yourself are being judged. This can make you procrastinate while doing the paper or become immobilized altogether."

It's important to realize that you are *not* your work, but that you are made up of an infinite variety of traits, strengths, weaknesses, feelings, and ideas. Realizing the diversity and innate value of who you are will help you to avoid the common tendency to have your self-image hinge totally on what you do and achieve.

Achievements may give you some satisfaction, but you don't need them to justify your existence. You would still be who you are without any honors and prizes.

Make Time to Have Fun   Fun is a vital part of your emotional health, so even if you think you don't have time, *make* time for fun, whatever that means for you. Taking time to relax, to pursue a hobby, read for pleasure, go for a long walk, listen to music, talk to a friend, meditate, write a long letter to a pen pal—whatever is fun for you—*must* be a part of your daily routine.

Work Out a Simple, Basic Daily Routine   With so many variables in your life right now, a little sameness and stability in your daily routine—things you don't have to decide constantly or things you can look forward to—can be soothing. Establishing a regular bedtime, a getting-up time, and a set study time; eating well-balanced meals on a regular schedule; and doing at least one thing for fun every day can greatly reduce the stress in your everyday life.

Exercise   Make some form of exercise a frequent habit. All forms of vigorous exercise—sports, running, walking, dancing—are excellent tension reducers.

Realize That You're in Control   You can choose to be nervous or choose to alleviate some of your stress. Taking responsibility for your nervousness and anxiety is the first step toward doing something positive about it. If, for example, meeting strangers is a stressful situation for you, saying "I get nervous when I'm with strangers" rather than "Strangers make me nervous" signals that *you* are in control and that you can choose to change this situation.

Use Your Imagination to Relax   Peaceful fantasies can be wonderful stress reducers.

Dr. Howard Newburger suggests two relaxation exercises he calls "Imaginary Place" and "Clouds."

• *Imaginary Place.* Sit down, close your eyes, and breathe deeply, trying to relax every part of your body. Then start to imagine a place where you would love to be, a place where you might feel especially peaceful. It might be a beautiful garden, a grassy slope overlooking a bubbling mountain stream. It might be a deserted beach at sunset, with the cool, frothy waves lapping at your toes. Or you might imagine yourself sitting on a hill, well above the clamor of the city, watching the twinkling lights below. Listen to the stillness. Feel the cool breeze on your face. Notice all the feelings you have in this imaginary place—sensations of sight, sound, and smell. Travel via your imagination to this peaceful place whenever you need to relax.

• *Clouds.* Close your eyes. Imagine that you're floating, nestled in a fluffy white cloud. You're safe, happy, and content. Stay there for a few minutes. Then breathe deeply and open your eyes slowly.

Let Others Help You   Don't suffer silently when you're feeling stress and anxiety. Talk with someone you trust. Sharing your feelings with others can help in a number of ways. You will feel less alone. You will feel relieved to get some of your feelings out in the open (sometimes they don't seem so unmanageable then!). Also, someone who knows you well may be able to help you explore ways you might make some changes in your life to lessen stress or cope with it more effectively.

MISDIRECTED ANGER

I have a problem with my temper. I always get mad at innocent people. Like if a teacher yells at me. I yell at my girlfriend later on. If I'm upset at my mom, I take it out on my little sister. Why do I do this and how can I stop?
Brad D.

I never get angry. That is, so people could see it. When someone does something mean to me, I stay calm and cool on the outside, but on the inside, I'm a nervous wreck! Sometimes I feel like shouting and screaming and telling the whole world off, but I never lose my cool. What can I do before I explode?
Sandi N.

Make a List of Things You Love in Life If you can't think of anything you like, think back a little, before boredom struck. What things have you enjoyed in the past? What could you—with a little effort—still enjoy? Making a list of these things may get you excited about life all over again.

Sixteen-year-old Ben tried making a list with the following results: "I love cold mornings, hot biscuits with butter and honey, riding around with Al and Mike, country-western music, hamburger pizzas, summer cookouts, swimming at the lake, going to ball games in Chicago, and driving fast by myself over deserted country roads!"

Jodie, who is also 16, came up with the following list: "I love the color blue, a guy named Ron, lemon cake, old convertibles, and putting on my headphones and listening to Fleetwood Mac full blast on the stereo. I love reading the newspaper on Sunday, going to the show or shopping, or taking a long walk with my friend Pam. I love listening to Jane Olivor, watching *M*A*S*H* and I just love Alan Alda for being himself. I love it when my parents trust me and take time to listen to what I have to say."

When you make your list of what you love in life, you may be amazed at the variety of things, people, foods, and activities that turn you on and make you feel glad to be alive!

Rediscover a Special Friend—Maybe a Friend You've Neglected for a Long Time "Take a risk," says Dr. Gordon. "Risk it working or not working. Maybe the neglected friend you'd like to get to know again is a parent. Some kids have difficulty coming to terms with the fact that their parents are nice people. Try talking to one or both of your parents. Start discovering each other. The ultimate high in life is getting to know—really know—somebody dear."

In getting reacquainted with someone who is special to you, you may also rediscover meaningful and lovable aspects of yourself!

DEPRESSION

It's taking a lot of effort for me to write this, so I hope you can help me. I feel tired, hopeless, and out of it. This has been going on for a while—about two months. I can hardly drag myself out of bed in the morning. In case you think I'm old, I'm not. I'm 17. What's the matter with me?

Jill Y.

I've been feeling depressed lately and nothing is going right for me. I feel bad because my parents are divorcing and my dog got run over two weeks ago and now we're moving and I'll be going to a new school. What can I do to feel better?

Paula-Jean T.

I've been getting into lots of fights with friends and have been in a down mood lately. I don't know how to shake it. All of a sudden, I'm not interested in anything. My grades are falling because I can't keep my mind on my work. I'm not sure why I feel this way or what to do about it.

Brian H.

Depression is a major problem for *all* age groups—striking from 14 to 23 million people this year with varying degrees of severity, according to the latest estimates from the National Institute of Mental Health.

But depression can be a particularly painful problem for teenagers. Depression is often an emotional response to significant changes and loss—and as an adolescent, you're experiencing changes and losses all the time.

Growing up brings with it some natural losses: the loss of a familiar way of being as your body and your family and social relationships change, and the loss of unlimited options as you face the challenge of choosing an educational plan, a career, and a basic lifestyle by late adolescence. In making some choices, we lose others forever.

You may also experience the loss of a boyfriend or girlfriend, the loss of a friend who moves away, the loss of your intact family if your parents divorce or if a parent dies, the loss of your old home and community as you move to a new one, the loss of a beloved pet.

Growing up and meeting your goals may also give you a sense of loss mingled in with your joy and satisfaction. As you become more independent, you lose some parental protection. When you realize your goal of buying a car, getting into the college of your choice, getting married, or moving into your first apartment, you have *lost* that goal and may feel a touch of sadness, a feeling of "What now?" as you try to find some new goals.

Loss and change are not the only reasons for depression.

Some people who habitually hold their feelings—especially anger—inside often become depressed.

Many women feel low during the drop in hormonal levels each month just before menstruation.

If you take certain drugs like barbiturates or

amphetamines, or drink a lot of alcohol, you may be more prone to depression.

If your daily diet includes a lot of sugar-laden junk foods, you may become depressed, some researchers believe. Although their findings are still somewhat controversial, some experts do think that there may well be a link between excessive consumption of junk food and depression.

There are also theories that some depression may have a genetic link. In many cases, of course, it is hard to tell whether one's depression stems from genes or from a depressed (or depressing) home environment. Some studies have found, however, that children and teenagers who are depressed sometimes have parents who have recently suffered a bout of depression, too.

Depression can be brief—or a prolonged ordeal. It can last a day or go on for months. It can make you feel temporarily down or it can absolutely overwhelm you. It can be linked to a specific problem or situation or it can be a vague, increasingly overwhelming feeling of hopelessness and helplessness that takes over your life.

According to psychiatrist Helen De Rosis, many teenagers experience simple *situational* depression—a reaction to a romantic breakup, a failure to attain a goal, a put-down from someone who matters, or some other significant loss.

"These feelings are reactions to an immediate situation and usually don't last a long time," she says. "You may do a lot of talking and complaining, too."

In what Dr. De Rosis calls a *true* or *significant* depression, you are immobilized, often for a long time. "Significant depression is slower to develop," Dr. De Rosis says. "You may feel that you're constantly falling short, that you're inferior, that you're helpless to change your situation. You may feel intense anger, guilt and self-hate, and hopelessness. When you attempt to keep these strong feelings inside (when you keep them *de-pressed)* *you* become depressed and feel totally numb."

Some people know that they are depressed. Others have a feeling that all is not well or may feel physical symptoms—like being very tired—but don't connect these to depression.

How can you tell if you might be a victim of depression? "Yes" answers to a majority of the following questions may indicate that you're depressed.

- Do you dread getting up in the morning?
- Do you always feel tired, no matter how much sleep you get?
- Do you have trouble falling asleep at night?
- Are you unable to eat? Eating too much?
- Have you lost interest in everything—even things you used to enjoy a lot?

- Are you having trouble concentrating on anything?
- Are your grades falling?
- Are you skipping classes or whole days of school?
- Have you stopped caring how you look, feeling that good grooming is too big a bother?
- Do you feel that doing *anything* (even phoning a friend) is more trouble than it's worth?
- Do you feel you've lost the power to make a difference in your own life?
- Do you find lately that you're having trouble making any kind of decision—even small ones?
- Do small annoyances sometimes make you fly off the handle?
- Do you say "No" to all suggestions of activities and all social invitations even if you have nothing else to do?
- Do you suffer from physical symptoms like stomachaches, headaches, and constipation?
- Have you lost a lot of weight—without even trying—in the past few months?
- Do you find yourself unable to express your feelings?
- Are you sometimes not quite sure *how* you feel?
- Do you see the future as a hopeless, unchangeable extension of today?
- Have you found yourself crying a lot without really knowing why? Or unable to cry—feeling *beyond* tears?
- Have you thought of taking your own life?

If depression is a problem for you, there are a number of ways you can help yourself.

Make Small Changes in Your Daily Routine Do something out of the ordinary for you. If you're allergic to physical exercise, start taking long walks or maybe even jog a little. Force yourself to accept an invitation or suggestion from a friend. Call a friend. Ask yourself what you'd be doing right now if you weren't depressed, then *do* it!

Release Pent-up Emotions in Safe Ways You might bicycle furiously, throw yourself into an intense racquetball game, cry, or complain to friends. You might try expressing anger more directly when this is possible and practical. Learning to express your anger in constructive ways and finding nonhurtful ways to deal with your angry energy is a major step in overcoming depression.

Don't Anesthetize Your Feelings With Drugs or Alcohol When you're feeling blue, it can be a huge—and understandable—temptation to look for an escape via drugs or alcohol, but these can only deepen your depression and postpone any solutions to your problems.

"Remember that dealing with your feelings is an opportunity to grow," Dr. De Rosis points out.

Plan a Treat for Yourself Every Day You need something—even a very small thing—to look forward to every day. Maybe you can reward yourself with a hobby you enjoy, a visit to a favorite place, a talk with a person you especially like, a special food, a hot shower or bath . . . anything that pleases you and makes it possible for you to get up in the morning and look forward to a new day.

Don't Criticize Yourself for Being Depressed Depression is a natural reaction to loss, to pent-up feelings, to a poor self-image and feeling of helplessness. Instead of getting down on yourself for being depressed, try to understand *why* you feel this way—maybe by writing out your feelings, maybe by talking with family or friends—and how you might make some helpful changes in your life.

Seek Help if Your Depression Persists If, despite your best efforts, you're still depressed, ask for help. A parent, family member, friend, school adviser, or favorite teacher might help you sort out your feelings and your alternatives.

It might also be a good idea to get a physical checkup to make sure that there is no physical condition that might be contributing to your depression. You may wish to talk with your doctor, too, or to a counseling professional—a psychologist, family or youth counselor, social worker, or psychiatrist—especially if you've had suicidal feelings.

You can also find help via telephone crisis hotlines and suicide prevention center helplines across the nation.

It's important to realize that asking for help doesn't mean that you're crazy or weak. It just means that you need more help right now than you're able to give yourself. Help is there—from caring family, friends, and counseling professionals—if you will only reach out for it. Asking for and receiving help can be a real turning point in your efforts to overcome depression and can make a significant and happy difference in your life.

HAPPINESS WITH YOURSELF AND YOUR WORLD

Sometimes I think about the future and wonder if I can be happy with inflation so bad and good jobs so scarce. I want to be rich even though my parents aren't. I think I'm fairly intelligent and could do well if I got the chance. I'm the sort of person who wants it all—success, money, a nice home, great car. You know, the old American Dream. What chance does a person my age (15) have to be happy in a future that seems pretty uncertain?

Scott L.

Career success coupled with financial security are often seen as the key to happiness. But a goal of happiness based on these two factors can often be elusive. You can lose a job or inflation can seriously diminish your wealth—and your happiness is gone. Or maybe you're never able to acquire the level of financial security or career success that you had hoped—and you never know happiness.

We all define happiness in very personal ways. You may find happiness living in the country close to the land, or in a small town where everybody knows your name. You may find happiness in the clamor of a large city, feeling that you're part of its excitement and vitality. You may find happiness in shared activities or in quiet moments alone. What comprises happiness for you is a part of who you are as a unique individual.

There are some constants, however—some basic goals and choices that many people overlook when they dream of fame and fortune. When dreaming about the obvious and often elusive elements that we believe are necessary for real happiness, we often forget these constants.

Happiness Can Mean Simplifying Your Life: Knowing What's Important to You and What Isn't It can mean not getting so caught up in moving ahead that you lose sight of the loveliness of today. Pausing to savor a special moment, watch a beautiful sunset, really listen to someone you love, or reflect on your life as it is right now, thinking of all the things you enjoy about it today. All of this can make happiness a more immediate possibility instead of a distant goal.

Happiness Is Having Enduring Relationships and Sharing Who You Really Are With Others It means not only enjoying the love of your family and your friends, but also working at your close relationships, nurturing them, sharing growing pains, disappointments, secrets, tears, hopes, and dreams with these special people throughout your life. You will meet many people in your life—growing closer to some and growing away from others. But the relationships that can endure time, changes, and knowing one another as you *really* are—with no games, no pretenses—can be a very special joy.

Happiness Is Trying New Things This might mean taking up a new sport, doing volunteer work, getting to know and appreciate someone who is much younger or much older than you. It can mean taking a night class in something you know nothing about—like art appreciation, Chinese cooking, or auto mechanics! It may mean walking or driving home via a different route one day. It means developing a curiosity about the world around you, asking questions, and being open to all kinds of new experiences.

Happiness Is Making Peace With Your World It means accepting the limitations and the advantages of that world and the people in it. It means finding a balance between your growing independence and your parents' continuing concern (often expressed via rules, restrictions, or unsolicited advice). It means learning to live with the things you can't change: your best friend's eccentricities, your Aunt Millie's laugh, your loved one's penchant for country-western music, the fact that you face growing responsibilities. When you accept these unchangeables, you may even come to appreciate and enjoy them! Happiness means accepting the fact that plans, people, and circumstances change, that things don't always go the way you thought they might. And happiness is knowing that you can cope somehow with whatever may come your way.

Happiness Is Making Peace With Yourself It means being as gentle in accepting your own limitations and as generous in acknowledging your assets as you would be with your best friend. Happiness is knowing that you can succeed or fail at a project, win a prize or not win a prize, be rich or be poor—and still be *you,* a valuable, unique person. Happiness is knowing that your definitions of who you are and what makes you happy will change somewhat as you grow. For self-discovery is a lifelong process and happiness is not dependent on a single goal reached at one particular time. You will be finding new clues to your identity and new ways to be happy throughout the years to come!

CHAPTER TWO

"My Problem Is . . . My Parents!"

My dad and I were very close until recently. Now he ignores me and we hardly ever talk anymore. I feel like killing myself or tearing up the photography book he gave me for Christmas last year. But I don't really want to. What else can I do?

Donna A.

My parents don't think I love them anymore because I'm hardly ever home and don't agree with their taste in clothes and music and I don't ask Dad for help with my homework the way I used to. (I don't need his help anymore. I'm smart and can do fine by myself now.) But I love them very much. How can I make them understand?

Tom T.

I feel like I'm losing my family. My brother, who's 19, is engaged and spends all his time with his fiancée. My parents are spending less and less time at home, too. They're always going off somewhere for weekends, just the two of them, or going off to play tennis or to dinner with their friends. We used to do everything together as a family, but I guess they think I'm old enough to take care of myself and that I don't need love anymore. But I do! How can I make my family close again—just like the old days?

Terry M.

I love my parents. They're pretty good people, but at times I get so burned up at them when they don't trust me or treat me like a baby or embarrass me in front of my friends. We've been fighting so much lately, it's like we hate each other, but we don't really. Is it possible to love and hate your parents? Does this mean I'm terrible or normal? Help!

Confused

As these letters—and possibly your own experiences—indicate, adolescence is a confusing time for both teen-agers *and* their parents.

It's a confusing time for your parents because you've grown up and changed so much in what seems to be

such a short time and, at times, your parents may not know quite how to be with you.

Some fathers, especially, may withdraw in confusion as their daughters grow from little girls to attractive young women. They may face a number of conflicting feelings, such as a natural admiration and attraction for their daughters' youthful beauty and, at the same time, a rush of fatherly protectiveness.

Parents in general may rejoice in your youth, your energy, and your many life options; may be deeply concerned that you make wise decisions about these options; and at the same time may envy you a little for your youth, your strength, and your many opportunities.

Your parents may also have some conflicting feelings about the role they play in your life right now. For years, they've protected you, cared for you, taught you, and provided you with necessities for survival. For a long time, they were the most important people in your world. Now your world is expanding and other people—particularly your friends—are beginning to matter a lot to you. Your parents may be happy to see you getting more self-sufficient. They may be delighted to have more time to themselves and the freedom to come and go, knowing that you are increasingly able to take care of yourself. Yet, they may sometimes be fearful that you're trying to grow up too fast and will get hurt. They may feel a little left out of your life. They may not always know exactly when you need to be independent and when you need their help and protection again. It's not easy to know when to let go—or to let go at all. Your parents may be happy and proud to see you grow, but sad to see you grow away and not need them as much.

Your feelings, of course, are a series of conflicts, too. You may feel both love and hate for your parents as you alternately struggle for independence and then turn back to your parents from time to time for help and reassurance. You may fear being a baby forever yet also fear the aloneness that full independence brings. You may hate still needing your parents as much as you do and yet feel frightened and upset if you feel they aren't there for you. You may be struggling to find your own values while feeling influenced by theirs. Sometimes it may seem that the only way to become separate from your parents is to rebel and to reject their values, ideas, and in some instances, the reality that you must still depend on them in many ways. You may deliberately adopt values, ways of dressing, and activities that differ from and even clash with those of your parents—then feel angry when they don't agree with you. Of course, if a parent *does* agree with you—if one or both start dressing like you and your friends or if your parents start *really* liking a boyfriend or girlfriend of yours and encouraging you to pursue the relationship—you may get angry, too, feeling that they're invading your territory, encroaching upon your separateness.

All of these confused feelings are entirely normal for you and your parents. Some families feel the conflicts more intensely than others. If, for example, your parents are extremely protective and can't see you as a separate and growing individual, you may feel a stronger need to rebel than others whose parents are willing to let their teens take some risks and learn. If your parents—like Terry's—tend to overestimate your independence a bit, you may feel more of a need to be protected than some of your friends whose parents are constantly there for them.

In coping with these conflicts, it's vital to understand that adolescence is a rough time for most teens and their parents. Your conflicting feelings—*and* theirs—are not bad, not indicative of a lack of love or caring. It's important to be concerned not with the rightness or wrongness of *feelings* (since feelings are neither right nor wrong; they just *are),* but with *actions.* It's important to try to act in ways that will help you to feel good about yourself and that will also help to cut down on some of the confusion you and your parents may be feeling.

For example, Donna, who wrote about her father's emotional withdrawal from her life, is feeling so angry over the loss of their closeness that she entertains notions of destroying either herself or a precious gift that he gave her in order to catch his attention again and make him aware of her grief. It would be more helpful to both Donna and her dad if she could simply share her feelings with him, without accusing him of not caring anymore. She might tell him that she has been feeling lonely, angry, confused, and left out. She could add that she misses their closeness and that, while she knows that this is a confusing time for everyone, she needs his love, reassurance, and guidance more than ever now. This approach might also work well for Terry, whose parents are spending less and less time with her. She

might tell her parents that she still needs them and needs a little family time with them, time to share feelings and experiences. They may have assumed that Terry would want to spend most of her time with her friends. They may be happy to set aside some special time—each day or several times a week—to be together and do things together as a loving and growing family.

Being honest and nonaccusatory in reporting your feelings can help your communication with your parents and can ease some of the inevitable transitions that are taking place within your family as you become less of a child and more of a young adult.

Sometimes—as in Tom's case—parents are the ones who feel abandoned. Tom can express his love for his parents in little ways—by trying to be around for a family activity now and then, by asking his parents' opinions on subjects not likely to flare into a heated controversy, by praising his father for past help with schoolwork ("You helped me understand algebra so well that math is easy for me now!"), by sharing some of his efforts and ideas with his parents, and by saying—on some occasion when it just feels right—"I love you."

Some teens are afraid that if they love their parents too much or agree with them too often, they will never really grow up. This is not the case.

When you are truly separate and independent in spirit, you will feel a new sense of freedom. You will not *need* to base your ideas or preferences on your parents—either by agreeing totally and never questioning or by disagreeing for the sake of disagreeing, which is just as dependent as accepting everything they believe without question, since you are *reacting* to them instead of acting on your own convictions.

When you're truly free, you may disagree with your parents and accept the fact that you probably won't agree on certain things. Such disagreements do not mean that you or your parents are being unfair. Disagreeing can simply mean that you are different, separate people—each with the right to your own point of view.

You will also feel the freedom to agree with your parents when it seems right to you, to make some of their values your own. This doesn't make you a child again. It means that you're a young adult exercising his or her own right to choose. Just because a value, an idea, or a choice happens to coincide with someone else's doesn't mean that it's not your own.

The option to express love—without the fear that your growth toward independence will be threatened—is another aspect of this freedom. The more separate and independent you become, the more love you may feel for your parents.

This sense of separateness and freedom doesn't happen overnight. Many families don't feel this freedom and peace until adolescence is almost over. Others, who try to ignore their conflicts and who avoid sharing their feelings, may never experience it. It is a growing process that doesn't usually happen without some pain, some tears, some anger, and a lot of caring. This is a time for you and your parents to mix as much understanding, love, and caring for one another as you can in between the inevitable struggles, conflicts, growing pains, and tears.

RULE CONFLICTS

I'm 16 and living in a jail—or it feels like one! My parents never let me see my friends outside of school and although they don't say for sure that I can't date, they go out every weekend night to see THEIR friends and make me babysit with my little brother. I never get to go anywhere or do anything. I don't think that's fair, do you?
Cecilia R.

My parents are overprotective. Everytime I want to go anywhere, I get a cross-examination. You know, where are you going, with whom, and for how long. It's getting to be a hassle to go anywhere. What can I do?
Rich O.

I'm a 16-year-old dude with an unusual problem: my parents are divorced, I live with my mom (who works) and she tries to make me do the dishes, a lot of the cooking and laundry, too. I don't think I should have to. I have enough to do with homework, football practice, dates, and time with my friends. I don't think I should have to do all that work, especially when it's basically women's work anyway. I'm thinking of asking to live with my dad and his new wife. What do you think I should do if they don't want me with them? How can I change my mom's mind?
Lance

Even though I'm almost 15, my parents treat me like a baby. I don't have any more freedom than my 10-year-old sister and it makes me mad. I think my parents should trust me and give me more freedom!
Stuck at Home in Ohio

Some rules are a necessary part of life for all of us. We have federal, state, and local laws, school regulations, and family rules as well. Rules of some sort are necessary to keep order in any household. Even when two adults are living together, they abide by certain

rules—e.g., if one will be late coming home from work, he or she will usually call and let the other know, or if one person makes a mess, that person usually cleans it up. In any situation, rules make living together easier.

But rules can also be a problem during adolescence. You and your parents may not always agree on how many and what kinds of rules there should be, which rules are reasonable and fair and which ones aren't.

Some teens resent *any* rules and rebel against all restrictions. However, it's important to learn to live with some limitations since you'll be facing these—in some way or another—all your life. Compromise and consideration are vital living skills. The choice, then, is not between no rules versus life in "jail," but between having too many unfair rules imposed on you versus having a voice in deciding what boundaries and limitations work best for you *and* your family.

Most young people realize (sometimes grudgingly) that parental rules and restrictions can be a sign of loving concern. Your parents care enough to ask where you're going and with whom, to risk your wrath by saying "no" on occasion. But parents aren't always sure when it's best to say "Yes" and when they should say "No." They can't always estimate how much responsibility you're able to handle. They can't always know which rules are really fair and which ones might not be—even though they probably *try* to be fair most of the time. Ideally, the rules in your house are—or can be—the result of open discussions and compromises between you and your parents.

While family lifestyles and needs vary widely, there are certain basic ideas that tend to work for most teens and their families—when given a chance. When you're trying to come to some sort of compromise about house rules—if you haven't already—you and your parents might consider the following.

Life Can Be Easier for Everyone When All Family Members Cooperate and Participate in Running the Household As a young adult, it seems fair that you do your share of household chores—your share being a matter of mutual agreement or compromise between you and your parents. Learning to cook, clean house, do laundry, and make minor repairs can be valuable to you when you're on your own—whether you're male or female. (With more mothers and wives working outside the home by choice and by necessity these days, the old assumption that all household, cooking, shopping, and child-care chores are "women's work" is not fair—if, indeed, it ever was!) By sharing chores and responsibilities, *all* family members will have more time for fun.

It is also reasonable to expect a little give-and-take—

and you will find yourself giving, too. With rising living costs these days, few families, for example, can afford a private phone or a car just for your use, so it's reasonable to learn to share by not tying up the phone for hours, not keeping the car out any longer than agreed (or bringing it home with an almost-empty gas tank!). You and your parents might compromise on which days or times you can have the car or what time limit should be put on most phone calls. If you have an income from a part-time job, you might come to an agreement about your paying for a second phone or for gas you use and the insurance you need when you drive the family car.

It is also fair to expect to give your parents some information about where you're going, with whom, and what time you expect to return. You may notice that your parents and other adults often give each other such information when they go out separately. Such questions—and curfews, too—are motivated by love and are for your own protection. Answering truthfully with no arguments can keep your parents from worrying about you unnecessarily. If you start balking at answering such questions or dragging in an hour after your agreed-upon curfew, however, your parents may become alarmed and suspicious and you could lose some of your freedom to come and go.

There Should Be a Balance in Your Life Between Work and Fun While it's reasonable for your parents to expect you to participate in some specific household and family responsibilities, it's only fair that—if you hold up your end of the responsibility bargain—you should have free time to have fun with hobbies, friends, and dates, or to just sit around and read or dream. Cecilia's parents, for example, are not being fair to her if they expect her to stay home and babysit *every* weekend night. They might consider getting another babysitter one of those nights, or staying home (so Cecilia can go out) alternate nights or weekends. Or they might take their small son with them on occasion. There are a number of ways they might find a fair compromise.

You Need a Gradual Increase in Responsibilities and Freedom as You Grow A 15-year-old should not have to live with the rules and restrictions appropriate for a 10-year-old. Likewise, a 10-year-old should not be expected to carry the responsibility load of an older sibling. Some parents try, with all the best intentions, to avoid showing any favoritism by treating all their kids alike, with the same rules and restrictions for all regardless of their ages. If this is the case at your house, it might be helpful to point out to your parents (quietly and tactfully) that children of different ages have very

different needs and that you as a teenager need to learn—gradually—to take more responsibility so that when you are on your own eventually, you'll know how to care for yourself and make independent decisions. Don't just agitate for more privileges. As you get older, you should have more privileges *and* more responsibilities. If you agree to take on more of the latter, you may find that your parents will allow you more freedom as well.

How Do You Approach Your Parents About Rule Conflicts?

Family counseling experts suggest trying to talk with your parents when they are relaxed and have time to listen and discuss the matter with you. You might take care to make it clear to them that you recognize the necessity of rules and that you want only to discuss a possible change in a rule. It helps if you have solid reasons for such a change and ideas for a compromise in mind.

For the past few weeks, Suzanne and her parents have been arguing about her 10 P.M. weekend curfew. After some fruitless arguments ("But, Mom, everyone else is allowed to stay out until 11 or 12!"), Suzanne decided to try a new approach. One night after dinner, she sat down with her parents and told them that she realized how much they cared for her when they set limits. "I also feel bad that I've disappointed you lately by getting in half an hour to an hour late on weekends," she said. "The problem has been that the show doesn't usually end until close to 10 or 10:30 and it's hard to leave near the end of a movie or to make it home in time if I stay to the end. A lot of kids don't have to be in until midnight and lots of our activities together are geared to that. I can accept the fact that you may feel that midnight is a bit late for someone my age. I'd be happy to compromise with a new curfew of 11 on weekends. Maybe we could try it for a week or two. I'll make every effort to be home right on time."

If, like Suzanne, you show a willingness to try to work out a problem, to compromise, your parents may be more willing to listen to your ideas and to give you a chance to show them how responsible you can be. Of course, it's crucial not to violate their trust. If Suzanne starts coming home late again, her parents will have a harder time trusting her the next time she asks for a rule change. She will have lost some of her power of negotiation by violating a rule she had a voice in making.

It's also important to know what's negotiable and what isn't in your family and to decide which limitations you can live with and which ones you really *need* changed, since you won't always get everything you want. For example, Mark, whose parents are devout Catholics, realizes that although he doesn't particularly enjoy going to Mass every Sunday, to go or not to go is not a matter of negotiation right now. "I'm not that religious and when I'm on my own, I probably won't go to Mass regularly," he says. "But I go now because my parents expect it. Period. It's OK by me as long as we can reason with each other on other things that matter to me. My parents are really good about giving me a liberal curfew and accepting my friends, who are welcome here any time. Those are two things that are really important to me."

Knowing what matters a lot to you and what doesn't can help you to decide when to work with your parents on trying to change a rule or situation and when to simply let it pass.

NEED FOR PRIVACY

My mom snoops around my room when I'm out. She reads my mail and diary, listens in on my phone calls, and has to know everything that happens at school, on dates, and in conversations with friends. I don't have anything to hide, but it bugs me when she goes through my things without asking and I don't always feel like telling her everything. Am I wrong?

Judy P.

I like being alone in my room sometimes, just listening to music or reading or thinking. No one else in my family likes being alone and they think I'm strange for feeling the way I do. They're always coming in without knocking, of course, and bothering me. I don't have any privacy at all. What can I do?

Chris C.

My dad is a school counselor. Before you start thinking "How nice. He must be real understanding!" let me tell you something: he's driving me crazy!!! See, he's very open about his feelings and talks a lot to us about what he thinks and feels and he expects us to be just as open with him. Well, I can't be. I'm a more private person or something. I like to keep some thoughts and feelings to myself. There are some things (not bad, just private to me) that I wouldn't tell my best friend, let alone my dad. How can I make him understand?

Eileen L.

The need for privacy is an important part of your growing separateness.

How much privacy you want and need, of course, depends a great deal on your personal preferences—whether you tend to be a loner, would rather be with people all the time, or find yourself somewhere in between these two extremes.

Privacy, of course, means more than simply being alone sometimes. It means that those around you respect your right to keep some thoughts, feelings, and aspects of your life to yourself when you choose. These feelings or thoughts or events may be potentially controversial *or* completely innocuous. The point is, they are yours and you don't feel like sharing right now.

It may be difficult for some parents to accept and live with your growing separateness. Some parents may snoop through your room or barrage you with questions because they feel they're losing touch with you. This can turn into a vicious cycle, with you needing privacy, what privacy you have being challenged or violated, and then you further withdrawing into your private self.

Reinforcing your right to privacy isn't always easy. Maybe most of your family is comfortable with nonstop togetherness and no secrets. Maybe they find it hard to understand your differing need for privacy. Maybe your parents think that if you're "secretive" you're up to no good. Maybe they feel hurt about your need for privacy, feeling shut out of your life.

It could be, too, that you might explore your definition of privacy. Maybe you feel that privacy means never having to tell your parents *anything* about your life, that nothing you do, think, or experience is any of their business.

This really isn't so, of course. In a family, we *all* touch each other's lives in many ways. It's important to make a choice between what you feel you can share with your parents and what you prefer to keep private.

What can you do if your parents are overstepping your private boundaries?

Try talking with them—calmly, without arguing. Explain that you love and respect them but need to have a little of your own life private, that it is part of growing and discovering who you are. You might reassure them that they are important in your life, that you value their opinions about some major problems and decisions you may face, but that in order to grow as an individual, you need some privacy, some space.

For example, Judy might explain to her mother, "I feel upset and embarrassed when you go through my things and read my diary. As you can tell, I'm not trying to hide anything major from you. Maybe you feel that we're not as close as we were and you want to get close again. I want to be close, too, but I'm growing up and need some privacy. If I knew we could respect one another's privacy, maybe I could feel comfortable talking to you more."

Chris might say something to his family like "I know it probably seems strange, but I'm a person who right now needs to be alone some. Maybe we could work it out so I could get some time to be by myself without interruption. I like sharing things with the family, but I also need to be alone sometimes."

Eileen could match her dad's openness with some of her own. The next time he asks "What are you feeling?" she could answer "I'm feeling a need to be by myself a little, to have some space and privacy. I like the fact that we can all be so open and that you care so much about how I feel. But I need to keep some feelings to myself. I need some space to grow."

These answers take a lot longer and a bit more effort to say than "Get off my back" or "Leave me alone!" but when said calmly and in a reasonable way, they can be much more effective.

It might be that your parents cannot—and will never—accept the notion of your right to privacy. They may feel that they have an absolute right to know everything—trivial and otherwise—about you, and they may feel angry and insecure when you talk about separateness. This is a problem for them that, hopefully, they will work out in time as you grow closer to full adulthood.

In the meantime, you may be able to satisfy some of your privacy needs by taking a walk when you need to be alone or by enjoying your private thoughts and dreams, accepting them as normal evidence of your separateness and knowing that someday you *will* be on your own.

PARENTS VERSUS FRIENDS

My father died five years ago when I was not quite 10. Since then, my mom and I (I'm an only child) have been super close. Like sisters, as she says. I like doing things with Mom, but now that I'm in high school, I really like being with my friends (who are my own age), too. Mom is very critical of all my friends and gets mad if I don't want to spend 99 percent of my time with her. I don't want to hurt her feelings, but I don't want to spend most of my free time with her. What can I do?

Shelley C.

While Shelley's situation is more extreme than most, there are some elements in her conflict that are shared by a number of teens and their parents.

Some parents may feel a bit rejected and left out

when their teenagers suddenly want to spend a lot of time with their friends. This may hit some parents harder than others. A mother like Shelley's, for example, who never developed her own interests, hobbies, and friends separate from her role as a wife and mother, may be hurt and bewildered when her children start to grow away. She may feel competitive with her daughter's (or son's) friends. And the teen may feel guilty about needing time apart and angry about parental interference, hostility, and competitiveness toward his or her new friends.

This situation is not an easy one to resolve, but a gentle, compassionate approach might be best: "I enjoy spending time with you. We have a very special relationship. But I feel that we *both* need our own friends, too. We can't be everything to each other." You might encourage your parent to pursue long set-aside hobbies or interests, to go back to school, or to get involved in groups and activities where she or he is likely to make new friends. Although you might still enjoy some special activities together, it is important for all concerned to learn to enjoy others as well as time alone. You can't fill all of each other's needs all the time. It's not fair or realistic to expect this of someone else.

I have a problem: my parents hate my friends! Every time a friend calls or comes over, my dad gets upset and is rude to them. It is very embarrassing. He and Mom can't find anything good to say about my friends. They say that Dave's hair is too long, Joe is too loud, and Mike is too dumb. (Dad calls Mike "Unconscious" because he thinks he's so stupid.) I like my friends, but am afraid I won't have any if my parents aren't more understanding.

Ron K.

My folks are real strange. They used to let me have my friends in the house to watch TV or listen to records, but they don't anymore. Now if we want to visit, we have to stand out on the front porch. This isn't exactly helping my popularity. Last night, me and this guy I like stood outside talking for half an hour and nearly froze to death! How can I get my parents to be more reasonable?

Fourteen and Frozen in St. Paul

If your parents seem to hate your friends, it might be helpful to try to discover their reasons for feeling this way and see if you can't help alter their opinion in some way.

The fact that "Frozen's" parents once allowed her friends in the house but no longer do is a clue that something might have happened to change their feelings. "Frozen" might examine the past behavior of her friends—if she's not aware already of the reasons behind her parents' front-porch edict. Maybe her friends took over the house, ate everything that wasn't frozen solid, moving, or nailed down (few family budgets can stretch far enough to feed a mass invasion too often these days), and disrupted the family's regular routine a little too often. It might help if "Frozen" could talk with her parents, discover their objections to the gang, and draw up some rules and agreements about the days and time her friends are welcome, where they can gather, and what they are or are *not* allowed to eat, drink, or smoke. Then she could make these restrictions clear to her friends—as a possible alternative to shivering on the porch.

Maybe your parents object to a friend or some friends because of negative gossip or family ties. Beth's mother, for example, was not pleased to find Beth spending time with Ellen, whose older sister was in a juvenile correction institution. Beth and her mother argued about this a lot and the problem wasn't resolved until Beth's mother actually spent a little time getting to know Ellen and discovered what a good person she was. Rushing your friends in and out of the house with no family introductions—or refusing to let your parents meet your friends—can raise their suspicions and fears to troublesome levels.

If your parents know your friends and dislike them, it may help to reflect on their complaints and criticisms to discover why they feel the way they do. Maybe your parents are supercritical of everyone and your friends are an easy target. Some people vent their hostility and anger by finding fault with others—a problem that can cause a lot of pain because it keeps them from being close to other people.

If this is the case with your parents and/or if they make fun of things that a friend of yours can't help, tell them as calmly as you can that it hurts you when they criticize and make fun of people you like. If they are rude to your friends, you might say quietly (preferably when you're alone together) "I felt very hurt and so did my friend about what you said." When you make it clear how much this is hurting *you,* your parent may make an effort to be more considerate.

It could be, however, that your parents' dislike of a friend or friends is motivated by a clash of preferences and philosophies or by genuine concern for you.

Ben's parents dislike any of his friends who have long hair or facial hair or who are not high academic achievers. Since his parents *are* polite to all his friends, Ben accepts their dislike of his buddies as their own separate choice. "I think it's too bad that they can't see past their prejudice over beards and see a nice person behind that, or that they can't see that there are all kinds of people worth knowing, not just people who share the same ambitions," Ben says. "But what can I do except think how interesting it is and how much I enjoy knowing a variety of people?"

If some of your friends have been in trouble with the law, seem to encourage you to engage in dangerous or destructive behavior, or have serious drug problems, your parents' dislike may be based on their concern for you. While you have a right to choose your friends, keep in mind that you are separate from them too, and don't have to mirror their behavior. Remember, too, that your welfare is a high priority for your parents, so you can understand—even if you disagree with—their dislike for anyone they feel might harm you in any way.

I'm so embarrassed by my dad, who insists on wearing a dumb Hawaiian shirt and baggy, knee-length shorts (with sandals and black socks yet!) around the house! He says he has a right to be comfortable, but my friends laugh when they see this getup and I could just die! He doesn't care if people laugh! What can I do?

Debbie S.

This is an awful problem. My mother weighs over 200 pounds and is just gross to look at. She's a nice person, but she eats like you wouldn't believe, especially when she's upset, which is often. What's really bad is that my friends make fun of her to me. They snicker and call her a "porker." I think they're being mean, but I'm even more upset with Mom for letting herself get that way. It's terrible because I think the other kids look down on me because of her.

Wendy W.

What your friends think is vitally important—especially in early adolescence. You may be very sensitive about any criticisms or comments they may make about your parents because it's easy to feel that this reflects on you in a negative way. You may also feel hurt for your parents when others make fun of them. You may criticize or try to wish away a parent's accent, way of dressing, weight problem, or whatever else may make him or her different. Or you may agonize when your friends notice a critical family problem—like an alcoholic parent. (This and other crises of family life are discussed later on in this chapter.)

It may help to keep in mind, however, that in the instance of parental eccentricities, these may be much more noticeable and important to you than they are to your friends. Your friends may giggle when they see your dad in a strange outfit because they don't know what else to do, or maybe they're thinking of some of the crazy leisure-time getups their own parents may wear. Chances are, however, that they will giggle, then forget.

If your friends continue to make fun of one of your parents, you might tell them how this makes you feel. Just say "I feel uncomfortable when you mimic my dad's accent. I don't think that's kind or fair," or "I feel really bad about the fact that Mom has such a weight problem. It makes her feel bad, too. It really hurts me when I hear you making fun of her. Please—as a friend —try not to do that anymore, OK?"

If your friends start to put you down because of your parents, it can be a particularly tough situation.

Julie, whose divorced mother has a drinking problem and a less-than-ideal reputation in their small town, says that the way she handles negative comments is to say simply, "Look, I'm not my mother. Don't judge me by what you think she does."

Wendy reports that since she wrote about her problem, she has encouraged her mother to join a weight-loss club and helps her to find other ways to deal with her frustrations besides eating (like taking walks, calling a friend, and keeping a diary). She's proud of the fact that she's helping her mother to overcome a problem that has caused grief for both of them.

In *any* situation, realizing that you are a separate person and are not responsible for your parents' alleged shortcomings, problems, or eccentricities may make you less edgy about your friends' reactions to your parents. Realizing your separateness, too, will help you to be more tolerant and compassionate about the very human shortcomings and problems your parents may have. They are not perfect, but they still probably have a lot of good points and a lot of love to give.

HIGH EXPECTATIONS

I'm a "B" student and have to work very hard for my grades. But my parents are convinced that I'm a genius and every time I get a report card, I get punished for not doing better. They won't listen when I say I'm doing the best I can. Now I'm grounded for the entire year with no phone, radio or TV privileges. What's the point of working so hard if I just get punished for it?

Thirteen and Miserable

My mother is an etiquette freak and it's ruining my life. Last week, when we went to dinner at my aunt's, I forgot and cut my bread with a knife instead of breaking it up. You'd think—from the scene my mother threw when we

got home—that I'd killed somebody. I can't keep up with all those rules. I try to be polite and stuff, but it's never good enough for her.

Tina B.

I'm having a problem being my own person. I think my dad needs to have me fill his dream of being THE perfect son and also live his life for him. He always wanted to be a varsity football player in high school and later be a doctor, but he didn't make the team and his college grades weren't good enough to get him into medical school. Now he wants me to achieve what he couldn't. I'm okay in sports, but I don't care for football and I don't know if I have either the brains or the desire to be a doctor. I'm really more interested in photography and filmmaking. How much do I owe him anyway?

David H.

If your parents are like most, they have high hopes for you and want you to do your best. Such encouragement, given in a loving way, can help you to achieve some of your goals and dreams.

However, when parental expectations bear no relation to reality and/or to your abilities and desires, they can hurt.

If your parents expect you to be an "A" student even though your best efforts bring a "B" or "C" average, if they expect you to be perfect or to live out all their own unfulfilled dreams, these expectations can be a threat to your self-esteem and can cause a lot of confusion and guilt.

It's important to remember that your value as a person is not linked to your grades, whether or not you win prizes, or any other visible achievements. You are a worthwhile person with or without any of these things.

It's important to realize, too, that some people who have very high expectations of others—especially their children—may not feel very good about themselves. Since they are not happy with themselves, they can never be completely pleased by anyone else. It could be that, as hard as you try, you'll never be able to please them. Their standards and rules will always be a step ahead of your achievements.

Alan, who had to work hard to get a "B" in math, sought to please his father by getting an "A" the second semester of his sophomore year. He worked overtime and neglected his friends, hobbies, and other studies. With great effort, he earned an "A-minus." When Alan proudly showed his dad the report card, his father shrugged. "Your other grades have all gone down, and besides, an 'A-minus' is not an 'A,'" was all he said. Suddenly all the joy was gone for Alan and he felt the old sense of failure and fury at his father for not appreciating his efforts.

If this could be *your* story, it's vital to set your own goals and to do your best for *you*. If you know that you're trying and that you're working for reasons and goals that are entirely your own, a parent's unrealistic expectations might not hurt quite as much. You might even be able to regard your perfectionistic parent with compassion—as someone who is unable to share so many joys and so many kinds of victories with you. That parent is missing a lot!

If you find yourself being punished despite your best efforts, try talking with an adult who might be able to help you and to intercede for you. This might be another parent, your favorite teacher, your school counselor, a caring relative, your clergyman, your physician, or a family counselor. Someone else who cares may be able to help your parents to encourage you in more realistic and constructive ways or, at least, to help *you* feel good about yourself despite your parents' unrealistic expectations.

Many teens feel torn between parental expectations and what they want for themselves. Some, like David, ask, "What do I owe my parents?" We owe our parents respect and a listening ear. You can respect their desire for you to do well. You can listen to their dreams, ideas, and goals for you. But, in the final analysis, you owe it to yourself to choose what's right for you and to do the best you can—for *you*.

HURT FEELINGS

My parents are always telling their friends about my so-called funny reactions to little, but important, private things. And these friends of my parents tease me about these. I've asked my parents to stop, but they say I should be able to take it in order to have a sense of humor and a good personality. What do I do?

Upset

I want to be a writer and have won several writing contests, but here's my problem: my dad is always telling me that I'm going to be a nothing and that I'm nobody. I think everyone—including myself—is somebody special, but he's hurting me a lot!

John Z.

I'm writing about a friend of mine I'll call Jamie. She's 14 and her mom is always calling her "tramp" and "prostitute." It's not true! Jamie doesn't even go out with guys yet. She doesn't smoke or drink or take drugs of any kind.

She's a real sweet kid and it just kills her when her mom says those things to her. Please help!

Sara G.

I feel so bad because I have this habit of making fun of my folks in ways that hurt them, I think. I don't know why I do this or how to stop.

Frank L.

Criticism, derision, or rejection from those we love hurts the most—and we may hurt each other in a number of ways.

You or your parents may be hurt by barbed humor or ridicule. Often this has little to do with the subject at hand and a lot to do with unexpressed feelings of competitiveness, hostility, and anger. If you find yourself having fun at someone's expense, stop and ask yourself what you're feeling and trying to express. Then you might try to find a more direct and constructive way to say how you're feeling.

If you—like "Upset"—find yourself the victim of constant teasing and violated confidences, you might try telling your parents how upset and embarrassed you feel. Anything that hurts so much is *not* funny and certainly no personality builder. You develop a good personality (including a sense of humor) by having the sense that you're loved no matter what and by feeling good about yourself. Only when you feel secure in this way can you laugh at yourself. Having others laugh at you, reinforcing your growing pains, is quite another matter. If talking with your parents doesn't help, enlist the aid of a caring relative or show your parents this section and talk about it—how your situation may be similar and how you feel about it. Your parents may not really mean to hurt you so much with their jokes. They may simply forget that perhaps you don't yet have enough experience and self-confidence to laugh at yourself a lot.

If your parents are extremely critical and even cruel in their comments—like saying you're a nothing and will never amount to anything, keep in mind—as John is trying to do—that *everyone* is somebody special. So are you. If you have a very negative, critical parent who seems to have a need to tear you down, this parent is probably suffering a bout of self-hate and, because he or she sees you as an extension of himself or herself, can't see anything good about you either. Realizing that this is a serious problem—an unrealistic, unfair observation on your parent's part—may help keep your self-esteem intact. You might try looking to others for encouragement—your other parent, a close friend or relative, a favorite teacher. There are a number of caring people in your life who can give you some of the loving affirmation that a troubled parent might not be able to give.

If you find yourself being very critical of a parent, stop and think before you say something. Maybe your dad tells dumb jokes or your mother's singing is just awful—in your estimation. If you have the urge to say something hurtful, ask yourself what purpose it would serve. It might be more constructive to say nothing. Alicia's mother, for example, loves to play the piano and sing most afternoons. She isn't very good at either, but it's a way to relax and unwind after work and she enjoys it. Alicia has learned to bite her tongue and keep quiet. "Mom enjoys singing and I guess it doesn't *really* matter whether she's good or not," Alicia says. "Personally, it bugs me to hear her singing off key, but I don't say anything about it anymore. I just smile and then disappear into my room, put my stereo headphones on, and turn the volume up and escape! That way, no one feels bad!"

Unfair labels can be a particular problem for teens—especially girls whose parents label them in ways that suggest that they are sexually promiscuous. What these labels are doing is expressing your parents' fears that you *will* do such things. Unfortunately, these labels *can* be self-fulfilling. That is, some teens, feeling hurt and angry that their parents don't trust them, may act in ways that make such labels reality—as long as they're getting the blame for such actions regardless. This kind of negative acting out, which is not a positive choice, but a reaction against parental labeling and lack of trust, can be hurtful to all concerned.

Unfair labeling can be a difficult problem to confront, but if your parents start to do this to you, it might help to express your feelings and your understanding of the fears behind their labels. For example, Jamie might say "I feel really hurt when you call me a tramp. I feel you don't trust me. I get the feeling that you're afraid that I'm sexually active or promiscuous. I'm neither. I appreciate your concern for me, but I wish we could express caring in ways that don't hurt. I need you to trust me."

Parents and teens can hurt each other, too, by an inability to express loving feelings. If you can't always *say* what you feel, you can still show love in little but important ways—by being thoughtful, by being there for each other when it counts, by being gentle with each other's feelings.

FIGHTING

I don't get along with my parents. We fight a lot. I have to admit I'm terrible with them—mouthing off a lot. But

they have this habit of nagging and yelling. What can we do?

Troubled

My mom and I usually get along and enjoy each other. But she'll get mad over little things from time to time and not speak to me for days! She won't talk to anyone when she's upset. What can I do when she's like this?

Les A.

I have a problem with my dad. He's been a terrible grouch since being laid off. It's impossible to get along with him. What can I do?

Bonnie C.

My parents and I sure fight about enough things—everything, in fact. But we never seem to solve anything with our fights. How can we start to solve some of our problems?

Jed F.

My mother and sister are always picking on each other. My poor dad—who's a hardworking doctor—tries everything to get them to be more loving with each other, but he's starting to get sick of the whole thing. I'm scared that my parents might break up over this. What can we all do?

Sally S.

Fighting can cause everyone in your family a lot of grief. Although it isn't usually possible to live together without disagreeing or irritating one another at times, it *is* possible to break a hurtful and nonproductive cycle of fighting.

Some people feel that fighting signals a lack of or breakdown in communication. Actually, people who fight with each other *are* trying to communicate. The people—and families—in deep trouble are those who don't try to express their feelings in *any* way. Families who fight just need to learn more effective, constructive *styles* of communicating.

If, like Jed, you and your parents go around and around about a number of topics and never resolve anything, you need to break this pattern of faulty communication.

The best way to do this is to agree—in a calm and cool moment—to do it. Sit down together and think about things all of you may be doing to keep fights going. Everyone probably has habits that trigger and perpetuate fights. Maybe you complain and fuss or whine. Maybe your parents nag you a lot. Maybe you're all in the habit of yelling and reacting without really hearing each other.

If you can identify problem habits that spark fights and try to change them, that's an important first step.

What if your parent has a fight-provoking habit that you've noticed and want to discuss? Bring it up tactfully. For example, Les might start a discussion of his mom's "silent treatment" by telling her how much he likes their closeness but how distressed he feels when they can't seem to communicate. Asking her how she feels when she is silent for so long rather than criticizing her behavior may help him to understand why she reacts this way and help her to see how this affects her son. Talking honestly in this way may help you and your parents, too, to start communicating in a more constructive way.

After discussing problem habits, you might try to list problem issues that have been the subjects of frequent battles. Each person should get a turn to talk about his or her feelings without being interrupted. Maybe setting a timer for five minutes each—and making a huge effort not to interrupt one another or stop listening—can help bring some controversial issues to the *discussion* level and everyone's feelings about these out into the open.

Next, try to see an issue from the other's point of view. There are several ways to do this. Family counselor Sheri Kesselman sometimes asks her clients to reverse roles.

"In one instance, a mother and daughter had been fighting about the fact that the daughter had come in two hours late the previous Saturday night," says Ms. Kesselman. "So we did a little role-reversal. The daughter played her mother and the mother played the daughter coming in at two A.M. from a date. Suddenly, the daughter saw the conflict from a new perspective. She had always seen her parents' concern for her as a bother and a curtailment of her freedom. However, when she was playing the role of her mother, things looked very different to her. She worried about the possibility of an auto accident and so on—like any mother would. This gave her a new understanding of how her mother felt and why she reacted the way she did."

If you choose not to try role playing, you might simply decide to ask "How do (did) you feel when I came in late?" or whatever the issue happens to be.

Once your feelings are out in the open, you can work at some sort of compromise. For example, if your parents promise not to nag, you might agree to do the dishes without complaining. Some families find it helpful to draw up a formal contract to deal with a recurring problem.

Counselors Carol and Andrew Calladine (who have several teenagers and have written a book called *Raising Siblings*) suggest that contracts can be helpful in settling conflicts over use of the stereo, family car, or television, or the assignment of chores.

The Calladine family, for example, has developed a special contract for use of the stereo. It allows an hour a day use for each family member with a weekly sign-up sheet to ensure each person a specific time slot. Those who violate the terms of the contract lose use of the stereo for a week.

"We save contracts for repetitive problems or cooperation issues," says Carol Calladine. "When it is used, then we all know that we mean business."

Some of these techniques may *seem* very contrived and artificial, but they may help your family break old patterns and habits and start getting through to each other. If you try these exercises with an open mind, you may be amazed at how well they might work for you!

It's important to realize that *some* fights are expressions of feelings that have little—if anything—to do with the issues at hand. For example, Bonnie's dad, who has just been laid off, may be feeling depressed and worried about the future and about finances. He may tend, because of this, to overreact to small problems or irritations. If you have a parent who is going through an emotional crisis, try not to worry or upset him or her needlessly. Being sensitive to each other's feelings during difficult times can help stop fights and start better communication.

It's important to realize, too, that you and your parents can't always solve your own problems, even with the best intentions. When fighting is terribly disruptive and repetitive—as it is with Sally's mother and sister—it may be time to seek professional help, such as family counseling, to resolve the matter. Sometimes in a crisis, we are not able to help those we love most. An objective, skilled professional counselor can make a great difference, helping your family to find new hope and peace.

PARENTS' MARRIAGE PROBLEMS

My parents are always fighting. I'm sure they hate each other. I wish sometimes that they'd get a divorce and stop all this. Do you think I should suggest to them that they get a divorce or should I just butt out?

Confused

My mother is always trying to confide in me about things I don't think I should know about—like how she can't stand to have sex with my father and how they can't communicate. It embarrasses me to hear all that stuff and, being only 17 and never having been married, I don't know what to tell her. I told her she ought to talk to a doctor or counselor or someone, but she said we shouldn't take our problems outside the family. But I don't want to HEAR any more about her sex life. I can't handle it, yet don't know what to say to her.

Kimberly J.

I know almost for a fact that my dad is messing around on my mom. What's worse, it's with a lady who pretends to be Mom's best friend! I won't go into all the details here, but I'm fairly sure Dad and this woman are lovers. Nobody knows that I know. Should I tell Mom? I'm upset and don't know what to do.

Bruce W.

If your parents are having marital problems, it can be a confusing and stressful situation for everyone in your family. You may be wondering what you might do to make things better—whether you should try to act as a mediator in their battles or leave well enough alone. Or you might be toying with the idea of unifying your parents with problems of your own (like school hassles or running away).

In most instances, it is best to stay out of your parents' relationship problems as much as you can. In the first place, it's impossible—even for you—to know what's really happening in their marriage. Some couples go through growing pains on the way to a new level of love and understanding. Strife can bring necessary changes. Some couples are trying to decide whether or not to stay together. Some couples who fight a lot may really love each other deeply and have no intention of breaking up. Others who never fight may grow apart and surprise everyone with a divorce. So you never know what the needs of a couple—even your parents—are.

Carol, who used to wonder why her mother ever stayed with her tyrannical, demanding spouse, has slowly come to realize that her mother is a very dependent and submissive person who doesn't have the desire to change and who actually wants someone to tell her what to do all the time. Although the marriage seems terrible to Carol, it seems to be meeting her parents' needs. So you can't really tell—from the outside looking in—what your parents' best alternatives might be.

Second, if you try to intervene in your parents' marital problems, you may find yourself more involved than you'd like to be. Then, if things don't go well, *you* may feel responsible. Your parents might begin to blame you for the problems that are really all theirs. (That's easy to do in stressful moments.) Or they might avoid or postpone seeking professional marriage counseling, possibly until it's too late for such counseling to be of any help.

What if your parents try to involve you, by asking your opinion or telling you more than you'd like to hear about their intimate problems? You might try being gentle but firm in your refusal to give advice or get involved. For example, when Kimberly's mother tries to confide in her again about her sexual problems, Kim might say "Mom, I'm really sorry that you're feeling so upset. I care about your feelings, but I feel uncomfortable hearing such intimate details about you and Dad. I know you feel strongly about keeping such problems in the family, but they're not getting solved. It might help change the situation if you could talk with our doctor or with a family counselor. He or she could help you much more."

If your parents try to get you into a fight that's really between them, refuse to take sides. Saying something like "I love you both and I don't want to keep you from working out your problems your own way" might help.

A third reason for keeping a low profile in parental disputes is that your involvement might precipitate a crisis. For example, if Bruce tells his mother about his father's alleged infidelity, it could unleash a number of problems Bruce can't anticipate. Many marriage partners, for example, know that their mates aren't faithful, but for any number of personal reasons, choose not to rock the boat. Maybe Bruce's mother senses the situation but is choosing to ignore it, knowing that it will end eventually. Maybe she is keeping quiet to save face. If Bruce brings the matter to her attention, however, she may feel humiliated and/or compelled to do something—have a confrontation, leave, or file for divorce—that she would not especially want to do. It could be that Bruce's parents have a mutual agreement about looking the other way and ignoring infidelities and would resent Bruce's intervention into this private area of their lives. It could be, too, that Bruce has misunderstood or jumped to conclusions about his dad's relationship with the other woman, and telling his mother would bring both his parents a lot of unnecessary grief and maybe even damage their relationship beyond repair.

Although you can't realistically hope to solve your parents' problems for them, you can help by making as few demands on them as possible during this stressful time and by trying to understand if they seem a little moody or withdrawn at times.

If their fighting is really getting to you, try telling them—during a lull in a battle and in a calm tone—how upset you're feeling. You might suggest that your clergyman (or clergywoman) or a marriage counselor might be able to help them. But you can't insist that they go. When it gets to be too much for you, get out of the house. Spend time with friends. Get involved in after-school activities. Take a long walk or bike ride. Go to the library or movies. Talk with a caring friend or relative. In short, try to live your own life as much as possible while they work on theirs.

DIVORCE

My life is falling apart. My parents got divorced recently and I hardly ever see Dad and Mom cries a lot and yells at me for nothing. We had to give up our house and move in with Grandma (who bugs me about every little thing) and I'm in a new school where everyone is really stuck-up and hates me. Sometimes I wonder if it's all my fault and if Dad would have left if I'd fussed less or kept my room neater.

Marta M.

My parents are getting a divorce, which is kind of a relief after all the fighting they were doing. But they are both so hateful toward each other that each one gets upset if I have anything good to say about the other. I'm feeling torn between them.

Matthew H.

I'm really disappointed in my parents for getting a divorce. They didn't even try to work things out! I have this dream that they'll get back together and so I hate it when they go out with other people instead of each other. How could I help get my parents back together?

Amy Y.

If your parents are divorcing or have already divorced, you may be experiencing a myriad of feelings.

You may feel pain at watching the love between your parents fade and at losing your family as you've always known it. You may also be wondering whether, if your parents can cease to love each other, they might also cease to love you.

You may feel guilty, wondering if you might have caused some of your parents' problems.

You may feel confused and afraid of what the future might bring.

You may resent some of the changes in your life: less money, more responsibility, less time to yourself or less time with either parent, a move to a new home and/or new school, the loss of certain luxuries.

You may feel angry at your parents for not working their problems out in a way that would allow them to stay together or for being so caught up in their own pain that they can't always see yours.

Or you may feel relieved that your parents have finally split and that the sullen silences, heated battles, and high tension are no longer part of your daily life.

You may be wondering if there's still a possibility that all this could be undone—and your parents could be happy together again.

"Many teenagers have a difficult time accepting the reality of a divorce," says Dr. Randi Gunther, a psychologist noted for her work with teenagers. "They can't give up their dreams of the family being reunited. They feel that wishing might make it so."

Wishing rarely makes it so, however, and this realization can be especially painful.

Accepting and dealing with your parents' divorce can take time. This process of acceptance involves working through your grief and anger in several stages—much as you would do with any major loss in your life. Some of these stages may occur close together. Some may happen before your parents actually divorce. But all are normal reactions to the losses that divorce can bring.

"The first stage is *denial*," says Dr. Gunther. "Here, you can't face the fact that this is happening to your family. You may think about all the good times you've had together and may dream of somehow getting your parents back together."

When you realize that this probably isn't possible, your reaction—*rage*—signals the second stage of your grief. You may have fantasized that your parents split because of you and that, as a result, *you* might have the power to reunite them. Now, as you realize that you're powerless to change the situation, you may feel hurt and angry. You might feel some hate for your parents and vow that you'll never, ever make the mistake of loving or needing someone again, only to be hurt.

"It's important to accept the fact—eventually—that there will be times in your life when you won't always have power over your own destiny," says Dr. Gunther. "If you can't accept this fact, you may tend to keep avoiding emotional involvements."

As your rage subsides a bit, you may start to reflect quietly about your situation. "At this stage, you may grieve about a lot of things," says Dr. Gunther. "You may grieve about growing up and losing your childhood as well as about losing your family life as it once was. You may feel new resentment about your lifestyle changes and see the divorce in terms of what it's costing you."

Gradually, you may feel more energy and a frenetic desire to get involved in outside activities and/or to rebel, maybe provoking some fights with one or both of your parents to get some separateness from them.

Depression may follow the rebellion phase. "This can

be a painful time, but it means that you're on your way to adjusting to and accepting your situation," says Dr. Gunther. "You may think, 'Why me?' You may find yourself questioning the loyalty of friends. But as you go along in this phase, you begin to really accept what has happened."

Not everyone, of course, moves through this process quickly, easily, or alone. If you're like most people, you'll need the support of your family and friends, and maybe an understanding relative, teacher or counselor to help you sort out your feelings.

In coming to terms with your parents' divorce, you may come to realize that your parents can lose their love for each other without ceasing to love you, and that if one parent doesn't seem to love you anymore, it doesn't mean that you're not lovable. You may also realize that this experience, however painful, may contribute to your personal growth.

"I grew up a lot and realized that I couldn't always have my way," says 16-year-old Jim. "I began to realize that my parents were people with a right to have lives of their own. Before, I had just seen them as *my* parents. When I saw them as more human, it made it easier for me to feel independent from them and yet care a lot for them too."

Fifteen-year-old Diane observes: "I used to be pretty helpless, like a lot of my friends, but now I've learned to cook, shop, budget, and make lots of decisions on my own. I've done a lot of thinking, too, about how I want my life to be. I don't want to be in my mom's spot ever: divorced with three kids and no work skills or experience, 36 years old and working at a boring, low-paying job. I want to get a good education and have a career whether or not I get married. I don't think I'd get married right out of school like my parents did. I want to have a life of my own."

What do you do when your parents are divorced and try to use you to get information about each other? I'm going bananas!

Tanya S.

My mother has been dating a certain man for several years. I don't especially like him, but my mom does a lot. Yesterday I was emptying the trash and found a used condom that was apparently used by my mother and her boyfriend. I'm so upset and ashamed. They could at least get married—not that I'd approve of that either, though.
Cynthia R.

My parents are divorced and remarried and I don't belong anywhere. Technically, I live with my mother and her

husband who ignores me (which is okay by me) except when his two brats (ages 7 and 10) come to visit every other weekend. They bug me a lot, but he always takes their side! It isn't much better at my dad's place. His new wife is only 22 (I'm 14) and she tries to act big and do a mother act. Either way, it's hard to take. Any suggestions?

Bob M.

Adjusting to the realities of your parents' divorce can mean facing new and confusing situations.

Your parents—like Tanya's—may attempt to use you as a go-between. If this is the case with you, remember that it takes three to play this game. You may be able to stop this hurtful game by refusing to go along with it. You might say that you love them both and would like the freedom to enjoy them both without spying on one or being interrogated by the other. Your parents probably don't mean to hurt you in this way, but are so caught up in their own feelings of anger and grief that they don't realize how you might be affected by such game playing. It may be up to you to *tell* them how you feel.

You may also find yourself faced with adjusting to new people in your parents' lives. Sometimes you may not agree with their choice of dates or may disapprove of their sexual activities. It may help to remember that your parents are separate from you. Their choices do not reflect on you and they—like you—are entitled to some privacy. It may help to concentrate on your own friends and your own social life, develop your own separate world, living according to *your* own choices.

When a parent—particularly the parent you live with most of the time—remarries, it can be a big adjustment. A new stepmother or stepfather and maybe stepsiblings as well can mean a lot of changes in your life, less privacy, more aggravation. But there is also the potential for new discoveries, new love, and new joy. When faced with a parent's remarriage, remember that your situation will probably not match any stereotypes you have in mind. Few stepmothers (or stepfathers) are truly wicked and few are the answer to your dream of having an ideal new parent. If your own parents are less than perfect (an almost certain possibility!), it isn't fair to expect perfection of a new stepparent. Most will have a lot of adjusting to do—not only to a new marriage, but also to you. It may take you a long time to get used to living with each other. You may end up being very close—or you may not. But you *can* learn to tolerate one another.

If you have stepsiblings, you might feel intense rivalry with them, especially at first. You may feel jealous when their natural parent takes their side in an argument or betrayed when your own parent—in an effort to get to know them—shows them a lot of attention and seems to favor them over you. "You may feel that there isn't enough nurturing to go around," says Dr. Alayne Yates, a psychiatrist whose thirteen children include seven of her own and six live-in stepchildren. "Unless your parents are Super-Parents, there probably *isn't* enough nurturing right now. You might look to grandparents, other relatives, and friends to fill the gap during this transition."

Dr. Yates feels that family meetings can be very helpful for families brought together by parental remarriage, especially when stress and rivalry may run high. "With a regularly scheduled family conference, you can share feelings and discover problem issues," she says. "Some parents feel a lot of stress, especially when the kids are divisive, taking sides against the stepparent or stepsiblings. And many kids feel jealous or a genuine sense of loss when there are suddenly more people sharing their parent's attention and love. Talking about these feelings with each other and setting up rules together can help. It may help to remember, too, that this stress is common at first and that time will help. In my own family, it took about three years for everyone to adjust and accept one another. In the meantime, family conferences, which give everyone a chance to be heard, can help a lot."

FAMILY CRISES

Alcoholism

My mother is an alcoholic. I almost never see her sober. It's bad because I can't talk to her about anything and am afraid to invite any friends over because I don't know how she'll be. My dad works all the time and I feel very alone. What can I do?

Anne B.

Dad drinks beer from the time he gets up until he falls into bed dead drunk at night. He thinks he isn't an alcoholic because he just drinks beer and he says he can handle his liquor. But he can't! He's great when he's sober (which isn't often), but when he's drunk, he gets mean and yells at everybody. Mom is afraid he's going to lose his job because of his drinking. I suggested that he go to Alcoholics Anonymous, but he started yelling "I'm not an alcoholic!" All I know is, things are really bad and I don't know what to do.

Rick D.

Life is undeniably painful for the son or daughter of a person with a drinking problem—whether or not that person will admit that he or she is an alcoholic.

You may miss the companionship of your parent. You may feel stress over family fights caused by his or her drinking. You may feel too ashamed to invite friends over because of your parent's unpredictable behavior. Your parent's irresponsibility may force you to assume extra responsibilities early in life. You may be hurt when a drunk parent turns on you and says terrible things. Even the tearful apologies later (if they ever come) don't completely ease the pain. You may wonder what you can do to help change the situation.

"Wanting to help and to solve the problem is a common reaction," says family counselor Doris Lion. "However, it's important to realize that *you* can't help the alcoholic in your family. The more you try to help by making excuses for that person or defending him so that he doesn't feel the consequences of his actions, the more you maintain the problem. The alcoholic has no motivation to change unless things get very, very bad for him or her."

It takes motivation and an admission that he or she is an alcoholic to get a person with a drinking problem to go to A.A.—which does a lot of good for the people who are able to reach that point.

In the meantime, seeking help for yourself can often be more constructive. Help is available for families and children of alcoholics through A.A.-related organizations called Al-Anon and Ala-Teen. Both are nationwide groups which should be listed in your local telephone directory.

Doris Lion observes that "these groups can help you to realize that we are all separate and that we can only be responsible for our *own* behavior."

In such a group, you can learn to act in ways that *don't* encourage and reinforce your parent's drinking habits and, at the same time, share your feelings with other people your age (at Ala-Teen) who really understand because they are living with the same situation. Knowing that you are not alone and that you *can* cope with this very difficult situation can be a great consolation.

Serious Illness

My mother has cancer. She's in and out of the hospital a lot. We don't have much money. I've had to take over everything—cooking, cleaning, and taking care of my two little brothers as well as going to school and doing homework. What's bad is I have no life of my own. I can't go out with my friends because Pop wants me home with the family. I can't have them over because he thinks they might make noise and bother my mother when she's trying to rest. I really love my mother, but this has been going on for over two years! She isn't getting particularly worse, but she isn't better either. I cry and feel bad for her, but I feel bad for me sometimes, too.

Lynda N.

A serious illness can affect a family in very stressful ways—with worry, grief, financial strains, and added responsibilities for everyone. While you can't change the reality of illness in your family, you *can* possibly find ways to change some aspects of the situation.

Talking with someone outside the family—a hospital social worker or counselor (many hospitals and cancer treatment centers have these to help families cope with the stress of serious illness), your clergyman, or a youth or family counselor may help you to resolve some of your feelings of grief, anger, and guilt. He or she may be able to help you to explore ideas for changing your situation in small but important ways.

It may help, too, to talk with your parents about your feelings of wanting to help yet needing to have some time of your own. Lynda, for example, might be able to invite one or two friends over to visit on the condition that these visits not coincide with her mother's rest periods and that they keep the noise level down.

Relatives, too, may be able to ease the burden of the immediate family by helping out, from time to time, with cooking or babysitting chores or just by listening to you talk about your feelings.

Talking about your feelings and finding compromises that will let you have some free time can give you an important morale boost. You may feel a renewed spirit of love and commitment to helping your family through the crisis of a major illness.

Physical, Sexual, or Emotional Abuse

I'm scared to death and don't know what to do. My father can't control his temper, even over little things like dinner not being right on time or one of us not moving fast enough to please him when he asks for something. He beats Mama, my brother Ted (who's 10), and me. I have bruises all over and Ted got beat so bad last night he couldn't hardly catch his breath afterwards. I've begged Mama to leave and take us somewhere else, but she says she's too scared, couldn't get a job, and besides he'd find us wherever we went. I'm afraid he'll kill us sometime. I'm only 13 and. . .

Desperate!

You've got to help me. I feel like killing myself because last night when my mom was at church, my stepfather raped me. He said he'd do worse than that if I told anyone. I'm scared to tell Mom anyway because she wouldn't believe me or would think I encouraged him (I swear I didn't! I've never even liked him at all. Now I can't stand the sight of him.) I'd rather die or run away than have him touch me again. Help me, please!

Patti F.

I've been depressed and wondering where I'm going in life and my parents aren't making it very easy for me. They think I'm worthless because I was the "mistake" that caused them to get married. They blame all their problems on me. Dad says I'd be better off dead and offered to lend me his gun. I wouldn't kill myself to satisfy him, that's for sure, but I don't know how to help myself either.

Sam J.

As these letters show, there are several general types of abuse: physical, sexual, and emotional. While these examples represent extreme family crises, they *are* real letters— and there are many teens in similar situations who are not able to ask for help—even in a letter. Such serious family problems are the exception rather than the rule, but are still a lot more common than anyone would like. When you're growing up in such a family situation, the experience can be devastating.

All of these abuse situations represent family problems that are too serious and complex to be handled or resolved within the family. Outside professional help is vital.

"Ideally, this would mean counseling for the whole family," says Doris Lion. "You might take the first step by encouraging one or both parents to seek out help. Or, if this isn't possible, ask for help yourself. Talk with a teacher, school counselor, clergyman, or to a hotline for emergency help and referrals."

Many teens in such circumstances—especially if physical or sexual abuse is involved—are afraid to ask for help, fearing that help will not be there and that their parents will abuse them even more, turn against them, or even kill them, or that they will be put into foster care and face an uncertain future.

However, alternatives are growing. For example, with the advent of shelters and halfway houses for battered wives and their children, people like "Desperate" and her family don't have to stay in an intolerable situation. There are no easy answers to coping with and protecting yourself from abuse. But you *can* find help and support if you take the first step and ask someone to help you.

"Keep in mind that you must try to protect yourself,"

says Ms. Lion. "You may be able to get help for your family and to change the situation. In the case of physical abuse, especially if both parents are abusive, you may have to get out of the family setting."

In the case of sexual abuse (which will be discussed in more detail in Chapter Eleven), there are also a number of possibilities for help. If you feel you can't tell your other parent (or if that parent doesn't believe you or is not supportive), you can tell some other adult—a teacher, neighbor, counselor, or concerned relative—who might help you. You can also call an emergency hotline for referral to appropriate help in your community, or call (or ask an adult friend to call) your local Children's Protective Services Agency, which should be listed in your telephone directory or available through Information. Do seek help. There is no reason for you to live with abuse of any kind.

Dealing with emotional abuse can be particularly difficult since it doesn't leave visible scars and doesn't always have the shock value to others that beatings or sexual abuse do. But constant emotional abuse is no less harmful.

As in other forms of abuse, you may come to assume the blame for your parents' obvious problems and may feel that you deserve to be abused.

This is *not* the case! With help from a caring youth or family counselor (often available at free clinics, youth clinics, or your local Family Service Agency for little or no money) plus support from other relatives and friends, you may come to see that an abusive parent is a troubled person who may have been abused, too, in his or her youth and who can express anger, hostility, and frustration only in abusive ways.

"It can be difficult to see that, when abuse is heaped on you, it is due to a parent's problem, but that's the way it is," says Ms. Lion. "Counseling can help you to get some distance from the situation and help you realize that your abusive parent is troubled and, most important, that *you* are not to blame!"

Living through and with such a family crisis can leave your feelings in a turmoil. You may wonder if you'll ever be able to love and trust anyone or if you'll ever be happy.

While some people may live lives scarred by pain and bitterness, others survive the worst possible home situations to live happy, normal adult lives. You can, too. Your attitude about your present crisis can have a huge impact on your life in the years to come.

There are three things you need to keep in mind when you're trying to survive and overcome of the pain of abuse, according to Doris Lion.

First, there are some elements in your home life that can't be changed. You can't cure or wish away your parent's problem, make everything fine for someone who won't seek help or face his or her problems, or transform someone who, for a variety of reasons, is unable to love. You can, however, make changes in yourself and in your life . . . changing the way you cope with your problems and knowing that it's possible to grow beyond your present pain.

Second, realize that your parent's problems are NOT yours. "You must see yourself as separate from your parents," says Ms. Lion. "This letting go may take time, but you *must* let go of the dream of changing a parent and realize that their problems are their own. When you're feeling separate, you may be able to forgive them and then go on with your life."

Third, in order to be free, you must forgive your parents. When you're having so much pain, it may be almost impossible to think of forgiveness. Instead, you may feel an urge to strike back at your parents and to hurt them as they have hurt you.

Unfortunately, prolonged feelings of revenge can keep you tied to a painful situation for years—even after it has ceased to exist! Some people lead bitter, unhappy lives, sometimes sabotaging their own dreams and goals to get back at their parents for long-ago problems. They only succeed in perpetuating their own pain.

Blaming ties us to the past. Revenge can hold us back from doing what we really want to do and need to do in order to grow past our pain to new, more positive experiences. In order to grow and go on, you must let go of your past and forgive.

"It's important to see your parents as people who made mistakes," says Ms. Lion. "Sometimes their mistakes hurt you. Instead of being bitter, tell yourself that your parents did the best they could at the time. Then let it go."

Forgiving does not mean denying or minimizing what happened or the pain you're feeling as a result, but it will eventually free you to find your own ways to be happy.

"You may always feel some hurt, but forgiving your parents sets you free to value yourself and to live for *you*—not them," says Ms. Lion. "You will be free to reach out to others, free to trust and free to love."

GROWING TOWARD BETTER COMMUNICATION

My parents and I don't communicate. They don't understand me at all. How can we start to talk to each other instead of just arguing?

Michael K.

Good communication with your parents takes a lot of time and effort to work out. There are no easy, instant steps to good communication, but there *are* some ideas that may help you begin to work out some solutions to the communication gap in your home.

Better communication begins with mutual respect for each other as people. You respect your individual differences. You have realistic expectations about each other. It is not reasonable to expect that your parents will ever be perfect, all-giving, always patient, and always wise. If you can see them as people who just happen to be parents as well, you will see two individuals who are capable of both wisdom and mistakes, who are sometimes patient and sometimes short-tempered, who can be resourceful in some instances and fearful and uncertain in others. Perhaps they can begin to see you, too, as an emerging individual who shares their lives but perhaps not all—or any—of their values, convictions, hopes, and dreams. If you can accept your separateness and agree to disagree with as much gentleness and respect as possible, you're on your way to better understanding and communication.

You may disagree—sometimes intensely. You may cry and rage and laugh together through the changes the next few years will bring. You may have very different ideas, very different lives, but if you can accept these facts, you and your parents may find that in spite of—or maybe even *because* of—your differences, you will always have much to share with each other.

CHAPTER THREE

Sibling Rivalry and Beyond

My problem is my obnoxious, spoiled-brat little brother. He gets away with everything. If he does something wrong, I get blamed! He's always innocent because he's Mom's precious little baby (age 9!). I can't stand it anymore!

Seething in Scarsdale

I have this older sister who thinks she knows it all. She's five years older than me and tries to boss me around all the time. How do I get her to leave me alone?

Kevin G.

I'm nobody's favorite. My dad and brother are real close and Mom and my sister tell each other everything! I'm all alone. Nobody even notices when I do something good, but my mom especially yells at me a lot. She says I have a stubborn streak just like her.

Hilary L.

Sibling rivalry is a fact of life for most families as siblings struggle for parental attention, personal space, and separate identities. Sibling battles can escalate in adolescence when your needs for space and attention are ever-growing—and ever-changing.

Psychologists are quick to point out that sibling rivalry *can* be useful.

"It is like a preview of the competitive situations you will encounter as an adult," says psychologist Dr. Arnold Dahlke. "With your siblings, ideally, you first learn how to negotiate, cooperate, and compromise."

"You learn early on that you will not always get your way," adds family counselor Doris Lion. "You learn techniques for getting what you want at least part of the time through assertiveness or persistence."

Sibling battles can be particularly intense if you and your brother(s) and sister(s) are close in age and/or if you're part of a large family where private space and time alone with parents are rare commodities. There can also be a lot of friction as you struggle with your own identity search and developmental changes. Once you feel more secure with your own changes and your own individuality, your fights with siblings may decrease.

Right now, however, you may be facing daily struggles. Maybe you feel that your parents favor a sibling and pick on you. Maybe you feel bossed around or bothered by a brother or sister. Maybe you feel that you get all the responsibilities and they have all the fun.

None of these feelings or situations is unusual. Although most parents love all their children deeply and try not to have favorites, it's difficult nevertheless to treat each one in exactly the same way. Your age, your individual temperament, and your parents' reactions to any number of traits you have can influence the way they relate to you, which can be quite different (though not necessarily less loving) from the way they treat others in your family.

If your parents relate to you in a different way, try to avoid falling into the trap of feeling unloved and worthless. Parents treat their kids differently for any number of reasons—most of them having nothing to do with lack of love.

For example, unlike most people in her family, who are very talkative and outgoing, Denise is quiet. It's harder for her to express her feelings. As a result, her parents don't talk with her as much and sometimes she feels lost in the shuffle. Denise's mother says, "Denise is a special person, but it's hard to know at times how she really feels. And I don't know the right questions to ask. She's so different from the others, but this doesn't mean that we don't love her just as much."

If Denise wants to feel more a part of her family, she needs to reach out in small ways. If she feels uncomfortable talking in larger gatherings, she might try asking for some private time to be with and talk with a parent or sibling.

If you have a parent—like Hilary's mother—who gets impatient with you because you're so like him or her, you're facing a very common problem. We often get most angry at others who share the traits we dislike in ourselves. If you and a parent or sibling are both stubborn or quick-tempered or moody in the morning, for

57

example, you might feel better about yourselves—and closer to each other, too—if you could talk about this shared trait and exchange ideas about how to cope with it. Asking each other's advice and trying to find ways *together* to compromise can ease a lot of tension between you.

THE BIRTH-ORDER FACTOR

If you have a bossy older sibling or a bothersome little one or if your parents expect you to be more responsible than the others *or* treat you like a baby and don't give you credit for being so grown-up, these frequent family conflicts could have a lot to do with your birth order.

A number of studies have been conducted recently on birth order—whether you're the firstborn, in the middle, or the youngest child in your family—and its impact on the way your parents treat you and the way you see yourself.

Birth order can often be a major factor when siblings differ greatly from each other despite having the same parents and the same basic home environment. Of course, temperament, physical traits, and other genetic traits matter a lot, too, and people can't be pigeonholed into strict categories, but a number of scientific studies are showing that your birth order can make you experience your home environment in a different way and that your parents may respond to you in unique ways, too.

If you're a firstborn child, you had your parents to yourself for *at least* most of your first year of life and probably somewhat longer than that. You got their undivided attention for a while. They probably talked to you more and fussed over you and expected more of you than they have of your younger brothers or sisters. Your parents may continue to ask a lot of you—expecting you to help out more, perhaps. You're more likely, because of your early attention from adults, to have more highly developed verbal skills and to be very responsible, a hard worker, and an achiever. On the other hand, you may also be a worrier, may be somewhat bossy, and may get really upset when you don't meet your own expectations, which tend to be high.

If you're a middle child, you may feel lost in the crowd or you may be a natural diplomat and good friend, having learned to cooperate and compromise early in life with your siblings on either side. A lot depends, of course, on your family size—whether you're the middle of three or the fifth of nine. Your sex can also be a factor. If you're a middle child, but an only son or daughter, you may get a lot of attention. If, on the other

hand, you're a middle child with same-sex siblings, you may get less than your share of attention. Dr. M. H. Kraut, a genetic psychologist, found in his studies that the middle child of three females may get the least attention and affection of all.

As a middle child, you probably have acquired a balanced view of authority. You can give or take orders and may be more outgoing and socially able than your other siblings.

If you're a youngest child, you may be babied or criticized, admired or ignored. Again, a lot depends on the size of your family and the age gap between you and your other siblings. You may get a lot of extra attention from everyone, but it could be, too, that the other members of your family are so busy with their own lives that they forget you at times. People may put you down as a baby—even when you're not—or may expect more of you than is reasonable. Maybe your parents don't make quite as much over your achievements because they've seen it all before and take it for granted that you'll be an achiever, too. Maybe you feel special or maybe you feel inadequate because everyone else in your family is bigger and more able right now. You may fluctuate between playing the role of the baby of the family and wanting to grow up fast. On the positive side, you may have a lot of creative talents and a strong sense of security and well-being. On the negative side, you may have trouble taking responsibility at times because less may have been expected of you.

These categories are just generalizations, of course, but you may be able to see some of yourself in one of them. Also, they may help you to understand how and why life is really different for each sibling in your family.

What can you do if you feel that you're being left out because you're older or younger or in-between?

Talking with your parents can help. "Don't approach them with angry accusations that they favor a brother or sister over you," suggests family counselor Dave Pounds. "They would probably just as angrily defend themselves. Instead, report your feelings with 'I' statements. You might say something like 'I feel left out sometimes' or 'I feel that I'm not valued.' Sometimes when parents constantly admire the beauty or grades or cuteness of one child, they really don't realize what they're doing to the others. Most parents won't say 'Hey, kid, you're ugly!' but they need to know how you feel and to be reminded that *you* need encouragement, attention, and praise, too. When you simply say how you feel, your parents won't be as defensive and may be very understanding."

If you have a bossy or bothersome sibling, you may also try talking with him or her in a nonaccusatory way.

With a know-it-all, for example, you might say something like "I appreciate the fact that you want to help me, but I need to learn to make my own decisions and do things for myself." Or if you feel jealous of a brother or sister, you might admit it and say why. You may be surprised to find that your sibling is also jealous of you—for some strong points and advantages you didn't know you had!

SIBLING COMPARISONS

Everyone in my family is better than me. My brothers are smarter, more athletic and popular, too. They win lots of honors and stuff. I'm just nothing compared to them.
                                                    Bill N.

I feel like half a person. I have this handsome, smart, and really NICE older brother that my parents treat like a king. They're OK to me, too, but you can tell they think John's really the special one. What bothers me most is that they call him by his name, but they never call me by mine (Cathy). Instead, they call me "Sis." It's like I'm not ME. I'm just my brother's sister. How can I start to feel better about myself?
                                                    Cathy C.

Sibling comparisons, whether they are made by your parents *or* by you, are not fair. You are a separate, unique person with your own array of positive and negative points. If you or your family haven't discovered yet how special you are, it's easy to make such hurtful comparisons. Perhaps a sibling wins more scholastic honors than you do and you feel like a nothing. It's important to realize that winning honors is something he or she does, but those honors do not define that person or make him or her better than you are. Your strengths may be in different areas. You may be very sensitive and wise in terms of people, for example, knowing how to comfort someone who's upset or how to make someone else feel good. Maybe, even though you don't have a lot of friends, the ones you *do* have are very close and special.

Getting stuck in the rut of making comparisons can be painful. Comparing yourself with someone else, it seems, usually ends up with you as the perpetual poor second (because you don't know as much about the other person and it's easier to idealize his or her life). Constant, usually unfavorable comparisons don't make you feel better and take energy and time that could be better spent finding out what's right—instead of wrong—with you!

"Remember that being different does *not* mean being inferior," says Dave Pounds. "There is something special about you. It may take time to accept yourself and to discover all your special qualities, but it's well worth the effort."

Your parents and siblings may be able to help you in many ways if you ask them.

Cathy, for example, might explain her feelings about her nickname to her parents and confide in them—and her brother—that she's having trouble feeling good about herself. She might even ask her brother—since they seem to be cordial with each other—"What do you think makes me special?" Her family probably feel that Cathy is very special in her own way and love her dearly, but may not feel it necessary to point this out to her . . . unless she makes her needs clear to them.

It may help to keep in mind that, because you *are* separate, unique, and your own person, your siblings' achievements don't really take anything away from you.

If your parents tend to label you and your siblings—like calling you "the smart one," another "the good-looking one," and another "the social one," it might help to talk with the others about how such labeling makes all of you feel. While many parents who do this do so with the best intentions (trying to make each child feel special), it can backfire and make everyone feel that they lack whatever the label doesn't include. Labels are usually too confining and inaccurate to be used on people. If you talk the matter over with your siblings, you will probably find that they resent being limited by their labels, too. After all, if your label says you're "smart" and your sister is dubbed "the pretty one," she may feel that your parents think she's dumb.

Then, separately or together, you might talk with your parents about how being categorized makes you feel. Communicating your feelings *can* make a difference!

CLINGING SIBLINGS

My little brother won't leave me alone. He bugs me constantly even though he knows it makes me mad. What can I do? My parents say he'll grow out of it, but he's driving me nuts!
                                                    Bugged

My 11-year-old sister wants to go everywhere with me, to the point of begging, crying, bribing, and screaming until she gets her way. Mom insists that I take her everywhere which can be a REAL DRAG!
                                                    Jennifer A.

Your siblings, like all of us, go through phases, and some of them (which may begin to look like permanent personality quirks for a while) involve annoying ways of seeking attention and trying to be close to you.

A brother or sister who bugs you a lot and who is always underfoot or a perpetual tease is often trying to get your attention the only way he or she knows how. The more you try to ignore him or her, the worse he or she gets. There are no absolute answers to this annoying problem, but taking time—occasionally—to give the sibling your undivided attention and perhaps planning a special outing the two of you can enjoy may help your sibling to feel secure enough to leave you alone at times. It may help, too, to tell him or her honestly: "I enjoy being with you sometimes. You're a good kid. I like you. But right now, I want to be left alone."

A younger sibling who wants to go everywhere with you—especially when he or she has the consent of your parents—can be a special trial. But here again, a compromise with your parents might ease the situation. Try to explain to them that, while you don't mind spending *some* time with your sibling, there are times when you would like to do something on your own or with friends your own age. If you offer to include your brother or sister *some* of the time, your parents are more likely to accept some sort of compromise.

SIBLINGS VERSUS FRIENDS

My brother has a habit of bugging my friends so much when they come over that no one wants to come over here anymore. He throws snowballs at us, makes rude noises, and tries to go through my friends' purses. It's just awful!
Jodie G.

My sister is only a year younger than I am and is very possessive of her friends. When one comes over and I say more than "Hi," she gets mad and starts telling me to stay away from her friends. I don't try to steal her friends! I'm just nice to them. SHE talks to all MY friends when they come over and I never get upset. What's the matter with her?

Puzzled

Rivalries over friends can be especially intense in the teen years—when friends are so special and important.

If you have a sibling (especially one of the opposite sex who is fairly close to you in age) who teases your friends relentlessly, it could be a (somewhat immature) bid for attention from your friends. He or she may find them attractive yet not know quite how to relate to them—except by teasing and being a pest. Or it could be that your sibling is jealous of your friendships.

Whether jealousy or attention-seeking is his or her

motivation, low self-esteem may be what is prompting your sibling's feelings and needs. Talk with your parents about this and try, too, to help build up your sibling's confidence so he or she can learn to respect your privacy and to relate to others in a more mature and reasonable way.

Low self-esteem can also cause a person to be very possessive of his or her friends. If a brother or sister feels threatened when you socialize with his or her friends, you might start trying to help him or her to feel more confident. Praise your sibling's good points. Let him or her feel valued, not only as a sibling, but also as your friend. As his or her confidence grows, he or she may be less afraid to share friends a little. Of course, it's important to watch your own behavior, too, to make sure that you don't try to take over a friend or exclude your sibling in any way while you socialize briefly. If you can show your good intentions and help your brother or sister to grow in confidence, new trust may flourish between you.

SIBLINGS VERSUS ROMANCE (YOURS)

My sister always steals my boyfriends and I hate her for it. She never keeps going with them. She just swipes them and then drops them after a few dates. Why does she act like this and what can I do about it?

Burned Up

I have a great boyfriend. So does my sister, who is a year younger than I am. We four double a lot and I'm getting to think I prefer her boyfriend to mine. How can I tell everyone this without hurting anybody?

Cece S.

Competition in love can be a particularly painful form of sibling rivalry which, in many cases, has little to do with the disputed loved one.

When a person like "Burned Up" 's sister has a continuing need to ruin a sibling's romances, it can indicate, once again, that that person's self-esteem is so low that he or she seeks constant reassurance—via competing for and stealing dates—that he or she is attractive and desirable. This form of one-upmanship, building oneself up at the expense of another, rarely if ever satisfies that feeling of inferiority and loneliness. So the person feels the need to compete again and again.

In the long run, such ploys can hurt one's reputation. (One 16-year-old girl with a boyfriend-stealing sister reports—with some satisfaction—that "a lot of guys at our school are beginning to realize that she's two-faced and they don't want to be *used* by her.") Hurting others can also be hazardous to a person's self-esteem, so while striving in hurtful ways to build herself up, this sibling is actually diminishing her self-respect.

If you're the victim of such a scheming sibling, it's vital to let him or her know how you feel. Keeping your anger locked inside may lead to a lifetime of resentment.

Counselor Dave Pounds recalls a client of his—an elderly woman—who often grumbled about her long-dead sister, remarking bitterly, "I never had a boyfriend that she didn't take away!"

"These feelings of hurt and anger have been with her for years, causing her a lifetime of unhappiness," says Pounds. "She never confronted her sister with her feelings. Instead, she locked them inside where they've been festering all these years like a deep wound."

You might point out to your sibling that she is not really helping herself by acting in this way and that she is certainly hurting you. Even if you can't get your sibling to see the error of his or her ways, you may feel better for having said something to let her know how angry you are.

Sometimes, a person may be so thoughtless and self-centered that he or she doesn't really consider how much he or she could hurt others while breaking up a sibling's love relationship.

Cece may well be one of these. If Cece happened to be your sister, telling her how hurt and angry you would feel about her desire for your boyfriend might be something of a revelation to her and might make her more aware of what *acting* on her impulses could involve.

If you find yourself identifying with Cece, wondering how to bring up the subject to all concerned, you might consider not saying anything at all . . . or doing anything either. Think about the relationship and what could happen if you intervene. Chances are, your sister would be hurt, her boyfriend could be embarrassed, and you could be rejected. And even if you "win," you really lose. You have hurt one or several people. You have lost the trust and possibly the love of someone who is really very important in your life. And you could lose a lot of self-respect as well.

If you are bored with a love relationship, try looking beyond your sibling's friends for someone new. If you feel a competitive need to win, try channeling it into an activity that won't be hurtful to anyone concerned.

SHARING THE SAME ROOM

I have to share a room with my brother, who is a total pig. I like things neat and hate it when my friends come over and see our room because of him. We live in a two-

bedroom apartment, so separate bedrooms are out of the question. I nag my brother to pick up after himself, but it isn't doing any good.

Steve H.

I'm embarrassed because I have to share a bedroom with my brother. I'm 13 and he's 11 and I get mad because he laughs at my bra and goes through my things. He's a number-one smart-aleck and I get no privacy. I want to sleep on the couch of Dad's den, but Dad says "No." What can I do?

Janet P.

While your own room is the best alternative, it isn't always possible in today's space and housing crunch. Like it or not, you may have to double up with a sibling.

(However, many psychologists believe that you should NOT share a room with a sibling of the opposite sex under any circumstances, especially in the teen years when both of you feel a great need for privacy. Some experts suggest that parents sacrifice a den, family room, or even the dining room to give their growing children of the opposite sex some space of their own and some privacy.)

If you're fated to share a bedroom with a sibling, there are ways you can keep problems to a minimum.

You might use room dividers, high bookcases or dressers, or even a curtain to mark off and define your own territory. You might make an agreement with your parents and sibling that each of you is responsible for decorating and cleaning his or her own territory only. That way, if you're stuck with a sloppy roommate, you won't get punished and penalized for his or her messes. (You also won't have to look at the mess as much if you get a good room divider!) And if *you* are the slob, you won't have to put up with all that nagging and hassling from your pristine roommate. You and you alone are responsible—for better or for worse—for the way your side of the room looks.

If room dividers don't give either of you the privacy you want or need sometimes (like when friends visit and you want to talk confidentially), you might come to an agreement—perhaps via a family contract—about a schedule that would allow each of you some private time—alone or with friends—in your room minus your sibling/roommate. If you make an effort to cooperate, giving each other the right to separate territory and private time, you can avoid a lot of fights and misunderstandings.

SIBLINGS IN TROUBLE

I'm worried about my brother, who drinks too much, which my parents don't seem to realize. He comes home late at night and throws up a lot. He also seems depressed and not at all the same person he used to be. Should I tell our parents? How can I help?

Wondering

Sometimes, parents who anticipate all kinds of conflicts in adolescence may think that a sign of serious trouble is just another phase. If you notice that a sibling seems severely troubled, it may help to bring it to your parents' attention—without necessarily going into any details about the sibling's behavior. You might just mention that your brother or sister seems to feel a bit depressed and wonder if your parents have noticed or know a way to help.

Better still, try talking with your sibling first. Express your love and concern as well as your willingness to help in any way you can. Sometimes a troubled person just needs someone to listen and try to understand. If a sibling has a drinking or drug problem, try to help him or her explore the feelings that might be causing him to try to escape. Even if your sibling angrily tells you to mind your own business at first, knowing that you realize a problem exists and care enough to mention it can help. You might encourage your sibling to seek help from parents or from counseling professionals. You can help, too, by just being there—loving, supportive, and willing to listen.

My older sister got pregnant when she was 16 and now I'm 16 and paying for her mistakes. My parents are very protective of me because of her. I'm not allowed to date at all . . . until I'm 18! I feel like I'm missing out on everything! What can I do about this?

Deb R.

When your family has experienced a crisis with a sibling, your parents may be twice as protective of you. Fear and concern make parents tighten restrictions and rules. If you feel—like Deb—that you're being made to pay, in a sense, for a sibling's mistakes, try talking with your parents and work toward a compromise.

Instead of accusing your parents of being unfair, emphasize *first,* that you appreciate their concern for you; second, that you are *not* your sibling but a separate individual; and third, that you are willing to discuss a compromise that everyone can live with.

For example, Deb might suggest that she be allowed to date on a limited basis—such as having a boy over to do homework, watch TV, or listen to records when her parents are home; going out to special dances, parties, or proms; double-dating with friends; or having an earlier curfew than most. While her social life might still be more restricted than that of the average 16-year-old, Deb might at least *have* a social life if she could show her parents that she's willing to live with some special restrictions.

A willingness to compromise (even at times when you'd rather not) is a sign of maturity. If you're willing to get your way in small steps, you may reach your goal of freedom sooner than if you rebel against all special restrictions, and you may earn your parents' trust along the way!

My brother is really spoiled because he just got diabetes and all the attention around here goes to him. I'm not allowed to have candy around because it might make him cheat on his diet. I'm mad!

Mary-Lee L.

My younger brother has cerebral palsy. He's a good kid, but I think our parents coddle him too much and don't let him do things for himself when he really could. Brett's doctor is always saying he should do as much for himself as he can, but he doesn't get a chance. Should I try to say something to my parents? They'll probably think I'm jealous of the attention they give him, but I'm not.

Allen D.

If a sibling of yours has a chronic illness or handicap, you may face some unique conflicts.

Maybe your parents devote so much attention and time to your brother or sister that you feel angry and neglected—and guilty for feeling that way.

Maybe your parents tend to be overprotective of your sibling, preventing him or her from utilizing his or her full potential—and you don't know how to help.

It could be, too, that your ill or handicapped sibling has become something of a tyrant, using his affliction or your parents' protectiveness to get his way all the time.

If you're feeling left out, it's important to think about your alternatives. If a sibling has a newly diagnosed illness like diabetes, things could settle down in a little while after everyone gets used to the special food and routines that he or she must follow. In the meantime, participating as much as you can in your sibling's care can get you involved and cut down on conflicts. Fixing special permissible snacks and helping a sibling exercise or care for himself or herself can help your family *and* make you feel good about yourself, too.

If your sibling will require constant care and you feel that you are always pushed aside, talk about your feelings with your parents, a close relative, or the hospital social worker. Your parents might be able to find a way—by taking turns or getting special help from relatives or health care aides—to spend some time alone with you when they realize that you need it so much.

If your parents are overprotective of your sibling, not allowing him to do some things for himself (including fending for himself in some sibling disputes, learning like everyone else to compromise), this could do more harm than good.

"Doing for a handicapped child what he could do himself or shielding that child from the reality of life, including sibling conflicts, can be a mistake," says Dr. Dahlke. "It's a way of keeping that person handicapped. It's best to allow a handicapped child or teenager to have as normal a life as possible."

Encourage your parents to let your sibling be as independent as possible. Offer to help teach your brother or sister a vital skill—with a lot of praise for his efforts. Talk with or encourage your parents to talk with your sibling's doctor or physical therapist to learn which tasks your sibling might master—and how these could best be taught.

UNDERSTANDING YOUR DIFFERENCES

I can't believe how different my sister and I are. I'm very loving and open. I love to hug and touch people. My 12-year-old sister turns off to physical affection and she calls me a weirdo when I'm open like that. Yet she is loving in her own way. She's a nice person. But why is she so different from me?

Jackie W.

People have different ways of showing they care. Some—like Jackie—can be very open, talking about their loving feelings and touching to show affection. Others are uncomfortable with such demonstrativeness and are embarrassed at times to say how they really feel. Some show their love by being thoughtful, doing favors for others without being asked. Others use gifts as a sign of affection. Still others tease and joke with those they love.

Realizing that we all show love in different ways, you may be able to recognize the various love styles of people in your family, and you won't feel put down if they don't respond to you in quite the way you do to them. It is important to respect their differences and appreciate

their efforts to show their love for you in whatever way they can.

GETTING AND STAYING CLOSE

You may think this is pretty stupid, but it's important to me. My older brother went off to college a month ago and I miss him a lot. I'm afraid he'll change and not be the same after this and that we won't be close anymore. What do you think could happen? Can two people still be close even when one changes?

Jeremy U.

I'd like to be close to my brother and really talk with him about feelings and such, but I'm afraid he'd make fun of me. Then I'd really feel bad. I'd like to be close, but I don't know how. Should I just give up for now and wait until we're grown up maybe?

Michelle S.

You and your siblings are in a state of constant change, and will probably change a great deal more between now and adulthood. Whether these changes bring you closer together or cause you to drift apart can depend, to some extent, on the ties that you establish now.

You can't always wait for siblings to grow up before you try to communicate with them because childhood hurt and anger may simply grow along with them.

You may be afraid to take the risk of calling a truce or sharing your honest feelings with a brother or sister. You may fear that your reward for your openness will be jeers, derision, or indifference. That could happen, family counselor Dave Pounds admits, but it is a risk worth taking.

"Love requires openness," he says. "While sharing tenderness and telling someone else who you really are can put you in a position to be hurt, *not* sharing your feelings can hurt you even more. Take small steps toward closeness with your siblings. Risk a little at a time. Tell one person, in some way, that you care each day. Try for five minutes a day to be honest with a sibling—and you'll learn to love each other a little more each day. When you share what you really feel, the most frequent response you'll probably get is 'I understand . . . I feel that way, too, sometimes. . . .' Your act of sharing invites openness and allows the other person to take the risk of being honest and loving with you, too."

This does not mean, of course, that you and your siblings will necessarily stop having disagreements and misunderstandings and feeling competitive with each other at times. These feelings are all part of growing up and part of living with another person. But you may be able to build a unique love and trust that can survive many years and many changes.

One young woman—now in her twenties—looks back on her relationship with her sister and smiles. "We spent our growing years fighting, crying, forgiving, and laugh-ing together," she says. "I also know that we can count on each other when it really matters. We know each other very well—and we still love and *like* each other. What more could you ask?"

With some risks, some caring, a lot of effort, and some time, you too may discover in your own brother or sister a loving rival and lifelong friend who is very special and very dear.

CHAPTER FOUR

The School Scene

ADJUSTING TO A NEW SCHOOL

I've been crying my eyes out the past week ever since I found out about my dad's transfer. We'll be moving to another state this summer and I'll have to go to a new school in September. I hate the idea. I'm not Miss Popularity here, but at least I know some nice people and always have someone to eat lunch with. I can't stand the thought of starting over somewhere else. Everyone will have their own cliques and friends and I'll be totally out of it. My parents say I'll adjust but I won't! What can I do? I'm thinking of running away.

Crying

The last two weeks have been absolutely miserable because my family moved from Texas to California. Now I'm stuck at this horrible school with some of the biggest jerks you ever saw. I was popular and active in everything at my old school, but everyone here is unbelievably stuck-up and conceited. All the school activities are childish or dumb. If I have to spend the next two years of my life here, I think I'll die!

Leahnna L.

The challenge of adjusting to a new school can seem like the last straw when it comes on top of the stress of a family move. What can be especially frustrating is the fact that you might not have had much of a choice in making the decision to move—and now your world is being turned upside down.

As much as you might like to, you can't usually convince your parents to call off the move or to leave you behind. However, if you're in your senior year or just about to be a senior, your parents *might*—depending on your feelings and family circumstances—consider letting you stay on with relatives or friends for the year so you can graduate with your class. Many families are able and willing to arrange this.

In most cases, however, you're stuck with a move and a new school. And that means adjusting to new classes, new teachers, and most important, a new social scene. It isn't easy to be the new kid in school, especially when everyone seems to have all the friends they want or need.

While you can't change the fact that you are new, you might make this transition easier for yourself by keeping the following suggestions in mind.

• *Go in with an open mind.* Try to see a new school as an opportunity instead of as a catastrophe. "Easy to say, but hard to do!" you may be muttering. "I just want to go back where I have some friends."

Memories of your old school can help you a lot if you use them in a positive way. What do you miss most about your old school? The friends you left behind? The school spirit? The familiarity of the place? If so, give yourself credit for your ability to make friends, to care about a school, and to adjust (you were new at your old school once, too!). If you made friends and happy memories there, you can do the same in a new place. Don't let your memories stand between you and new experiences.

Dede, who just turned 16, was distraught last fall when a family move put her in a new high school. "Even though I gradually got involved in school activities and met some nice people, I talked a lot about how much I missed my old friends and old school and how I could hardly wait to go visit them in the summer," she says. "What really opened my eyes was when this girl wrote in my yearbook: 'Have fun with your old friends this summer, Dede, but don't forget your *new* friends here!' If I could give anyone any advice about how to cope with a new school, it would be to give the new people in your life a chance!"

• *Avoid making a negative first impression.* When you're new in school, many people will be indifferent to you at first. It takes time to break through this natural indifference. In the meantime, it's helpful if you can avoid getting off to a bad start.

How could you get off to a bad start? Perhaps by making constant (always unfavorable) comparisons between this school and your old one. You can also lose potential friends with constant put-downs (like saying that everyone is a snob or that the school activities are dumb or boring). It can be a big temptation—if you're anticipating rejection anyway—to reject the new people before they have a chance to reject you. It's easy to pin labels on people and activities when you're feeling very unsure of yourself. People can pick up quickly on bad vibrations and sense put-downs right away. Give them, the new school, and *yourself* a chance.

Another potential turn-off can be coming on too strong or trying too hard to be accepted right away. It isn't always a great idea—even if you have the nerve—to sit down uninvited with a large group in the cafeteria and try to take over their conversation, or to try to be the new class wit or cut-up. Instead, give yourself time to fit in gradually, to learn more about the school and the people around you.

• *Start small.* Instead of going up and talking to groups of people, try saying "Hi" to one or two new people a day—in the hall, before class, in the cafeteria line. Ask directions or questions. Try right now for some limited, nonthreatening contact with others.

• *Make an effort to join school activities.* Most schools have clubs and extracurricular activities, which can be a good way to get to know people who share some of your interests. Socializing in terms of interests and shared activities may help you get past some clique barriers and get to know a wider range of people.

• *If you move to a new town in time to attend summer school at your alma mater-to-be, do it!* Summer sessions, which are usually held in the mornings (so you won't have to contend with solitary lunches), usually more relaxed, and often less ruled by cliques than regular school sessions, can be a good way to ease into your new school. It may be less difficult to get to know people in this low-key setting. Also, you won't have to spend the whole summer dreading September since you'll get a bit of a head start toward learning your way around the school and meeting new people.

• *Pursue some nonschool activities in your new community.* Join and become active in your new church youth group, your community youth center, little theatre, or whatever else your town may have to offer. You might also try volunteer work that attracts people your age. This way, you have a chance to meet and work with some of your classmates in a nonschool setting. Shared experiences and interests may, again, make it easier to be friends.

• *Give yourself time.* Unrealistic expectations can hurt you most. Don't despair if, after a few weeks, you haven't made a lot of tangible progress. Be gentle with yourself. Adjusting to any kind of change takes time. Allow yourself time to cope and to adjust to the new people in your life. And give them time to adjust to you.

POPULARITY PROBLEMS

If You're Not "In"

In my high school, if you're not in the IN group, you're nothing, even to the teachers. The IN crowd runs everything. The rest of us are considered nerds. I'm not ugly and have a nice personality, but I'm still not IN. What can I do?

Feeling Low

The school I go to is full of cliques. I'm not part of them. I don't fit in anywhere. I have no friends to speak of and no one to eat lunch with. How can I stop being lonely?

S.P.

"In" groups and cliques loom large among the school problems of many teens. If you feel out of it and powerless because the in group runs everything at your school, if you wonder what it is that makes people eligible for this magic circle, you have lots of company!

In fact, high school in groups have been the subject of a number of studies by social scientists! Sociologist James Coleman, for example, interviewed thousands of teens and found that in general, athletic ability, followed by cheerleading, physical beauty, coming from the "right" family, a winning personality and smile, and nice clothes are common traits shared by in-group people.

Ralph Keyes, who has taken a thorough and entertaining look at high school in his book *Is There Life After High School?*, observes: "Being 'in' has nothing to do with ability. Power is central to "in" status. This power comes from *givens*—like looks, family status, or clothes—things that are bestowed on a person rather than earned."

If this is the case at your school and if you don't seem to have these essential givens, it can be pretty depressing. You might think that life will always be this way, that you'll always be on the outside looking in. However, social researchers offer some encouragement.

First, believe it or not, being in the in group is no guarantee of happiness. Ralph Keyes points out that "since their status is bestowed rather than earned, they feel little pride in its attainment. And studies show that many in-group people don't feel especially popular. They may not like the other people in the group. They may feel people like them for their status and not for themselves."

One's memory tends to be very selective. It is often pain—rather than joy—that we remember most, and this is true for most people, regardless of their school social status. For example, in a major newspaper interview not long ago, actress Ali MacGraw remarked that she was out of it and never dated in high school. When the article appeared, a former high school classmate wrote in to say that Ali had been one of the most active, admired, and envied girls in the class. But, obviously, her struggles and her pain stayed with her long after her triumphs were forgotten.

The second point experts make is that being popular does not guarantee a lifetime of achievement and popularity. Some high school stars reach their peak senior year and spend the rest of their lives looking back wistfully on that time of glory. Some go on to further triumphs—as do those who had less notable high school experiences. Being out of it in high school is NOT a sign that you're a loser.

In researching his book, Keyes interviewed a number of celebrities and found that Dustin Hoffman was dateless and shy due to his acne, braces, and hairless chest when he was in high school. Famous model Lauren Hutton didn't have a date for the prom until a teacher fixed her up with one at the last minute. Isaac Hayes was a late bloomer with a squeaky voice whose classmates made fun of him and called him a sissy.

And there is a flicker of pain when best-selling author Nora Ephron remembers the high school dances when no one would dance with her and the time a blind date ditched her at a party. Nora, like many who have felt out of it, spent hours of her adolescence dreaming of being famous someday and showing everyone. She feels that her early pain helped motivate her to succeed. Over the years, however, her reasons for pursuing success have changed. Now she strives to please herself, not to show old high school foes.

Life usually does improve after high school, not because you are suddenly magically transformed, but because your environment and what works in this environment change.

"Unless you're a performer, physical beauty and a winning way don't count as much once you're out of high school," says Keyes. "On the other hand, qualities that could lose you status in high school—like brains, imagination, independence, quiet persistence, compassion, or aggressiveness—may be just the qualities you need to make it in the larger world where performance counts more than style. No study I've read has found *any* correlation between high status in high school and achievement as an adult."

So much for the future. "Terrific," you may be saying. "But what about life NOW? It hurts to feel out of it!"

One of the best ways to cope with your present pain is to think of all the qualities you value in yourself now, qualities that will help you grow now and in the future. Some of these are really more valuable than what counts most right now toward admission to the in group. You can lose the givens like looks, money, and family status, and even athletic prowess fades with time. But you can't lose yourself—your intelligence, sensitivity, compassion, creativity, or any number of other qualities that make you special. There are some people in your life—friends of all ages, and relatives—who can help you explore what your most valuable qualities might be. You can also help others who may be feeling out of it to discover their own assets and value as individuals.

Keep in mind, too, that relatively few people in any given school are true "Innies." You, as a person on the outside of that tight little in group, have a lot more freedom and flexibility to make friends of all types.

If your school is very cliquish in general, making friends isn't as easy as walking up to a particular group and introducing yourself. Make contact with individuals instead. Someone who is in a clique, yet who shares an interest with you (via a club, after-school activities, church group, or the like) may become a friend eventually. Even if you don't ease your way into a particular group, you can make some friends—who may or may not be part of cliques—if you follow your own interests and keep from putting yourself down as a social outcast. That, unfortunately, can be a self-fulfilling label.

"People who are self-accepting are attractive to other people," says psychologist Sol Gordon. "People who put themselves down as losers and who act in self-hating ways tend to repel others. It's important to be a real person and to accept yourself as you are. Then others will, too."

While you may envy those who seem to have it all right now, remember that *no one* ever has it all—and that if you can start to feel good about who you are at least most of the time, you'll have a lot going for you.

Feeling Disliked

Everyone hates me and I don't know why. I try to be nice, but I don't have any friends. What's wrong with me?
Upset and Unpopular

People are always making fun of me. I get teased for everything, including my looks, personality, and lack of intelligence. I'm not pretty, but I'm not stupid or ugly either. A guy I thought was nice actually BARKED at me the other day and called me a 'dog.' Some of the girls get together and make cutting remarks to me. Why do they pick on me? I don't do anything to them!

Gail K.

I'm nice, but people still don't like me. I don't get mad even if someone takes my dessert at lunch and I laugh at everyone's jokes (even when they're not funny). What am I doing wrong?

Kara W.

"Everyone hates me!" is one of the most frequent complaints of young people who feel unpopular. Taken literally, it can be an overwhelming feeling—one that might prompt you to draw the covers over your head each school-day morning, feigning deep sleep, illness, or temporary insanity to get out of going to school and facing another day of indifference, exclusion, or harrassment.

It is usually something of an overstatement as well. In many cases, people will be indifferent because they don't know you and are very involved with themselves and their own worries about being accepted. A few may dislike you. A few might want to know you better. But being disliked by everyone is just about as impossible as being liked by everyone.

It's important to examine your expectations about popularity to keep from being overwhelmed by feelings of rejection when someone isn't friendly. There will always be people who snub you or give you a hard time. These aren't *everybody*. These people, too, may not be acting out of real hatred for you, but reacting to some of their own feelings of insecurity, trying to build themselves up by tearing you down.

Examine your own attitudes. Do you walk around silent as a sphinx, with your eyes downcast? Are you defensive and angry, just waiting for hassles? Do you go around looking depressed, never smiling or saying "Hi" to anyone?

If so, people may feel you're unapproachable and a change of your behavior can help. Spend a day acting *as if* people liked you. Smile at everyone. Say "Hello." Give the impression of a good mood and of self-confidence (even if you're quaking inside!). You may be surprised at how much better you'll feel and how many more people will notice you and respond in a friendly way. This will probably not be any miracle cure for lack of popularity, but it's a start, a way to shake that feeling of being totally shut off from others.

If you're being tormented by taunts (usually from people who are very insecure themselves), it can help once again to examine your behavior. You may be, quite unconsciously, offering yourself as a safe and available victim. You may react quickly to taunts and teasing, with visible hurt and anger, giving others the response they wanted.

"Look at the situation," suggested Dr. Sol Gordon. "Is the person attacking you habitually nasty? Then his or her comments really don't mean much when you stop to think about it. Have you encouraged taunts by overreacting and providing a good show for your antagonists in the past? Could you be overreacting to what may be good-natured ribbing that everyone gets? Remember, too, that people sometimes attack others for things they're worried about in themselves."

If you're a frequent victim, keep in mind that the taunting may say more about your attacker than about you and that you can choose not to take seriously the opinions of people you don't respect.

The best way to short-circuit an attack, according to Dr. Gordon, is to ignore it or *agree* with your attacker, who may then feel suddenly silly and powerless.

"People who attack you usually do so when they have an audience, and the success of the attack depends on provoking you," Dr. Gordon points out. "If the attacker can't get a rise out of you, he starts to look silly in front of his audience. You can also neutralize an attack by going along with it. If someone calls you stupid, you might say 'Yes, you wouldn't *believe* how stupid I am' and then go on about your business. By doing something *unexpected*, you can block your opponent."

Maybe—like Kara—you find the reasons for your lack of popularity difficult to pinpoint. It might be that you're trying too hard, giving up too much of yourself, in order to be friends with others. If you never say "No," never offer any opinions, and always go along with the others, your classmates may have trouble getting a sense of who you are as a person. They may feel that you're not being honest with them. They may think that you're too good to be true (and to be close to!). They may think you're a doormat type with no backbone and no individuality. It's easy to get locked into such an image when you want so much to be liked.

It may help to try being more authentic—to say "No" when you want to (even if it's really difficult at first), to say when you feel upset or down, to offer an opinion on something that matters to you (whether the others agree with you or not). Friendship involves sharing positive and negative feelings, problems as well as good times. Real friends will respect your opinions, even if they differ. They're likely to respect you most for being yourself.

TEACHER TROUBLE

There's this teacher that scares me so bad I almost cry before class. She's my math teacher. She yells at people when they make mistakes. She hasn't yelled at me yet, but I'm afraid she will. I can't concentrate in class because I'm afraid she'll call on me or yell at me. I'm too scared to say so when I don't understand something. Help!

Cindy Y.

I got caught cheating earlier this year. This one teacher won't forget about it. Most people cheat. I just happened to get caught. But I get watched like a criminal now. The teacher also picks on me and blames me for any trouble in class. I'm not a troublemaker, but he thinks I am. How can I change his mind?

Russ G.

Our social studies teacher is a real pain. She thinks she knows everything and won't let anyone argue with her, even when she's laying her personal opinions about controversial issues on us. We don't think this is fair. What can we do about it?

Rusty and Dawn

My older sister is two years ahead of me and had all the same teachers I have now. One of them, the Spanish teacher, gives me an awful time. She's always going "Your SISTER was so good in Spanish, why aren't YOU?" This hurts my feelings a lot. How can I tell her so she won't be mad at me?

Sharon B.

Teacher trouble can come in all varieties and for a lot of different reasons. Sometimes a student will create his or her own trouble by cutting up in class, breaking rules, or handling any problems with a teacher by rebelling or mouthing off. But teachers can also make trouble for themselves—and you. Some are unkind and intimidating. Some aren't fair. Some are opinionated and overbearing. Some just seem to hate students—period.

The fact is, teachers are human, too, with faults as well as good points. Few, if any, set out to be (or consider themselves to be) *bad* teachers, but many can and do make mistakes.

"Ideally, teachers and their students should have good communication in order for the best learning to take place," says Dr. Thomas Gordon, a clinical psychologist and founder of Effectiveness Training Programs (including Teacher Effectiveness and Parent Effectiveness). "Some teachers—and students—block communication by threatening, blaming, criticizing, name-calling, or being sarcastic."

Many young people feel powerless to deal with teacher trouble, however, because all the power seems to be stacked in favor of the teacher. This feeling of helplessness can tempt you to act in destructive, communication-blocking ways instead of trying to work out problems reasonably.

What can you do if you're having trouble with a teacher?

"Look at constructive ways you might express your feelings and needs," says Dr. Gordon. "This might involve trying to get more student participation in school matters. It can mean trying to understand what is happening in your relationships with your teachers. If there is a problem, whose problem is it? And can it be resolved in a way that no one has to lose? Ideally, the student-teacher relationship involves openness, caring, and mutual needs-meeting."

A lot of student-teacher relationships are not quite ideal—as you probably know! Some teachers are used to talking, not listening. And some students sabotage themselves immediately by complaining about problems—often in front of other students—in an accusatory way, earning a trip to the principal's office instead of increased understanding and some sort of solution to the problem at hand.

Using the "I" method to simply report your feelings, and talking with your teacher in private (between classes or after school) can help you get through to most teachers in a nonthreatening way.

How can a method like this work—in real life?

Sharon might tell her teacher (who compares her with her sister), "I feel hurt when I'm compared to my sister all the time. It keeps me from doing my best."

Russ, whose teacher remembers past offenses and is keeping an eye on him, must work to regain his teacher's trust. Talking with his teacher might mean saying something like "I understand, because of past problems, that you want to keep an eye on me. But I feel sometimes that I get blamed for things I didn't do. I want very much for you to trust me more. If you give me a chance, I'll show you that I *can* be trusted!"

Cindy, whose teacher frightens her so much, might have a very tough time confronting her. But a quiet, respectful talk could help a lot. In fact, if her fear is somewhat evident while talking (in private) to the teacher, this might help make the teacher aware of the impact her yelling has on Cindy and possibly other students as well. Cindy might rehearse her speech before her meeting so that instead of blurting out "You scare me to death whenever you yell!" she might say quietly: "I'm the kind of person who gets very upset when voices are raised. I often feel scared in class and am afraid to give answers or ask questions or tell you when I don't understand something. I want to do well in your class. Do you have any ideas about how I can cope with my fear?" When Cindy admits that *she* has a problem hearing the teacher's yelling, the teacher may feel less defensive and, understanding Cindy's feelings, may try to behave in a less threatening way.

If you have a teacher who loves to pontificate and lecture, but who hates to listen and discuss class-related ideas, gently suggesting a discussion forum once or twice a week—where students can air their views about issues related to classwork—might help more than attacking the teacher's one-sided view of things or his or her ideas. If you suggest a class discussion with the idea that this will help all of you to realize more fully the importance of the class material, you may be able to make a compromise that everyone can tolerate.

At a number of schools, student powerlessness has been lessened via student-teacher advisory or review boards that get together to discuss and hear problems and complaints from both teachers and students. This system has been working well at a number of schools since the early seventies. It could work at your school, too, if you don't have such a board already. A group of student leaders or a student petition might inspire your principal to try the idea. Students at schools where such boards flourish report that they help student-teacher communication and trust a great deal.

Whether you try to solve a problem with a teacher via the help of an advisory board or by a quiet talk using "I" statements, making use of your own resourcefulness and power to help solve a problem with a teacher can help boost your self-esteem. When you realize that you can do something to help yourself and to change a bad situation, you're likely to feel new confidence and new hope.

If a Teacher Labels You

I have this teacher who calls me a "retard" since I don't learn as quick as the others. It makes me feel bad. Especially when people laugh at me.

Wayne F.

I'm really upset at my science teacher because he just assumes I can't understand anything and won't bother to answer my questions in class. He called me "stupid" once and is always saying that girls aren't ever as good in science as guys. Once I mentioned that I might like to be a doctor. He told me no way, that I don't have the brains. Well, now part of me is mad and says he's wrong. Another part of me believes him and feels terrible. How do I know what part of me is right? I really don't think I'm stupid.

Betty C.

Constructive criticism is one thing—hurtful labeling quite another. While hurtful to students, such labeling is really a sign of a problem within the teacher. The teacher may be impatient and resort to name-calling out of frustration. He or she may feel inadequate and try to gain a sense of power by diminishing the self-esteem of others. Some teachers, too, are victims of their own prejudices—feeling, for example, that female and/or minority group students are generally less able.

It *may* help to approach the teacher with comments like "I feel hurt when you call me names and the others laugh" or "I feel angry and upset when you call me 'stupid' and make fun of my dreams for the future. I'm trying as hard as I can and feel I should get some credit for that."

However, if you have a teacher who tends to label or ridicule students, his or her habit may be so firmly established that the teacher may not really hear or take to heart what you or any other student may say about feelings.

If you're the target of such a teacher, it's difficult, but important, to look to others—like other teachers, parents, family, and friends—and to *yourself* for encouragement. Don't be quick to believe that what this one teacher says is right and lose your confidence or your dreams. Teachers are often wrong in their labels and assumptions about students—sometimes in a spectacular way!

For example, when the mathematical genius Albert Einstein was in high school, a math teacher advised him to drop out of high school "because you'll never amount to anything."

Thomas Edison, inventor of the light bulb, the phonograph, and over a thousand other items, was called "a failure and a dunce" by *his* teachers.

Charles Darwin, who in later life was to shake up the world with his theories of evolution, failed to impress his early teachers, who called him "a disgrace."

Hurtful labeling and later triumphs are happening all the time. In June, 1980, for example, Michaele Christian graduated first in her class of 205 at Washington's Georgetown University School of Medicine, the first woman *and* first black to do so. Her achievement was particularly notable in light of the fact that her high school counselors had told her she had no aptitude for science, discouraged her interest in medicine, and expressed doubts that she could even survive academically in college. After all this, it took some time for Michaele to learn to listen to and believe in herself—and to go on to succeed far beyond anyone's expectations.

Michaele was fortunate. Somehow, she managed to believe in herself and to follow her dreams, even though others tried to discourage her. Countless others take hurtful labels to heart, losing their confidence and their dreams.

Remember that whether or not you have the potential or the desire to be a superachiever or whether you will lead a quite ordinary life, no one has the right to label you as "stupid" or as a failure. If that happens, try to separate yourself from the label as much as you can, seeing it as the teacher's problem. Although you may remember the hurt for a long time, try not to carry it with you inside after you leave that teacher's class. It may help to remember that no teacher can know you as well as you do. There are many famous, successful people and many more not-so-famous but happy people who are successful in their own way, who belie their teachers' early labels. You can, too.

"Teacher's Pet"

I have a problem. My English teacher has become a good friend. She encourages me to write a lot and we have lots of interests in common. Sometimes I stay after class or after school to talk with her, not because I'm trying to polish her for grades, but because I want to show her my poetry or just talk a little. The trouble is, the other kids are calling me her "pet." That's upsetting. Should I stop talking with her because it upsets my friends?

Louise M.

"Teacher's pet" is a label often reserved for someone who is known as an apple polisher or classroom politician. It can also be the cry of students who feel jealous and left out. They may long for extra attention or friendship from a teacher, too. Or they may fear your friendship with a teacher is threatening their friendship with you.

If you have a problem like Louise's, realize that jealousy can be behind such name-calling. At the same time, try to resist any temptation to make your friendship with your teacher obvious in class by monopolizing his or her attention or asking for special favors. If the teacher shows obvious signs of favoring you in class, talk with him or her about it. It might be best to save special talks for lunchtime, class breaks, or after school. During class time, your teacher's attention should be more evenly distributed.

It can help, too, to reassure your friends that they are special to you in a way that an adult friend *can't* be, but that, in growing we need friends of all kinds and all ages.

Crushes on Teachers

Help! I'm in love with my history teacher! I think about him day and night. He's about 26 and is very nice to everyone. He's not married and I have daydreams about us being in love and maybe getting married someday. How should I let him know I love him? Do you think we could make it work, even if I'm 13 and he's 26?

Julie N.

I'm 14 and have this weird problem: I have a big attachment to my basketball coach. He's strong, smart, and tough, yet cares about people, which is how I'd like to be. I admire him a lot. I'd rather be with him than a lot of my friends. I also don't date much yet (even though I like girls). Do you think this means I'm queer? I don't think about having sex with him, but I sure think about him and what a great guy he is a lot!

Don H.

My science teacher and I are in love. I'm 13 and he's 29, married and has a baby boy. During recess, we make out in the classroom. A so-called friend of mine saw us through the window and told everyone. Now he says we ought to cool it so people won't talk, but I still love him and can't live without him. I don't care about his wife and baby or those stupid people who talk. I just care about him. What can I do?

Patti W.

Crushes on teachers are common, especially in early adolescence, and can be a useful part of growing up. Your intense love and admiration for a certain teacher can be a special experience for you in a number of ways.

For Julie, her crush on her teacher is a way of learning what it means to love a man. Right now, she may be looking for someone "safe" (who is unavailable to her because of age and position) to love and to fantasize about sexually and/or romantically. When Julie feels ready emotionally to face and act on such intimate feelings, it is likely that she will be attracted to someone closer to her age, someone who can offer real prospects for romantic involvement. But her early love for that special teacher may remain with Julie as a bittersweet memory or tender learning experience for a long time to come.

Many young people like Don admire and want to be like a teacher of the same sex. This is not at all unusual. In adolescence, you are looking for role models outside your immediate family and it's very normal to feel intense love and admiration for someone of your own sex who, perhaps, has many qualities you'd like to develop. Feeling such love for a same-sex friend may be a very necessary part of loving yourself. If you can't get close to other men (or women) and reject them as friends or role models, you're rejecting yourself in a way, too.

Finding some special teacher or friend to admire can help you discover and strengthen your good feelings about yourself. This love doesn't have to have anything to do with sex. Love and sex are not necessarily one and the same. You can love someone very much as a friend and never have sexual feelings. The ability to be emotionally open to people of the same—and the opposite—sex is a valuable one for your growth as a caring person.

Sometimes, though, your trust and love for an older person—a teacher, perhaps—may be exploited. This is the case with Patti. While romantic attention from a teacher can be very flattering and may seem like the fulfillment of your most cherished fantasies, the situation can eventually be very hurtful.

Fantasies about a teacher can be fun, but reality is usually somewhat different. If *you* are tempted to try to change these fantasies to reality, keep in mind that you may lose a good friend in the process. Be aware of what the consequences might be for the person you love and the choices you may be asking him or her to make. There are, of course, laws prohibiting sex between adults and minors under the age of 18, and school regulations about teachers' behavior as well. A sexual relationship between you and a teacher could jeopardize the adult's job and existing love relationships and could end up with legal actions as well. In view of these consequences and the realization that acting on your fantasies at this point may not be best for *you* emotionally or physically, a teacher is likely to discourage any sexual or romantic invitations from you, even though he or she may find you attractive and like you a lot. So keeping your fantasies to yourself—and continuing to enjoy them—can be a good way to avoid rejection!

If a teacher doesn't decline your suggestions *or* starts coming on to you, with or without encouragement, this can be bad news. Considering the odds of professional, legal, and personal trouble plus the prospects of hurting you deeply, a teacher who displays the poor judgment to become sexually involved with a young student often has deep problems requiring professional help. As much as you think you can't live without him or her—you can! Protect yourself by refusing to get involved. Encourage the teacher to seek help. If you are being constantly harassed and/or the teacher is threatening to use his or her power over you (via grades or recommendations) to force you into doing what he or she wants, talk with your parents, your school adviser, another teacher, or your principal. This can be very difficult, but may be necessary if you are being threatened.

If your teacher is not harassing you, but you are still having trouble dealing with your feelings, try talking with a counselor at your local free clinic or Family Service Agency, or your clergyman or clergywoman. Sharing your feelings with someone who is caring yet objective can help a lot.

If a teacher is rejecting *or* exploitative, remember that this doesn't mean you're unlovable. It may mean that a teacher cares enough about you to say "No," or that a teacher isn't capable of a generous, giving, nonexploitative relationship—and that's too bad.

But it doesn't mean that you're not valuable or worthwhile, or that you won't grow and go on to love others and, most important, to love and value yourself.

Getting Attention Versus Getting Along

I'm new in this school and want to get on the good side of all the teachers. I got lots of new clothes and a new hairstyle and am really turning on the smiles. What else can I do?

Missy J.

Using flirting or flattery as a means of getting on a teacher's good side is manipulative and often useless. A lot of teachers resent the fact that a student thinks he or she can impress them into giving good grades on the basis of superficial considerations like personality, clothes, or looks, instead of ability, interest, and hard work. This ploy may work on a few teachers, but will be a turn-off for most (not to mention the hatred it will inspire in fellow students!). Trying to get special attention and favors by manipulative means can work against you in other ways, too, by channeling energy and attention away from studies—not only blocking your learning, but inviting a large share of teacher trouble as well!

Getting along with teachers and developing good communication is quite a different matter. You don't have to have beauty, great brains, or a fabulous wardrobe to do it. If you work and try as hard as you can in your classes—whether or not you're a top student—you can earn a teacher's respect. A teacher who knows you're honestly trying is likely to be willing to help if the subject is difficult for you. Competent teachers grade on demonstrated ability and on effort. Trying your best can have other benefits besides avoiding teacher trouble: it can help improve your knowledge and skills in a particular subject area and teach you how to work, how to organize your time and your thoughts. All this can provide benefits for you for many years to come.

ACADEMIC PROBLEMS

Poor Study Habits

If I don't do something to improve my grades, I'll never have any social life! My parents are grounding me until I pull my grades to a "C" average (I get mostly "D's" now). My trouble is getting things done on time. Also, I can't concentrate much. What can I do?

Trapped

I have bad study habits and I know it. So far, I get by OK because things are pretty easy in this school, but I'm worried about when I go to college. I know of some people who flunked out because they didn't know how to study. I want to get good habits and practice them now so I won't get into trouble later on. How can I do this?

Brad K.

Whether you're hoping to improve your study habits as a first-aid measure for bad grades now or simply to avoid an academic crisis later on, learning to use and organize your time can be very valuable.

The following ideas might help you to see what you're doing *right* or what you might do to change some of your study habits.

When You're At School

• Pay attention in class. It sounds elementary, but is easier said than done (especially on a hot afternoon when the teacher is boring and someone you really like is sitting nearby). But listening and taking notes on key facts and important information that you're likely to see on tests, plus facts that particularly interest you (or ones that are *least* boring) and things you don't understand, will make it easier for you to ask questions in class and to study for tests.

• If there's something you don't understand, ask for clarification immediately. Many people hesitate, fearing that they'll look dumb or that people will laugh. But if something isn't clear to you, chances are there are others who are confused, too. They'll be glad you asked. And the teacher will probably be more willing to give another explanation now—while he or she is on the subject—rather than later when your question might be a disruption. Also, if you clear up your confusion about something immediately, you'll be better able to understand later material, particularly in subjects like math, science, or foreign language classes. If you don't ask for help early on, your confusion and problems with the subject may only increase.

• If you have particular trouble with a subject, ask the teacher for special help outside of class. You might also ask a parent or a friend who is good in the subject for some tutoring. But avoid the temptation to let the other person do any of your work for you. It may be a short-term answer to getting homework done, but it won't help your understanding of a subject and is no help at all at exam time.

• Make use of extra time at school. If you think about it, there are many little moments during the school day when you could review class notes, language flash cards, or vocabulary lists. If you get into the habit of doing this briefly—while you're walking to class, waiting for the teacher to start class, or waiting for a friend to arrive for lunch—you'll discover that this "found time" can be very valuable. It doesn't have to mean shutting out all your friends. If you're like most people, you do have some moments alone in the course of the school day. Or you and a friend could review class material together. This doesn't preclude just relaxing or socializing, but finding a few minutes here and there to study and review notes can help you a lot.

At Home

• Decide on a study schedule and stick to it. While it may vary according to your daily activities and family needs, setting aside several hours of time *every school night* to study can help make homework a habit. Keep your schedule flexible enough so that a special event or unexpected crisis won't blow your whole study plan.

• Make it easier for yourself to concentrate by studying in a place with the least traffic and noise possible. If it's too noisy at home, you may have to escape to your local library. If you can concentrate better with the radio on softly, use it to help you relax and get into your studies. TV and studying usually don't mix.

• Make long-range study plans. One of the greatest problems that students have is anticipating big projects and exams in a way that will avoid last-minute panic, cramming, all-nighters, or failure to complete an assignment. Just about everyone has some problem with procrastination. You can overcome your tendencies in this direction by getting a wall calendar or desk diary at the beginning of the school year or semester and marking down the dates of midterms, finals, and other exams. Make notes about the due dates of term papers, essays, and research reports as they are assigned. Then set some intermediate deadlines for yourself so that you can do projects little by little and avoid feeling overwhelmed (which can inspire you to procrastinate) or last-minute panic. If, for example, you have a report due in three weeks, start the research now. Set a date for finishing your research and another for organizing and outlining your report. Set a final deadline for finishing the writing of the project itself. Taken in steps this way, a special project might not seem so bad.

• Don't try to spend hours studying one subject. That's a quick route to boredom. Even with high interest and excellent study habits, you would have trouble holding your concentration on one subject for hours. When you feel your mind beginning to wander, take a break. Talk a walk, meditate, or study something else for a while.

• Set aside one hour a week to *review* all your class notes or assigned reading from the previous week. This will make it easier to keep up in your classes and you'll be less likely to panic and try to cram all your studying into the night or two before finals.

• Reward yourself. Tell yourself that when you have finished studying for this one subject, you'll get up and stretch, listen to a favorite song, or take a short walk before hitting the books again. Or get as much studying done as you can before your favorite TV show and use watching the show as your reward. It's essential to make time in your daily life for fun, relaxation, and friends. If you deny yourself any rewards, you'll come to resent studying and find it harder to motivate yourself to work—if all you have to look forward to is *more* work! Good study habits can free you for even more fun time.

Exam Jitters

I'm a fairly good student, but I fall apart at exams. I get so nervous because I want to do well that I can hardly read or understand the test! Isn't that crazy? But it's true. I can't concentrate when I get nervous and tests make me nervous! What can I do about this?

Barb A.

While *some* amount of anxiety about tests can inspire you to study more, try harder, and thus do well, there is a point you can reach—as Barb has—where your nervousness gets in the way. You may misread directions or questions. You may go blank and be unable to concentrate. You may even feel physically ill.

Exam jitters usually hit people who expect a lot of themselves and who see every test as a crisis. If this sounds like you, there are ways you can help yourself.

• Work on getting a new perspective. Tests can be important, but you'll survive even if you *don't* do well. Even if you fail miserably, it won't be the end of the world. Tell yourself that you'll try your best and do as well as you can, but also give yourself permission to be less than perfect. No one is perfect—or has all the right answers—*all* the time!

• When you're taking an exam, listen carefully to any directions. Read over the entire test before you start to write. Sometimes answers in essay tests can be interrelated, and one can suggest answers or a way of approaching another. Also, looking at the whole test may help you to cope with that traditional student nightmare: sitting down to an exam and not knowing *any* answers, or waiting for that one impossible question to come up. Questions that look easy can give you more confidence to tackle the tough ones. If they all look impossible, you might pick the one that seems least difficult and start with that. By answering easier questions first, you can build your confidence and, while answering them, may think of solutions for some of the more difficult questions or problems.

• If you feel that old panic starting to take hold, stop what you're doing, close your eyes, and breathe deeply. Relax your shoulders and neck. Remind yourself that whatever happens with this one test, life will go on. Taking a small break for a minute or two of relaxation can make a big difference.

Being Smart Versus Being Popular

All the guys hate me because I'm smart. It isn't considered cool for girls in this place to be smart. My girlfriends (all two of them) say I should play dumb and even get bad grades so guys will like me. I want a boyfriend, but I'm not sure it's worth bad grades. What do you think?

Regina R.

At some schools, it's actually *in* to be bright, but at others, it can get you labeled a grind, a nerd, a scuz, or worse. Feeling that you have to choose between excelling academically and having friends is very painful. Girls experience this a great deal in instances where boys feel threatened by bright females or girls who are good in nontraditional areas (like math, science, or shop). In these instances, both boys and girls have listened to and taken to heart some myths and outdated ideas about intelligence. Studies have found, for example, that girls do just as well or better than boys in all subjects (including math) until they hit puberty. Then, suddenly, most girls develop an aversion to or fear of math and science. They start believing some of the myths—often reinforced by parents or teachers—that they can't really understand those subjects. And as acceptance by the opposite sex becomes more and more important, excelling in school diminishes in importance for many girls who hold on to the myth that if they can get a man, all will be well. (Present divorce statistics and the increasing number of couples who must both work to keep even with inflation point up more than ever the importance of a girl's getting a good education and developing excellent working skills, too).

Guys, too, of course, can also get the message from some friends that it isn't cool to study too much or to be too brainy.

If you, like Regina, feel faced with a choice between popularity and grades, there are some ideas you might want to consider.

• It *isn't* cool to brag about grades or to flaunt your intelligence with those who can't keep up with you. This can make friends resentful. Some people behave this way in order to build barriers between themselves and others. Maybe they think that their achievements are the only interesting and worthwhile aspects of themselves. Maybe they are afraid of getting close to others and keep others at arm's length by their bragging. If you find yourself falling into such behavior patterns, it may help to ask yourself "Why?" and to examine your feelings about yourself and your friends.

• Your friends are important, but so are you. A few friends might be friends for a lifetime, but many others will pass out of your life in the not-too-distant future. Friendships are rewarding, but the rewards you'll get (including increased self-esteem) from developing your best potential and doing your best right now may bring you lifelong benefits.

• If you're a bright girl and guys snub you, keep in mind that in adolescence, guys tend to lag developmentally behind girls by one or two years at least. The less developed and the more insecure a boy is in his masculinity and self-image, the more likely he is to be threatened by a bright woman. Give your male classmates time to grow and change. In the meantime, it might help to seek out friendships with guys a year or two ahead of you in school, especially those who put a high value on their own achievement. If a man feels secure about himself, he is less likely to be threatened and most likely to value you as an intelligent companion.

• Realize that playing dumb can be a turnoff. "People know you're bright, and if you play dumb, they'll resent this kind of reverse snobbery," says Dr. Sol Gordon. "This isn't fair to you. Putting up a front takes energy you could put to better use. And you *will* find people who will be interested in you and accept you as you are."

POOR SCHOOL DISCIPLINE

It's hard to learn anything at my school because most of the teachers are softies and classes get out of hand.

There's too much noise to study in the library or study hall. Going into the bathroom is hazardous. You can get robbed or hit and people are always smoking and taking dope. I'm no straight arrow type, but it's getting disgusting. By the way, I go to a school that's in a well-to-do suburb, not the inner city. What can I do—or a few of us disgusted students do? I mean, as long as we're having to go to school anyway, we might as well learn something.

Mark S.

If you, like Mark, are disgusted at the lack of discipline at your school and are sure that your feelings aren't typical, you might be surprised and reassured to know the results of a recent Gallup Poll. This survey of hundreds of teenagers across the nation found that, by far, the teens' number-one complaint about their schools was lack of discipline!

At some schools, in recent years, tuning out, disrupting classes and even attacking teachers and fellow students has been considered *in* behavior by some groups. But now, more and more, it is becoming cool and *in* to be more disciplined, to return to values of hard work and respect for others.

The problem is, some people are taking a while to catch on to this new trend. If discipline is still a problem at your school, you can help change the situation by talking with your teachers, principal, student council, and friends to find ways to bring more order to your environment. Rules that are clear to all students and that are enforced inspire discipline. So do well-thought-out punishments for breaking rules. Some school administrators, realizing that unruly students may see suspensions or special classes for troublemakers as rewards rather than punishments are, instead, banishing these students to special, closely supervised study areas at school. There they must work in total solitude until further notice.

Encourage your parents to add their voices to the demands for better school discipline. Help school officials develop ways to improve student-teacher communication and channel complaints in a constructive way. Studies have shown that the more personal interest a school's administration shows in its students, the less likely that school will be to have discipline problems.

Get together with people who feel as you do and start exerting some peer pressure on the others to settle down and listen in class. The more people begin to control their behavior, the less cool disruptive antics will be.

If you've had problems controlling your own behavior in the past, take some responsibility for doing that now. Don't expect teachers to control you. Take control *yourself* and try, for one day at a time, to be attentive and listen without disrupting the class. You may be surprised to find that you'll feel much better about yourself than you ever have before.

BOREDOM AND LACK OF MOTIVATION

I'm 15 and really turned off to school. All the classes and teachers are boring. I used to try to get interested, but forget it. School is so dull, I can hardly make myself go. Both my parents work, so sometimes I just stay home. If I didn't get into trouble over it, I'd skip school more often. I feel like it isn't worth the effort.

Jack C.

I used to be a good student, but I'm not anymore. I'm tired of school. None of my classes have anything to do with real life. They're irrelevant and boring. I think I can learn more about life by working, but since I'm only 14, it's not that easy to get a job. But if I don't do something, I'm going to die of boredom!

Michelle J.

If boredom with school is a problem for you, too, you have lots of company. Maybe you have trouble paying attention as your teachers drone on about subjects that seem to have little connection with the realities of your life. Maybe you'd like to do well, but can't quite get motivated to study. Maybe you're a former or present honor student who is feeling tired, discouraged, and burned out.

If you find yourself a bored underachiever (everyone says "You could do a lot better if you'd only apply yourself!") you may find it difficult to get interested enough in any classes to want to listen and to summon the energy to make yourself study.

"Try getting involved in something that's exciting and interesting to you," suggests Dr. Sol Gordon. "It might be sports, drama, religion, music—it doesn't matter what. The point is that the energy you acquire by doing what interests you may make it easier to apply yourself to the routine, boring stuff that most schools call compulsory education."

Your efforts—not grades—matter most, Dr. Gordon contends. "The most important thing about grades is what they can or can't get you," he says. "As long as you achieve in other areas, have friends and lots of activities and interests, bad grades don't mean there's something drastically wrong with you. But if you're an underachiever, have no interests, no friends, and terrible grades as well, you need to take some risks—like making a friend, finding an interest, and achieving in your area of interest."

Lack of motivation to try can be self-perpetuating.

The less you do, the less you'll feel like doing. "You don't have to be a psychologist to know that the process of not learning is exhausting," Dr. Gordon points out. "Students who fool around and don't learn much at school are tired at the end of the day. If you want to have more energy for after-school activities—learn, for your own protection!"

If you're a good student, but bored, looking for new challenges (instead of turning off to school altogether) can help. Take a course or two for credit at your local community college, or a summer program for high-ability high school students at a major university. Learn a new skill. Look into earning some advanced credit for college if you plan to go. You might even explore the possibility of going to college early. (See information in the next section on early college admissions and work possibilities.) Get a part-time job or pursue some new and interesting hobby.

If you're an achiever who is feeling burned out, this could be due to the fact that you've put pressures on yourself to excel all the time, haven't made time for fun, and are having trouble relating your studies to your goals in life. Making some changes in your outlook and behavior can help give you new hope and energy.

"Focusing all your energy in one place without any balancing factors in your life can make you burn out very quickly," observes Dr. Bruce Bongar, a psychologist who has done a lot of research on stress and burnout. "You can't go 200 miles per hour all the time. Learn to relax and make time for fun, for physical exercise. Give yourself permission, too, to learn from your mistakes. We learn from our failures as well as our successes. A mistake can teach you something important. It can signal a new beginning."

If you're upset that school isn't more meaningful, a new perspective can help. "School is not a meaning, but an opportunity," says Dr. Gordon. "When you see it in this way, a lot of possibilities will begin to open up."

Even though some classes can seem totally unrelated to your life and your anticipated future needs, this is not always the case. It may be very difficult to judge, while you're a student, what's relevant and what isn't. A major university conducted a recent study which polled current students in the communications department asking which classes seemed most and least relevant, and then asked the same question of a cross section of graduates who had been working in communications for at least five years. The results were surprising. The class that present students considered *least* relevant was voted *most* helpful in aiding career adjustment and achievement by graduates! So you never really know what might be useful to you later on.

The *most* obvious benefit any of your present classes

can give you, perhaps, is discipline. The discipline you develop as you work on listening to and absorbing material that may not be exactly fascinating can help later on. (No job, no matter how fulfilling, is fascinating all the time. Every occupation—from homemaking to movie acting to scientific research—has its tedious moments, and discipline can help you through them!) Also, making a habit of learning and expanding your skills can be useful all your life.

"Don't let bad classroom experiences turn you off to learning," says Dr. Gordon. "How can you fulfill yourself if you're opposed to expanding your mind and skills? Don't postpone learning for the future. What you do and learn now can determine, to a large extent, what will happen in your future."

DROPPING, SKIPPING, OR STOPPING OUT

I can't take school anymore. I want to drop out and get a job. This freaks my parents out. They say I'll never get anywhere in life without a high school diploma. If I stay here any longer, I'll go bananas. How can I convince my folks that dropping out isn't the worst thing that could happen?

Joe N.

I've always made all "A's" and am a junior. The problem is, I'm bored with high school. There's no challenge at all. I've been thinking about taking some college-level courses to get a head start toward college, but what I'd really like to do is actually go to college early. I've heard of that being done. How can I do it?

Jill R.

Please help me decide what to do. I'm about 95 percent sure I want to go to college, but I don't want to go on straight from high school. I want to take a year off to work and maybe travel a little. I need a break from school. Is this a good idea? If so, how can I talk my parents into it? (They don't think it's so hot.)

Denise H.

Although most students still choose a traditional four-year high school education, there *are* alternatives if you're restless, turned off, unchallenged, or eager to move on with your life.

Dropping out of high school—in the literal sense, without any further educational plans and no work skills—is almost always a mistake. Most jobs, even those requiring minimal skills, require a high school diploma. Dropping out of high school may guarantee very limited career choices and economic outlook. Most experts advise that you try to hang in there and finish your requirements for a diploma.

There are several ways you can do this—besides staying where you are. In many school districts, there are work-study programs that combine academic credits with credit for work experience (which takes place during the day—usually half-days). There are alternative schools and night classes that allow students to progress toward a diploma at an individualized pace, often allowing time for a daytime job combined with night classes. However you choose to complete your requirements, getting a high school diploma—if at all possible—can be important to your future.

If you're a better-than-average student, you may be able to get your diploma early by passing a proficiency exam if you live in a state (like California or Florida) that offers this option to students over 16. While the Florida test is generally considered quite easy, the California test is another matter. The first year it was given, only 30 percent of those taking it passed it. Now only students with better than average skills tend to try the test and slightly over half manage to pass. A California state official explains that "the test was designed as a law-abiding way to freedom for motivated students." Students who earn their diplomas this way go on to work, travel, or college. Several other states are presently considering similar tests for able students desiring an early exit from high school.

Bright students who either want to earn advanced college credit while still in high school or want to start college early have several alternatives.

You can earn advance credit by taking Advanced Placement Exams and cut the time and money you'll spend in college. You can achieve the same end by taking college-level credit courses at your school or a cooperating local college. The College Level Examination Program (CLEP) is another way to get college credit for knowledge you already have. Or you may choose to combine your last year of high school with your first year of college if you apply (in your junior year) to one of over 2,000 colleges across the nation that accepts outstanding high school seniors as freshmen. Generally, you'll earn your high school diploma (plus a year of college credit) after completing your first year at the college of your choice.

To explore these and other alternatives further, check with your adviser or guidance counselor.

Another alternative to the traditional education pattern that shuttles many high school graduates directly to and through college is "stopping out." This can mean taking time out to work or travel either before starting college or at some point in your college career. For some students, especially those who may not feel quite ready for college and aren't sure what they want to study, taking some time out can be very helpful. Time out can help you mature, take some risks, get in contact with the working world, discover your interests, explore personal goals, and earn some money toward college expenses.

Some colleges permit delayed admissions for students who want to take a break for a year or two between high school and college. Here you would apply as usual in your senior year, be accepted, and plan, with the college's permission, to start classes in a year or two. Colleges are also becoming more flexible about permitting students to take formal leaves of absence—with readmission assured—anytime during their college careers (with most taking advantage of this after the sophomore year).

Stopping out may not be for you. If you can't get a job or if travel plans fall through, sitting around for a year can be a drag. So it's best to have firm alternative plans before deciding definitely to stop out. This is not an all-around panacea for burnout and/or indecision, but taking a year off from school might give you a new appreciation for education, motivation to study, and new goals.

COLLEGE PROS AND CONS

I'm having a terrible time trying to decide whether to go to college. I'm an excellent student, but discouraged. College is so expensive and students work so hard only to come out and not be able to get the jobs they want most of the time. You see college graduates working as secretaries or in factories. It makes me wonder what's the point of all that education? It seems like a bad investment of money and time, yet I'm still not sure. Can you give me some ideas about the pros and cons of college to help me and my parents decide?

Stan R.

More and more young people today—maybe you, too —are sharing Stan's confusion. Soaring costs, a shrinking job market (in *some* career fields), and a new emphasis on practical education are all making students and their families have second thoughts about what used to be an almost automatic decision for bright students: going to college.

Here are some ideas—pro and con—that might help you explore your options and feelings to make a decision that's right for you.

College is no guarantee of a rewarding career. While a college degree *never* automatically promised a future of financial rewards and career fulfillment, the competition for interesting, rewarding, and/or creative jobs (particularly those in the humanities, journalism, teaching, and the like) has increased considerably in the past ten years. It is estimated that, by the mid-eighties, as many as 40 percent of college-educated workers could end up with jobs that have been filled traditionally by high school graduates. The highest professional demand areas for college graduates will be in technical fields like computer science and engineering.

On the other hand, college is an absolute requirement for some jobs like medicine, dentistry, engineering, and other professional fields. A college degree could give you more career flexibility. A number of employers seem to prefer to hire and train college graduates. If you end up changing careers once or more in your working life (as an increasing number of people are doing these days), a college degree may help. Without a degree, some career options will be closed to you forever.

College graduates don't earn more—and sometimes earn even less—than high school or vocational school graduates. It's true that going to college is not a sure route to the good life. A 1976 Census Bureau study, in fact, found that most men and women making over $20,000 a year were *not* college graduates, and that *half* of college graduates over 25 years of age made less than $13,500 in 1976. Another study, this one by the U.S. Department of Labor, estimates that 66 percent of humanities graduates and 75 percent of social science graduates end up with jobs outside their fields of study. Those who do get degree-related jobs often earn less than $10,000 a year to start. This is considerably less than starting salaries for many junior college, secretarial school, or vocational school graduates.

On the other hand, a college degree seems to offer some protection from unemployment. All factors being equal, employers tend to prefer hiring college grads, even for jobs that don't require such an educational background. This may be bumping some high school grads out of jobs that have been readily available to them in the past. Recent studies reveal that the unemployment rate for college-educated workers is much less than half that of people with high school diplomas only. On a national average, a high school graduate is three times more likely to become unemployed than a person with a college degree.

College is more expensive than ever and, viewed as a financial investment, has lost some of its appeal. It's true that college costs are soaring. Even a four-year public university can cost as much as $12,000, and the price tag for four years at a private university can go considerably above $30,000. Some, in arguing against college, add to these the costs of your lost income while going to school and of spiralling inflation, which can erode any higher earnings that college graduates may have since such financial advantages tend to come later on—rather than early—in a graduate's working life. Some financial analysts feel that, viewed strictly on a financial basis, the person who goes to work immediately after high school and makes a habit of saving and investing his or her money wisely has the best advantage.

On the other hand, you can't evaluate a college education strictly on a financial basis. Salary expectations, employment figures, tuition costs, and other financial considerations don't tell the whole story about the value or lack of value a college education could have for you.

Going to college can help you to grow both intellectually and emotionally. It can help you to be a more effective worker whatever you do. You will learn discipline, how to organize your thoughts and your work, how to think logically, write effectively, and how to get in touch with yourself in new ways.

According to some studies, college graduates, on the average, have happier, more stable marriages and devote more time to their families. They also tend to be healthier and to live longer than those who haven't been to college.

Of course, these are generalizations. As everyone knows, college can't prevent divorce, disease, and job dissatisfaction. But it can be an invaluable growth experience.

It's possible, too, to minimize some of the actual costs of college. Financial aid and low-interest loans (to be discussed in Chapter Twelve) help many students get through four years or more as full-time students. There are other alternatives—from attending college in the evening or on weekends, to getting college credit by examination or for work experience, to stopping out to work for a while and/or going to a community college for the first two years—that can cut some costs significantly.

The decision to go or not to go to college is a very personal one. (With all of today's alternatives, it isn't a decision that has to be made irrevocably while you're still in high school.) Whether or not you choose to go to college can depend a lot on your feelings and goals.

Maybe you really want to go to college. Maybe it's necessary in order to achieve a career goal. Maybe you're eager to use higher education to grow intellectually and personally. College could be for you.

But it isn't for everyone. Maybe you just don't flourish in an academic atmosphere. Your practical skills may be what you value most about yourself. You feel confident that you can grow best in another environment. You'll have many choices (which we will be discussing in Chapter Twelve) ranging from starting work immediately to attending a business, vocational, or technical school.

There are many ways to learn and grow all through your life. Whatever educational choices you make right now may be only the beginning. . . .

CHAPTER FIVE

Friends and Enemies

I think friends are a lot of trouble. But I don't like being all alone either. Lots of times I've trusted someone only to be disappointed. People can't keep secrets or know what it means to be loyal. It's at the point now where I hate to even try to be close to anyone.

Alone in Mobile

My best friend is fantastic and is always doing things for me, listening to me, and encouraging me. Sometimes I wonder what I can do for her or give her to pay her back. Any ideas?

Gail T.

Friendship is a basic human need. It is a particularly intense need in the teen years. As you're growing up and growing away from family ties, the people with whom you share your growing pains, experiences, and dreams for the future are very important and special to you.

Ideally, these friendships all share certain elements. You and your friends are, ideally, equal, with no one person winning or losing, dominating or giving in all the time. You respect each other's viewpoints, even when you disagree. You protect each other's secrets and vulnerabilities, never deliberately doing or saying anything that could hurt each other. You're comfortable with each other—able to be honest, to be quiet when you choose, to be sad, or to have fun without worrying what the other is thinking of you. You are there for each other—listening, caring, giving. And your friendship doesn't depend on being together constantly. Although you enjoy being together, you can be apart for a day, a week, or a summer or longer and pick up where you left off.

Of course, since no one is perfect, no friendship exactly fits the ideal. Friends love and confide and compete with each other. We get angry and disappointed with each other. We hurt each other. And yet some friendships survive.

It takes hard work and commitment—very much like any other love commitment—to build and keep a close friendship. It takes effort to try to understand and communicate with another person, to consider that person's feelings and best interests, to give as well as take.

But most people who have friends they treasure claim that all the rewards of friendship are well worth the effort, that no material gifts or monetary rewards can match the joy of sharing feelings, memories, and experiences with someone special.

IF YOU HAVE NO CLOSE FRIENDS

I don't have any girlfriends and since I broke up with my boyfriend, I've been alone a lot lately. I love to bowl, play tennis, and go horseback riding, but not alone! How can I make some friends?

Jodie M.

Every school year is the same. I have to make all new friends because by the end of the year, all my old friends hate me. Pretty soon, everyone in school will hate me. Help!

Scared

I'm 14 and the least popular kid in school. People are nice enough, but I have no close friends. Maybe it's because I used to be fat, ugly, and scuzzy-looking. But I've lost weight (I'm just a shade on the safe side of chubby and still losing) and when I started taking care of myself, I discovered I had good and bad points alike. But I'm still a social misfit. How can I make some good friends?

Sandi R.

I'm totally miserable. I'm 14 and things aren't going well for me. I've been depressed and down on myself a lot. To top it all off, I don't have any real close friends. By that I mean someone I can feel easy or calm around. I don't know what to talk about when I'm with anybody anyway since nothing good has happened to me lately. Even when I ask someone to come over after school, they have an excuse. Believe me, not having close friends hurts far more than a sickness or broken bone. It's like all of me is broken and it hurts terribly.

Miserable and Depressed

Having no close friends is a painful feeling, as these letters show. It can also be a self-perpetuating situation if a person starts to feel so bad about himself or herself that he or she becomes afraid to risk reaching out to others or if a person's depression and low self-esteem are so evident that others tend to shy away.

This may be the case with "Miserable and Depressed." She is feeling down on herself, depressed about her life in general, and especially upset about her lack of close friends. If she can start being gentle with herself, accepting her strengths *and* her problems as part of who she is, this self-acceptance may gradually draw others to her. It's important to know that feeling sad and lonely at times is part of being human and that these feelings can be shared with others. People sometimes withdraw when they're going through a tough time, reluctant to share any feelings but happy ones. But building friendships with others includes taking the risk of being vulnerable, sharing the whole spectrum of your feelings with those close to you.

Of course, coming on with too many intimate thoughts and feelings all at once may scare people away. Building a friendship is a gradual sharing process. First, work on self-acceptance, realizing that your feelings—positive and negative—are a part of being human. Think of the qualities you have that would make you a good friend. Work on appreciating these in yourself. The advice about being your own best friend has been repeated so often that it has become something of a cliché, but there is a grain of truth in it. If *you* don't like yourself, it will be that much harder for others to get to know and like you. When you're on good terms with yourself, others are likely to be attracted to you because you will exude more confidence, energy, and interest in others.

This doesn't happen overnight, of course. It takes a while to change your self-image and to learn to act in new ways. It also takes time for others to adjust to the new you. This may be the reason that, despite Sandi's weight loss, her social life hasn't suddenly blossomed. Often, when people lose a lot of weight or otherwise change their appearance for the better, they have unrealistic expectations about what these physical changes will accomplish. Miracles—like becoming popular immediately—almost never happen. The best thing about a physical change like Sandi's is that it can help her to feel better about herself and take good care of herself. In the long run, this can make a difference in her social life. What she might do now is to continue the good things she is doing for herself, avoid labeling herself a misfit, and instead take some risks—like talking to others, giving them a glimpse of her new confidence and assertiveness, sharing her joy. If she waits for others to come to her, she may wait a long time!

Jodie M. also needs to take the initiative in order to make friends. As many people do, she has neglected same-sex friends in favor of a boyfriend. Then, when she loses that relationship, she's all alone. If she wants to make some girlfriends—friends who will endure while dating relationships come and go—she might join a club featuring some of her interests or ask a girl she thinks she might like to go horseback riding or play tennis. Shared activities can be one way to get to know someone. Or if there is a girl she would like to know, Jodie might start initiating short conversations with her, maybe ask her to have lunch with her one day or to go out for a snack after school. It's important to view such a friendship as a long-term commitment that is very important in its own way—not just a friendship to be forgotten when the next dating prospect comes along. Friendships with those of the same sex aren't just for filling in time between dates. They are an important part of growing to accept yourself and can be an opportunity to build trust and share your feelings. Such friendships can be a joy all your life.

Some people like "Scared" make friends easily enough, but find that *keeping* them is another matter. While there are some friendships that don't last because they weren't meant to (the people involved didn't have enough in common or enough caring about each other to sustain the relationship through changes), if you have difficulty retaining *any* friends, it's time to examine yourself as a friend and look for ways that you may be sabotaging your friendships.

How could you be losing friends?

• You may be losing friends because you have a need to always be right—and anyone who disagrees with you is automatically wrong. You may be judgmental about others' feelings or actions, making it clear that *your* way of thinking and acting is the *only* way. In your relentless desire to win points and arguments, you may be losing friends.

• Maybe you neglect your friends—not just in favor of dating prospects, but also on a day-to-day basis. Do you wait for your friends to call *you?* To suggest activities? Do you expect them to do most of the giving in your relationship?

• Are you willing to share who you really are with friends—sad feelings as well as happy ones? If friends are taking the risk of revealing their feelings or of calling you with no similar sharing on your part, they may assume that you're not really interested in their friendship.

• Are you loyal to your friends? Do you care about them as people? Or do you tend to use them to gain social status or simply pass time? Do you find yourself using their confidences for your own gain (like getting attention by spreading an interesting but confidential story about a friend all over school)? Do you try to build yourself up at times by tearing a friend down? Do you take your friends for granted and feel that, even if you're mean and thoughtless, they'll forgive you (with no apologies from you) and keep coming around?

• Are you willing to give as well as take? Friendship doesn't mean trading favor for favor, but it does mean caring about each other. Do you use a friend as a sounding board for your own problems, but find yourself unwilling to listen to his or hers for very long? Do your friends mean enough to you to work out problems and compromises? Or do you drop a friend at the first hint of trouble?

Examining your own behavior can help you to start making lasting friendships by *being* a better friend yourself!

WHEN A FRIEND ASKS TOO MUCH

I have this buddy who wants to hang around with me all the time. I like to be alone sometimes, but he doesn't understand. Also, he seems to think that we should like to do all the same things if we're friends—like hunting, which he likes and I hate. I like this guy, but he bugs me when he tries to take over my life.

Roger H.

My friend Lisa is jealous of all my other friends. Now, SHE can have friends. That's OK. But the minute I go over and talk to someone else, she throws a fit. I've tried talking to her about this but she won't listen. What can I do?

Lori Y.

I have a friend who keeps me busy asking guys if they like her. It's embarrassing! My boyfriend says it makes me look immature. He gets mad because he says she's using me. But she gets mad if I don't go around asking for her. So whatever I do, someone is mad at me. How can I handle this?

Confused

All my friends copy my homework. I feel really used, but if I don't let them, I might end up with no friends at all. How can I tell them "No" in a way they won't get mad?

Upset

How do you say "No" to a friend? I have a close friend who is really great, but I find myself sometimes going along with what she wants when I'd rather do something else. Also, how do you keep some privacy? We talk a lot about our lives, but there are some things I'd rather keep to myself, only she gets hurt when I say this. She says as best friends we should share EVERYTHING!

Margie B.

Setting limits—saying "No" when you want to or need to—is an important part of friendship. Some people fear that saying "No" will cost them friends. In fact, setting boundaries can make you and your friends closer and more secure in your relationships, since you'll know how much you can ask and expect from each other. If you always say "Yes" (even when you'd rather not) friends may be unsure of your real feelings and may tire of trying to second-guess you. Since a good friend doesn't *want* to impose on you, he or she may simply stop asking anything of you—and this can stunt the growth of your friendship.

When do you need to set limits with friends?

When Your Needs Are Not Being Met and/or the Relationship Is Becoming Unequal Maybe you need to spend more time alone or with other friends. Maybe a friend is trying to run your life, asking you to give up too much of yourself.

When You're Asked to Do Something That Is Against Your Values Maybe a friend wants to borrow your homework or copy your test answers. Or it could be that a friend is urging you to experiment with drinking, smoking, drugs, shoplifting, or sex, for example—when you'd really rather not.

When You Feel You're Being Used If you're doing all the giving with no option for taking, or if you're asked to do things that may not be in your best interests (like things that make you look foolish, keep you from pursuing interests that are important to you, and the like) it may be time to think about changing both your compliant behavior and the pattern of the friendship.

Setting limits on friendships requires some assertiveness on your part. You don't have to come on strong—just be honest.

If a friend wants to share *all* your time and activities, you might say something like "I really value our friendship, but I need some time to be alone. People can be very close and yet not do everything together. This doesn't mean I don't like you. Appreciating one another's separateness is a part of friendship, too."

Making your feelings clear—"I really don't want to do that. But please go ahead if you want"—can help you and a friend understand each other better. If you let yourself get pushed into doing all kinds of things you don't want to do, the resentment you'll probably feel will put an emotional wedge between you and your friend.

If a friend resents your other friends—as Lori's friend Lisa does—it's important to realize your own power to act. Lisa doesn't have to "let" Lori see her other friends. If she keeps trying to come between Lori and her friends, Lori has several alternatives. First, she can try talking with Lisa again. She might say something like "Lisa, I really care about you. Yet I feel frustrated when you try to come between me and the others. Do you fear that I might get close to someone else and forget you? You're special to me. I don't see that happening. But I do need other friends—just as you do."

If Lisa doesn't care enough about Lori to listen to her point of view, it could be that she's not really a friend.

If a friend asks you to do something that is against your values, long speeches are not usually necessary. Just a simple "No, thanks!" or "I don't want to" may do. Most people try to be open-minded and aren't likely to react in a negative or pushy way unless you start lecturing them or unless they detect a wavering note of uncertainty (a hint of "Well, *maybe . . .*") in your voice.

If you find yourself being used, examine your own behavior. It could be that you've been trying to buy friendships with your superior academic abilities or by other special favors for people because you feel that giving answers or running errands is all you have to offer as a friend. Being used means inequality—with you at a disadvantage—and doesn't exactly do wonders for your self-esteem. Instead, think of other qualities you have that make you a potentially good friend. Maybe you're sensitive and caring. Maybe you are patient and level-headed, yet like to have a good time. Maybe you can inspire others to try new things or to do their best. You don't *need* to be anyone's homework supplier or errand runner.

It will take some assertiveness on your part to call a halt to your special services. If a friend asks to copy your homework, you might say "I'm tired of giving you answers all the time. I feel used. If you need help with your work, I'd be happy to help you, but I won't just give you answers anymore. That's not fair to either of us."

If you're resigning as an errand runner, you could say something like "I don't have time to go running around doing that. I care about you. But my time is important to me, too."

Being honest in this way may lose you some questionable friends. But those who care about you will come to respect you even more when you stand up for yourself and put limits on what you will do.

It can be especially difficult to set limits on matters of privacy. While you and a close friend can share many things, there may be some thoughts, feelings, or experiences that you'd rather keep to yourself. He or she may feel the same way. Needing privacy is OK and some people need more than others. Sometimes you can sense a friend's differing needs.

"I'm very open about my life and my feelings," says Lynda. "I tell my friend Jeanne about everything. But at the same time, I don't push her to tell me more than she's comfortable with. She doesn't like to talk about her relationship with her boyfriend too much. I respect her need to keep that private—even from me. She's just a more private person than I am. But she's a good friend!"

You can also get clues that you may be intruding when a friend changes the subject, hedges on an answer, or says "I don't want to talk about it." If you sense that your friend really *doesn't* want to tell you something right now, you may feel hurt and a little rejected. But respecting his or her right to privacy can, in the long run, help your friendship grow.

When *your* privacy is at stake, you may choose to use any number of ways to let your friend know, depending on what works in that relationship. Changing the subject may help, but it's best, whenever possible, to try saying directly but gently, "I feel very close to you, but I really don't feel comfortable talking about that right now."

Friends who matter will usually try to respect the boundaries you set. And you may find that, as you become sensitive to other people's limits and boundaries, your friendships will grow and deepen.

DATING/FRIENDSHIP CONFLICTS

Balancing Your Time

My girlfriend and I used to be very close until she got a boyfriend. Now they're always together. The only time I see her is at school and even then her boyfriend is right there. I know it's important for her to spend time with him, but does she have to ignore me completely?

Hurt

I'm losing my friends. I've been dating this guy who doesn't like me to see my friends, so gradually my friends have started dropping me. I don't want to give up this guy, but I'd like to keep some friends.

Worried

Finding a balance between time spent with dates and time with friends can be difficult, but is necessary if you want to keep your friends. It isn't unusual, in the initial excitement of discovering a new love, to neglect your friends. (This can be especially true for girls.) This can easily become a habit and, unless you change this pattern, you can lose some treasured friends. What you're telling your friends, in a way, is "You're not as important to me as the person I'm dating at the moment. . . ." The fact is, friends can be *very* important. Many friendships will outlast any number of dating/love relationships.

Even when you're in love and in a relationship that looks permanent, having friends—both separately and together—can enrich your lives a great deal.

If a boyfriend/girlfriend objects to your spending time with friends, gently discuss this, telling him or her that friends are—or should be—important to both of you, and that your relationship is very special and can only be enhanced by both of you having balanced lives, complete with friends. You might try to agree on times and days you will spend with friends. Spending some time apart can actually help your relationship, giving you time to think, to exchange ideas with other people and have experiences you can enjoy sharing with each other later on.

Quality of time spent with friends is also important. If your friends seem jealous, it could be that you're spending your time with them talking about the love of your life and not really *being* with them, interested in them and their lives. Most of your friends will probably be delighted to share your happiness, but since friendship *is* sharing, try to give them equal time and listen to what they have to say.

If you're on the other end—feeling left out and neglected—you might try speaking up to your long-lost friend. It might help to say something like "I feel hurt when you seem to ignore me. I know how important your boyfriend/girlfriend is to you and I'm happy for you, but I miss you. I feel I'm losing *you* in a way. I would like to be able to have some time together again."

It may take a while, but most friends, if they truly value you, will try to find some sort of balance in their lives—and start to include you more.

When Your Friends Are Too Helpful

My friends are too helpful. When I like a girl, they start hanging around her and saying "That guy over there has the hots for you!" It's an attention getter at times, but I'd rather approach a girl myself instead of being embarrassed. How can I tell the guys to cut it out when they're only trying to help?

Mark S.

A friend of mine is always trying to get guys to like me. I know she means well, but it's starting to annoy me. What can I do?

Beth W.

Friends who are a bit too helpful in promoting your cause with the opposite sex are a common complaint. While most friends mean well and can *sometimes* help, it is best to rely on your own rather than group efforts to attract the attention of someone you like. If a person is besieged by squadrons of your friends he or she may begin to feel overwhelmed and even annoyed. He or she may also wonder why you can't speak for yourself.

If a friend pesters others trying to *get* them to like you, these people can feel pressured and may react in the opposite way.

If you have a friend or a group of friends who have tendencies in this direction, ask them to cut it out—in a gentle but firm way. Explain that while you appreciate their efforts on your behalf, you would rather handle the details of your dating life yourself, since liking or loving is a very personal experience that a third person—however well-meaning—can't just *make* happen.

When a Friend Becomes a Rival

I went with this boy that I really loved for five months. During this time, my best friend started liking him and she called him all the time. Now my boyfriend has dropped me to go with her. I feel hurt because of what she did to me. I still love him, but don't know what to do.

Hurt and Mad

When a friend comes between you and a loved one, it can be a double betrayal. You may be hurt that your friend would do such a thing and angry that your loved one would go along with it.

Competition of this sort is quite common in adolescence and often has less to do with you than it does with a friend's need to prove herself (or himself) by "winning" someone away from you. It can say a lot about your loved one, too. Teens are particularly vulnerable to flattery by the opposite sex and most have a need to date and know a number of people. So, with no real evil intentions toward you personally, people you care about can hurt you deeply.

Such situations can be devastating to friendships. The hurt inflicted is not quickly—if ever—quite forgotten. If you find yourself vying for the attentions of a friend's date, be aware that, even if you "win" this attention, you will lose—possibly forever—a valuable friend. Your competitiveness may keep you from being close to anyone—which is a rather high price to pay. It is best to find other ways to bolster your self-confidence and to express your competitive feelings—ways that don't hurt others and that also make *you* feel genuinely better about yourself.

If you've been hurt in this way by a friend, there isn't always a lot you can do to remedy the situation in the way you might like (such as going back to the way you all were before the big crisis). Coming between you and your loved one was *not* a kind or friendly thing for this person to do, but he or she is not the only one involved in the decision. Your boyfriend/girlfriend also chose to leave you—possibly for a number of reasons. It may help to realize that your hurt and anger are natural reactions and that time will help ease your pain. You might also feel better if you could confront one or both people involved and tell them how you feel. Express your hurt and your anger. Bringing these feelings out into the open may give them something to think about and could make you feel better, too.

When Your Friends and Your Date Don't Get Along

I have a problem that seems to have no solution. My girlfriend hates my friends. She thinks they're real low-class or something. Actually, their interests are just different from hers. I feel bad that she doesn't like them and don't know what to do.

Bob L.

I'm 15 and hurt because my girlfriends keep laughing at my boyfriend because he's sort of shy, wears glasses, and has crooked teeth. They say he's a creep, but I really like him because he's so kind and thoughtful and helps me to have more confidence in myself. We really hit it off as people. I hate the feeling that my friends are making fun of me and calling me a creep, too, for going with him!

Cheryl S.

It can be painful when the people you care about most don't care for each other—but it happens all the time.

If your boyfriend/girlfriend doesn't like your friends, this doesn't mean that you have to choose between them. Just try to keep them as separate as you can—making time to see your friends minus your partner whenever possible. You might explain to your loved one that asking a person to give up all his or her friends is not usually a reasonable request. Each of you needs his or her own friends. Try to find a compromise guaranteeing each other that freedom *and* as much freedom as possible from social obligations with people you or your partner dislike. If you're willing to compromise, you can avoid a lot of hassles about friends. It's important to realize the fact that the two of you can love each other very much and still like very different people.

If your friends criticize or make fun of a date, listen carefully to their comments and try to find out what they're really saying, the real sentiments behind those comments. There could be jealousy and a fear of being left behind. There could be definite concern for you if the person you love has a reputation for hurting past loves. Or there could simply be values that don't match yours. Listen and decide whether your friends' comments make sense to you.

If you're hearing jealousy and fear, reassure your friends. Maybe they're afraid you'll no longer care for them. Maybe they're feeling left out and unpopular. Make an effort to reassure them that they are valuable, lovable people. Try to help them improve their own social lives. Their negative comments might stop if you show that you care.

If you hear genuine concern in their comments but don't agree that this person is wrong for you, telling your friends that you appreciate their concern but have decided that the love relationship is worth the risks it may carry might help get them off your back.

If your friends have different values, if—for example—they value looks or social status most in a date and you don't—remind yourself that *your* values are important and right for you. Many teens who feel insecure about their own attractiveness put a lot of emphasis on physical beauty in dates, feeling that if a date doesn't measure up to the group standard, it's a poor reflection on them. Part of maturity is realizing your separateness. You and your loved one have both strong and weak points. Neither of you can be perfect. Accepting each other as you really are makes it possible for love to grow. You won't feel that a partner's weak points diminish you OR make that person a less valuable human being.

As you mature and feel more secure, a friend's comments about your date's shyness, complexion, or crooked teeth won't have the same impact. You'll be able to say "Yes, he (or she) *does* have bad teeth and acne. So what? He (or she) is a good person and is someone I really care about." And you can feel fortunate that you've been able to grow past the point where superficial concerns matter so much to the point where who a person is matters most.

OPPOSITE-SEX FRIENDS

One of my best friends is a girl, which means I get some ribbing from the guys, some questions from my mom, and occasional static from girls I date because they're jealous. Nobody seems to think it's possible to have a real friend of the opposite sex without sex or romantic involvements entering into it. Joanne and I can talk honestly to each other in a way I can't talk to the guys, though I have some good male friends, too. We have no plans to date. Yet we're very close. It's hard to explain how much our friendship means. Do you think this is strange or unusual?
David C.

Traditionally, male-female relationships have taken on the rather limited tone of courtship. Male and female interests, pursuits, and psychological needs were deemed too different to allow platonic friendships to develop.

This has been changing in recent years, however, though some people are still confused over such friendships. Some wonder how friendship and love differ and if it's really possible to separate caring from sexual attraction. People who enjoy such friendships insist that friendship with the opposite sex *is* possible, that sex doesn't have to be a part of it (after all, we don't usually have sex with same-sex friends and yet can develop very loving relationships) and that male-female friendships can be very special.

"My friendship with Mike is just great," says Carol. "He sees me as a separate and equal person. We can talk about all kinds of things and we don't make the demands on each other that we might if we were dating. Our relationship is very easygoing. I really like getting to know a man as a friend—not just a dating prospect."

Many agree that platonic friendships with members of the opposite sex are desirable and possible—given certain ground rules.

As in all friendships, you and your opposite-sex friend must feel equal. Respect for each other as separate people who are not locked into traditional roles is a part of this feeling of equality. If the male puts the female on a pedestal or the female expects the male to take the lead in every way and be strong all the time, building a friendship could be difficult. It's important to see each

other as people—without "masculine" or "feminine" labels on feelings or behavior.

Accept the friendship as it is. If you initiate a friendship with the thought of transforming it into something else, you may never really become friends. While some lovers were good friends first, accepting each other as friends—with no other expectations at the moment—is important. If you're concentrating on a goal instead of the other person, it will be more difficult to get to know each other. It's important to accept the intrinsic value of friendship and the fact that it is *not* an inferior relationship. It's vital, too, to accept the limitations of friendship—knowing that it is not a substitute for dating relationships. Both are important.

Put sex in perspective. While sex can be a beautiful part of being close to someone, it isn't indispensable for intimacy. There are *many* ways to be loving and close to another person.

In a male-female relationship, sexual feelings cannot be denied or ignored—or they may become more important than they have to be. Talking about the reality of these feelings can be a way to diffuse their impact.

"My friend Judy and I talked about how we find each other attractive, but agreed that our friendship is the most important priority to us," says Tony, who is going steady with Ann. "We made a decision not to act on our sexual feelings if they should come up. You don't have to do everything you think about. I believe in being faithful to Ann. Besides, I wouldn't want to do anything to jeopardize my friendship with Judy."

Love brings with it certain responsibilities. It means —if you're committed to your friends and your dating partners—that you care enough to put the people you love into the proper perspective so that no one is victimized or hurt. Realizing and appreciating the uniqueness of each love relationship—whether sexual or nonsexual, with a person of the opposite or of the same sex—is a large part of the joy of loving. If you treat all your relationships with care they can add beautifully to one another.

A willingness to give and accept love in a myriad of ways can be freeing and rewarding. As more men and women begin to think along these lines, we may start to see a trend toward more love in friendship—and more friendship in love.

FIGHTS WITH FRIENDS

I can't understand why, but my best friend sometimes spreads lies about me doing things with guys that I DON'T do. It's terrible! What can I do?
Jill G.

If you're the target of false rumors and lies, the only things you can do are:

1. Confront your friend and talk about the problem. Try to find out why she does this. Is she trying to feel more important? Does she feel jealous of you in some way? Is it a way of expressing wishful thinking—that she could be more popular with guys? Together, you may be able to talk over the underlying feelings and find new ways for her to resolve them. Helping her to build up her confidence and other good feelings about herself can help you, too. Maybe then she won't feel a need to shock people with her lies. It can help, too, if you give each other the freedom to express feelings of jealousy and anger when they occur. If each of you can say to the other—out front—"I feel jealous!" or "I'm upset because I'm not that popular!" or "I'm angry when you tell lies about me!" you can get these feelings out in a nondestructive way and possibly even deepen your friendship.

2. Don't go around talking about the lies to others. This only keeps the false rumors in people's minds longer. Just keep acting and living according to your own values and people will probably eventually forget all about the lies.

I have a friend with a big mouth. I thought I could trust her, but I can't. I've told her some secrets and then she's spread them all over school. What can I do?

Cindy S.

My buddy Don is hung up on this chick Rhonda who could care less about him. I overheard her telling her girlfriend that she thought Don was a creep. The last time Don was going on about her, I said "Hey, come on, man. She thinks you're a creep. I heard her tell Sally. Why don't you start liking someone else?" Now he's mad at ME!

Paul R.

Sharing secrets can be a lovely part of friendship, but broken promises and confidences can mean broken friendships. If you have a secret you want to confide in someone, it's a good idea to be very selective. Some secrets are best shared not with a friend but with a professional helper (like a counselor, member of the clergy, physician, or hotline advisor). Some friends view secrets in a more casual way than you might, and in telling them, you may risk having the news spread. Some friends, too, want to keep your secrets, but can't—especially if the news is shocking or exciting. Others, however, can be trusted to guard secrets no matter what. If you really think about your friends as individuals, you will know which ones you can trust to keep secrets and

which ones you probably can't—no matter how close you may feel to them.

Being selective about your confidants and, in some instances, even keeping some secrets to yourself entirely, can help prevent situations like Cindy's.

Spreading gossip can also cause conflicts in your friendships. Don't be too quick to believe *or* to report verbatim any tidbits you hear.

If, like Paul, you hear the object of your friend's affection describe him or her as a creep, reporting back to your friend is *not* a good idea. As Paul has discovered, it is often the bearer of bad tidings who gets the brunt of the victim's anger. It's important to protect your friend, to help him or her and yet allow your friend to save face. You may find it best to wait for your friend to express frustration over a specific situation and then you can gently offer suggestions.

For example, it would have been more constructive for Paul to have gently encouraged his friend to discover other potential loves and to gradually shift his focus from the girl who doesn't respond to one who might—without an in-depth report of Rhonda's negative comments about him.

In another instance, Patti heard some girls talking about her friend Sharon, calling her a lesbian because she didn't date and didn't seem to show much interest in boys. Patti knew that Sharon liked boys a lot but was a shy, very private person who didn't reveal her feelings too openly. After Sharon complained about feeling isolated, Patti started encouraging Sharon to be more open about her feelings for boys. "It's fun to talk about liking boys and it will make people realize you're really one of them," she told her friend. "You don't have to reveal your deepest secrets, but give people a chance to know you a little better."

If Sharon had known about the rumors, she might have withdrawn further. With Patti's tactful encouragement, however, she is feeling better about herself and is taking the risk of revealing some of her feelings—including her desire to be noticed by boys and start dating.

I'll admit it: I'm a mean, awful person sometimes. I really like my friends, but when I get the least bit upset, I turn on them and put them down. I'm always sorry later. How can I stop this?

Paula M.

Some people deal with feelings of anger and frustration by turning on those they love most because it seems safe. A friend or relative is less likely to retaliate and more likely to forgive. (Of course, this isn't always the case.) If this is a habit with you, you may find yourself yelling at a friend when you're really mad at your English teacher, or trying to make a friend look dumb because you're feeling bad about yourself. Any feelings of relief that you get from this tend to be temporary. When you're mean to others, your self-esteem ultimately suffers, too, and you begin to wonder if you're a terrible person.

You're not a terrible person—just a person who needs to learn how to handle his or her feelings better. Next time you feel angry or frustrated or down on yourself, try talking about your feelings with a friend, taking a brisk walk, or maybe writing about how you feel. If you can share your feelings with your friends (instead of victimizing them) your friendships will be much more rewarding and long-lasting.

If you have a friend who tends to dump bad feelings on you, speak up and tell him or her how this makes you feel. Some people feel that, in the name of love and commitment, friends should be able to take any abuse and somehow understand. If your friend feels this way, it may be necessary to point out that abusing someone is never OK and can be hazardous to enduring friendships. Then help your friend find less hurtful ways to express angry feelings—from talking them out to working off angry energy at active sports.

Making Up

My friend Sue and I had a falling out last week. I'm sorry it happened, but I feel it was her fault in the first place so she should come to me first and apologize. How can I make her do this? I really miss her!

Shana O.

Forgiveness is an indispensable aspect of friendship. Caring for each other does not mean that you won't have fights and misunderstandings. It does mean that you'll have the will to work things out eventually. Friendship does NOT mean never having to say you're sorry. If you're like most people, you'll find yourself saying that many times in your life to the people you love.

Making up with a friend after a quarrel isn't something that can follow hard and fast rules. A conflict with a friend is not always a black-and-white matter where one person is 100 percent right and the other totally wrong. For the sake of your friendships, you need to be flexible. This doesn't mean letting people walk all over you or not telling them how you feel when you're angry or upset with them. It *does* mean keeping an open mind about being the first to call a truce and to express your desire for peace, even though you may feel that the fight wasn't your fault. You don't have to go overboard on apologies in this case. You might simply say "I miss

being with you and am sorry we quarreled. That's in the past. Our friendship is more important to me than any argument or misunderstanding."

If your friend tries to rekindle the argument by pushing you to admit that you were wrong—when you don't feel you were—you could say something like "At this point, the question of right or wrong is not nearly as important as our friendship. Let's say we both had a point. I'd rather forget the argument. What matters to me is getting back in touch with you."

If you were primarily wrong and know it, being able to say, "I was wrong. I'm sorry," can do wonders for your friendships, making some friends feel closer to you than ever.

When a Friend Isn't a Friend

How can you tell a friend from an enemy? It's hard for me. I know it's normal to have fights with friends, but when does a friend stop being a friend? When should you give up trying to be friends?

Karen K.

It can be difficult, at first glance, to tell a friend from an enemy. Friends can disappoint and hurt us. Friends fight with us and misunderstand us. So when is a friend NOT a friend?

The distinction between friend and enemy may be one of intent and consistency.

"To qualify as an enemy, someone has to hurt you in some way," says psychologist Dr. Howard Newburger. "This can mean diminishing your accomplishments, holding you back, minimizing your chances for happiness and fulfillment—on a regular basis. This can be very subtle at first. Your first clue may be your feelings after you see this person. If you feel miserable or get headaches after being with someone, that person may not be a friend."

Sometimes it takes a while to hear your feelings and to become sensitive to what's happening. Vicki, for example, always felt that Jane was her best friend. Vicki admired Jane so much that she took her put-downs as constructive criticism. When Jane made fun of the furniture in Vicki's room—calling it cheap and shabby—Vicki began to save earnings from her part-time job and, after a year of saving, bought a new desk that was perfect for studying and sewing projects. Jane was not impressed. "You paid $150 for a NEW piece of furniture?" she jeered. "Why for only a few hundred dollars more, you could have bought a nice little antique desk. That would have been terrific."

As hurt and anger welled up inside her, Vicki began to remember past put-downs: Jane's making fun of

Vicki's long-term dating relationships (she claimed it was boring to go with someone more than two weeks) and Jane's dismissing Vicki's ambition to be a newspaper reporter with the comment "That's the stupidest thing I've ever heard. Those people are awful and besides, you could never get a job." No wonder, Vicki told herself, she often felt depressed after seeing Jane!

At first, Vicki tried to confront Jane and tell her how she felt. But Jane didn't seem to care about Vicki's feelings or about Vicki—except as a perpetual victim. It was at that point that Vicki decided to end the friendship.

"I wanted to protect myself from being hurt," she says. "Jane didn't care about me. But I started caring about myself enough to stop hanging around with her. And I feel a lot better now."

If someone in your life—like Jane—hurts you and refuses to consider your feelings, even when you express them directly, it may be time to move on to people who will accept you and offer you genuine friendship.

IF A FRIEND NEEDS HELP

I have a friend who has a lot of problems. His parents are getting a divorce and his girlfriend just dumped him. He seems to be depressed and walking around with a chip on his shoulder all the time. I'd like to help him, but how?
Chris P.

Helping a friend in need—whether he or she is facing a minor problem or a crisis—can be a joy and a responsibility. It's satisfying to be able to help someone you care about, but it may be difficult to know how to help at times.

How can you best help a friend in need?

Dr. Ruth Michaelson, a clinical psychologist, suggests that you first must know yourself. "Know your strong points and your limitations very well," she says. "Feel free enough to forget yourself and concentrate on the other. Realize that, if a friend doesn't want to talk to you, he or she may not be ready for help yet. And when you do talk with a friend, don't rattle on about your own experiences or pretend to have all the answers. Listen to the other person without making judgments."

It's also important not to be too quick with advice.

"Raising alternatives is the most constructive way to help," says Bruce Tjaden, campus pastor at California State Polytechnic College. "Avoid giving direct advice. Advice presumes that problems can be solved with words. There is a difference between giving advice and giving information. In giving information, you present possibilities and let your friend make up his or her own mind. And if you can't think of alternatives, say so. And

try to think of where your friend might be able to find the kind of help he or she needs."

Experts agree that it's important to know your own limitations. If a problem is too severe and serious to handle alone, find someone to help—a counselor, teacher, clergyman or clergywoman, or doctor—anyone who can provide the needed help. Your friend may be too upset to seek this help on his or her own. As a caring friend, you might help him or her to find sources of information and follow through to make sure that your friend gets this necessary help.

In a crisis or, really, any time, the best thing you can do for your friend is simply to be his or her friend and show how much you care.

WHEN A FRIEND MOVES AWAY

I've been crying off and on since yesterday, when I found out that my best friend Alicia is moving away in June. It's awful because she's moving almost 3,000 miles away, so we can't visit often or even call since our folks aren't exactly rich. I hate writing letters and I'm so afraid we'll lose our friendship. We both want to stay close for life. How can we when we're living so far apart?
Heidi J.

Long-distance friendships *are* possible and can last for life if you give them proper nurturing and care. This means keeping in touch with each other often. You can do this in a number of ways.

• Writing letters can be a chore, but isn't so bad when you're writing to someone who is special to you. If you suffer from instant paralysis the minute you pick up a pen, imagine what you would say if your friend were with you. Speak your thoughts out loud and write them down. That way, you'll end up with a letter that sounds like you.

• If letters get tiresome (or prove impossible) try exchanging cassette tapes. Many small tape recorders are quite inexpensive now and talking to a friend this way can be fun. It can also be lovely to actually hear a dear friend's voice talking about feelings, news, and experiences with you once again.

• Be faithful about remembering his or her birthday and other special events. Try sending postcards or greeting cards with short messages on them for no reason at all—except to say "hi."

• On major occasions—like a birthday or Christmas—your parents may give you permission to call your friend long-distance. (If so, agree on a time, set a timer, and don't exceed the time limit!)

• Take the risk of sharing your changes with your long-distance friend. Both of you are likely to change a lot in the years to come. You may or may not grow apart. But keeping in touch will make it easier to grow with each other and accept each other's changes.

FRIENDSHIPS AND CHANGE

I'm 16 and have this really good friend who's 18 and has been close to me for two years. That is, until recently. The problem is that he tries to treat me like a kid, which I kind of was when we started being friends—but I'm not now. He doesn't like the fact that I've grown up so much, I think. What can I do?

Ted G.

My best friend and I seem to be growing apart. I can't say when it started to happen, but we just aren't as close as we used to be. We've developed different interests and new friends. But still it's sad. I keep wondering if any friends are forever and if it's part of growing up to lose touch with people who have meant a lot to you?

Beverly Q.

Sometimes—as you feel yourself growing apart from someone or when you feel a treasured friend starting to slip away—you may wonder if life means having to say "Goodbye" again and again.

You don't always end up saying "Goodbye" to friends. If you and a friend are drifting apart, it might be helpful to discuss why this is happening. Ted, for example, might talk with his friend, saying how much he values their friendship and enjoys the thought that he is growing up and able to be more equal. His friend may not be able to handle equality in a relationship, however. Some people build up their own self-confidence by seeking out unequal relationships, which usually don't stand the test of time. If you're in such a relationship, you might try reassuring your friend, telling him or her how much he or she means to you and adding "Let's find a new way to be together." And, even if things don't work out, you'll know you tried.

There are times when you will say "Goodbye." We outgrow some friendships. Time and circumstances weaken some ties. Different interests and new people can come between you and a friend. If this happens with you, don't put yourself down or feel that, if the friendship couldn't last a lifetime, it wasn't worth much. People pass in and out of our lives constantly—and our lives can be greatly enriched by them. You may have learned a lot and grown a lot and may have many happy memories as a result of some friendships that are no longer. As you think back, you might rejoice in the fact that you were able to be close to someone, that you were able to care. The ability to love and share with others is something you carry with you for a lifetime.

And there are some friendships that will last a lifetime. These relationships will represent a lot of shared joy and pain and a great deal of effort to keep up with changes in each other. But when you're fortunate enough to have some longtime friends, you'll realize the essence of friendship—a special, gentle form of love.

CHAPTER SIX

Dating Dilemmas

SHOWING THAT YOU LIKE SOMEONE

I have one question: how do you show a girl you like her without making a fool of yourself? I'd feel stupid coming on with some of the lines I hear other guys use. But I haven't exactly come up with any brilliant openers myself. What's the best way to show you like someone?

Gene B.

There's this guy who likes me. He looks at me a lot and smiles. What am I supposed to do besides smile back? He's sort of shy, but I like him. Should I go up and start a conversation or something?

Nancy J.

Showing that you like someone can sound easy in theory ("Show the person in little ways that you like him . . . make it obvious that you notice her . . . above all, be yourself!"). But what little ways, which obvious signs, and which true aspects of yourself can you show without risking ridicule or rejection?

Any time you try to reach out to someone, there is the possibility of rejection. It's possible, too, that who you are may seem silly to a person whose tastes run in another direction. What matters most is showing your interest in someone without embarrassing *yourself.*

There are two good ways to avoid this possibility.

Start Slow Don't expect instant miracles. Show interest and get to know the person you like gradually. Instead of plotting out the perfect opening line and putting yourself in a definite win-lose situation, show your interest at first in low-key ways. Smile. Say "Hello." Make little comments—before or after class—about the class, the weather, or whatever seems right at the time. Direct a comment—preferably a sincere compliment—to the person you like. Or ask this person a question about a subject of mutual interest *or* concern (like "How are you coming on your term paper? What did you decide to write about?" if the person you like is the studious type). Start with short comments and build slowly toward longer conversations. Get to know him or her little by little. That way, you'll be able to gauge his or

her interest in you, too. This way, too, you can avoid giving someone the wrong initial impression—for example, by coming on strong with a tired old line or in a way that seems phony and doesn't ring true for you.

Be Yourself That advice has become quite a cliché, but for a reason: it happens to be true. If you're *not* Mr. (or Ms.) Cool, you'll look foolish trying to be. If you look a little uncertain when you first talk to someone you like, if you stammer a little or blush a lot, that's less likely to turn someone off than a slick, phony line. In fact, some may find your vulnerability endearing!

If you're on the receiving end of this attention, it can be hard to know what to do. Maybe you wonder if you're misreading the signals. Maybe the person is just being nice and isn't interested in dating you—so you keep your distance and wait.

There are alternatives to waiting passively for the first person to make his or her next move. Dating doesn't have to be the main concern or goal right now. If someone is hinting that he or she likes you—by gazing in your direction constantly, smiling a lot, saying something now and then, or maybe even teasing you or clowning around when you're nearby—and if you want to encourage him or her, try meeting the person halfway. Help conversations along. Initiate some of your own. Tease back. Compliment the other person or make a nonthreatening observation like "You're really interesting and fun to talk with. I enjoy what you have to say." Maybe you could even make the first move and ask the person out for an after-school snack or study session or to an informal party—preferably a low-key situation where you'll have a chance to get to know each other better without a lot of pressures.

HOW TO TALK TO EACH OTHER

My problem is that I don't know what to say when I'm around boys. That's a big reason I think that I've never had a date even though I'm a junior. Help!

Annie B.

I feel bad about not being popular with girls. I'm not terrible-looking or anything. But I have trouble talking to them. Yet I talk to guys easily. How can I get over this shyness with girls?

Larry D.

I have a very hard time asking girls out. I get so afraid of being turned down that I often mess things up for myself. I mean, I ask girls out in a way that they almost have to say "No." How can I get better at this?

Brian K.

How do you talk with someone on a first date? I'm awful at it! I get so nervous I can't say anything and guys think I'm dull so they don't ask me out again. I can be very talkative and fun with my family and friends, but on a date, forget it! How can I keep from clamming up?

Diane U.

If you find yourself speechless around the opposite sex, you may be seeing them as a species apart—perhaps as a superior breed of people or maybe as simply mysterious. If you can begin to see boys—or girls—as people just like you, initiating a conversation won't be so frightening. Imagine for a moment that this person is not at all different from you. What would you choose to say? This might still be an appropriate question or remark. Men and women are just people with many of the same feelings, interests, and fears. Everyone wants to be liked and to avoid rejection if at all possible. Most people are nervous in unfamiliar situations. So it's not so unusual to feel nervous about talking to someone new, asking someone out, or conversing on a first date—whatever your sex.

It might help to share your nervousness a little. When you ask someone out, you might even admit that you're nervous. When Scott asked Lynn to a party, he said "I'm feeling kind of nervous asking you out, but I'd really like it if you could go to Jan's party with me next week. Would you be able to go?" Thinking back on the invitation later, Lynn admits that she found Scott's vulnerability attractive and that his openness helped her overcome a lot of her own nervousness.

Bob gets nervous asking girls out, too, but he tends to use his nervousness to put energy into his approach. "I used to get very intimidated and almost depressed because of my nervousness," he says. "I would say to a girl 'You wouldn't like to go out with me, would you?' That isn't exactly the greatest approach. It was too easy to say 'No, I wouldn't' if she was at all in doubt. But I started letting my nervousness raise my energy level so I would sound happy and excited when I asked someone out. It

isn't being insincere at all—and it works! I feel much better about myself now."

Nervousness doesn't have to mean dating disaster. It can be an opportunity to share your feelings with each other and become less threatened (or threatening) and more approachable. Mike, who could see during a first date with Sheila that she was at least as nervous as he was, remarked, "A first date is kind of nerve-racking, isn't it? Are you feeling as nervous as I am? Maybe we can help each other!" Sheila, relieved to see that she wasn't alone in her nervousness, began to relax immediately.

It's important to be easy on yourself and not expect to be brilliant, witty, and generally the perfect date. There may be some awkward silences. The evening may be filled with small talk. Or one or both of you may start talking compulsively out of nervousness. Those things happen—but the less you worry about them, the less awkward and frequent they seem!

HOW TO GET REJECTED

I have lots of first dates, but don't get asked out again much. I'm not someone who sleeps around and I'm not ugly either. Sometimes I think it's because I'm boring, but I'm not sure. Do you know what bugs guys that I might be doing?

Puzzled

According to a recent survey by *CO-ED* magazine, some habits and quirks that might stall your social life whether you're male or female include:

• Trying to act cool all the time
• Calling your date a name like "Baby" or "Sweetheart"
• Using obscene language
• Smoking a lot
• Dressing flamboyantly
• Not accepting your date as he or she is, but trying to transform his or her taste in clothes or personality
• Guys expecting girls to wash, mend, or iron their clothes
• Girls who always say "I don't care," leaving all decisions about where to go and what to do up to the guy
• Guys to try to pay for everything all the time or girls who *never* offer to pay for anything

In an informal poll especially for this book, another group of teenagers placed the following behavior types at the top of their list of undesirable dates:

• Someone who is poorly groomed and hasn't bathed in ages

• Someone who spends the evening bragging about how much money his or her parents have, how many material things he or she has, or how smart or popular he or she supposedly is

• Someone who talks on and on about other people he or she has dated—going on forever about how perfect the others were or how terrible they were—in excruciating detail

• Someone who is insensitive to another's needs to talk or to have a voice in making choices about shared activities

• Someone who is jealous and possessive—*especially* after only one or two dates

• Someone who comes on strong, expressing feelings of love and permanent commitment and expecting those feelings to be returned after only a few dates

If you see yourself in some of these examples, it may help to realize that much of this behavior stems from feelings of insecurity. Maybe you're not sure that you'll be liked as you really are, so you try to act cool, sophisticated, tough, or compliant in order to make a good impression on your date. Or you may talk about things like money, family status, other dates, or your achievements to show your date that you're special. Or you may expose many private feelings early on—from past hurts to feelings of growing love or jealousy—so that he or she might understand how much you need his or her love.

Unfortunately, trying too hard and needing too much from someone, especially early in a dating relationship, can bring disappointing results. Turned off by what he or she sees as bragging or phoniness, embarrassed by premature confessions and confidences, or feeling trapped by your neediness, the other person may start edging away from you.

Game playing—whether you're trying to be someone you're not, appealing to another person's guilt through your neediness, or never disclosing your true feelings—is never a good idea. Being yourself and sharing who you are—in stages—is the best way to get to know another person. This may mean, instead of trying to act cool in order to hide your insecurity, saying "Sometimes I get nervous, but I'm having a good time," or "I tend to be quiet when I'm just getting to know someone."

Being yourself could mean expressing an opinion about where you would like to go and what you'd like to do on a date, which can give the other person some clues about your interests, likes, or dislikes as well as the sense that you're a whole person in your own right—with separate ideas and opinions.

In many friendships, if you stop to think about it, you learn about each other gradually as you share personal information little by little until mutual trust has had a chance to grow. It's much the same in dating relationships.

It's important to remember, too, that there are times when you will not be asked out again—or will be refused—through no fault of your own. Many adolescents don't feel ready for a steady, long-term relationship, feeling the desire to date many different people. Others, often due to their own insecurities, are attracted to people they think will make *them* look important by association—very popular or extremely handsome or beautiful types, for example. When your own—and others'—self-confidence is shaky, dating can be difficult. As you and the people around you grow and begin to feel more comfortable with yourselves as you are, it will be easier to appreciate and value each other and to have relationships that last.

WHEN ONLY PERFECTION WILL DO

I can't stand to go out with a boy unless he's very good-looking. There are some guys I know who are very nice people, but they're not lookers. There aren't too many guys at our school who are male "10"s and those who are, everyone wants to date. Some of them are pretty stuck-up, too. How can I start getting more interested in the nice but not-so-handsome guys?

Joyce S.

What is it with guys? If you're not movie-star pretty, you're nothing to them, and if you ARE pretty, it doesn't matter whether you're dumb, have no personality, or aren't even a nice person—you'll have lots of dates. It's disgusting and unfair!

Upset in Georgia

Physical attractiveness and/or social status seems to have special importance in the dating scene during adolescence. Why?

Often, this is due to a young person's own insecurity—feeling that he or she is not so attractive or desirable, but may capture some of this magic by association, by basking in reflected glory. Since physical attractiveness is such an obvious asset—immediately apparent to onlookers—that tends to be of primary importance to insecure teens who try to tell the world "Hey, I must be attractive and terrific, too, if I can date this Beautiful Person."

If you insist that only the most beautiful or handsome person will do as a date, you may be more involved in proving yourself than in getting to know and enjoy another person. Some very attractive people do complain, in fact, that others often don't look beyond their beauty or handsomeness to discover who they really are as people. This can, in some instances, hurt as much as being rejected as a date due to lack of sufficient attractiveness. If you're hung up on beauty as reflected status, you might be missing some great opportunities to be close to others—who may or may not be beautiful.

How do you break this habit of seeking out physical attractiveness above all other considerations?

First, it's vital to work on your own self-esteem, realizing that your own assets are potentially much more valuable to you than any reflected glory. You have power over your own strong points. You can develop them further. When all your self-esteem is based on seeming to possess another person, the loss of that person can be devastating. If you begin to appreciate who you are, no one can take these good feelings away from you. Liking yourself helps you to like others—of all types and descriptions.

Second, start looking closely at others with no serious consideration about their looks. What *else* can you find to value? What do you appreciate—quite apart from what they might do for you? You may make some very happy discoveries!

WHEN YOU ALWAYS GO FOR THE WRONG ONES

I get hurt again and again by guys. Why? Because I go for the wrong kind. I don't know why, but I'm attracted to those who are kind of bullies and who don't respect women much. Every time I meet a nice guy, I think "He's nice, but part of me thinks he's a weak drip . . ." and I turn off on him. What can I do?

Tammy T.

What do girls want? I try to be sensitive and nice to everybody. I'm not a male chauvinist and I'm not ugly either. I'm not an outcast. I'm fairly intelligent and have a lot of friends, some of them girls. But when it comes to dating, so many of the girls seem to go for the real macho pigs—the ones who treat them like dirt. These girls are always coming to me saying how hurt they are by this guy or that one. Why do they go for that type? Why don't they get more interested in guys who try to be nice—like me?

Bob S.

Being attracted to people you know may hurt you or being rejected in favor of bullies can be a painful pattern. It can happen a lot in the teens, but is not uncom-

mon at other times of life as well. This pattern seems to be particularly common among women who find themselves attracted to men who aren't sensitive or even emotionally approachable.

If this sounds like the story of your life, you may be wondering why you have this preference. There are several possible causes.

Some young women have grown up hearing about how *real* men fit old stereotypes (always strong, unemotional, domineering, not particularly interested in women as people, prone to enjoy most times with their friends and likely to give their woman a hard time now and again). Such girls may feel that a boy who doesn't fit this old-fashioned formula is not really masculine. The fact is, of course, that the more emotionally secure a man is in his own humanity and masculinity, the less he will have to prove, the less he will feel he has to match old stereotypes. The more he likes himself, the more sensitive and kind he will be to the women he dates.

Some people—both male and female—seek out others who treat them badly because their self-esteem is so low that they feel they deserve to be treated in this way. A person who has little self-respect may feel undeserving of and even threatened by people who treat him or her well.

Working to improve your self-esteem—by yourself, with the help of family and friends, or even through professional counseling—can help you to break this hurtful dating pattern.

SAYING "NO" GENTLY

There is this girl I like as a friend, but she wants more than that. She'd like us to date. I'm dating several people right now and would rather not date Suzi because it might hurt our friendship. Besides, I'm not physically attracted to her even though I like her a lot. What should I do?

Jim K.

What do you do when a boy keeps calling and asking you out and he just doesn't appeal to you in that way? I like Terry OK, but I don't want to go out with him. How can I say "No" without hurting his feelings?

Katie L.

When you say "No" to someone who is interested in dating you, the risk and possibility of hurt are always there. The only thing you can do is to minimize the hurt by being as honest and as gentle as possible.

Some people, in trying to be kind, aren't specific and lead a person on. Or they may date people they don't really like for a short time to avoid hurting their feelings and then find the hurt increased in magnitude when they break up. Some give various excuses every time they're approached by someone they're not interested in dating. The old "I'm sorry, but I'm busy . . ." line may work with some people who get the hidden message by the second or third time, but what about the person who says "I know you're busy the next three weekends, but how about going out with me a month from next Saturday?" or the person who asks you out for New Year's Eve in July? Obviously, you need to be more specific.

If you can, it's best to express positive feelings about the person. You might say "I think you're a nice person, Terry, but I'd prefer we didn't date. I'd rather be your friend." If you're dating someone else, say so. You might try taking responsibility for the lack of chemistry between you, saying something like "I feel I'm not the right kind of person for you" instead of "You're not my type."

If a friend—like Suzi—wants to transform your relationship into something else, gentle honesty is also the key to minimizing hurt. Jim might tell Suzi how much he values their friendship and how he doesn't want to tamper with a good thing by starting to date. He might point out that their special friendship may outlast most dating relationships both will have. This approach does not guarantee instant understanding or no hurt on the part of the person who is being turned down, but it may decrease the pain and allow the other person to save face a bit and to feel that he or she is valued and appreciated in some way.

TIME TOGETHER/TIME APART

My boyfriend feels put down when I don't want to spend all my time with him. I love him, but I like time alone and with friends. How do I tell him this?
Marlene B.

I have a problem with my girlfriend. I'll call her Mary Ann. She is very dependent and wants to be with me constantly. Our relationship is her whole life. I care about her, but I also like to be with my friends and go out for sports, too. It's getting so she's like a burden and I hate that. How can I get her to see that her constant hanging on me isn't helping our relationship?
Jack D.

When one person is particularly dependent or when one has greater needs for time alone, it can cause a lot of conflicts and pain in a relationship. While there are no instant solutions to this—and a compromise may take

time to work out—it may help both of you to understand that people cling when they feel insecure about a loved one or about their own lovability. It may help to reassure a clinging boyfriend or girlfriend that he or she is very special and that spending time apart can be good for your relationship, giving you time to be alone or to enjoy friends on a one-to-one basis.

It's important to remember that liking or loving each other means more than needing each other. It means having enough faith and trust in each other to allow one another time to grow and experience all important aspects of life—including time alone and time with friends. It's vital to have a life of your own—with separate interests, solitary thoughts, and your own friends. When you're both whole people (instead of just two halves making a couple) you'll have that much more to share with each other.

NEW-STYLE DATING

Do you think it's all right for a girl to call a boy she likes to ask him to a party? Some girls I know do this, but my mom thinks it's tacky and doesn't want me to. My phone isn't exactly ringing off the hook and I really want to go with a certain boy to a certain party that's coming up soon.
Jennifer C.

There's a guy I like a lot who doesn't have much money. I think he's about to ask me out (he keeps hinting about it) and I want to pay my way on our date. How can I tell him this in a way that he won't be embarrassed?
Laura J.

In the past five or ten years, it has become more and more common for girls to call boys, to ask them out, and to share dating expenses.

Some of these new developments are a shock to the older generations. In your parents' youth, it was very rare for girls to take the initiative and call boys or ask them out. It was even more unusual for a girl to share expenses.

Today, however, traditional dating roles are being questioned. Although many still follow tradition, a growing number of young people are experimenting with new freedom in dating relationships. Being flexible in paying or asking each other out can ease a lot of frustration for both sexes. For guys, it can mean freedom from always having to pay; for girls, it can mean freedom from always having to sit forlornly by the phone waiting to be called. A number of young people appreciate such sharing.

"Paying my own way a lot of the time gives me a feeling of power in the relationship," says Shari, a 17-year-old senior. "My boyfriend and I feel more equal. And also it means we can go out and do more things now that he isn't stuck with all the expenses."

Sixteen-year-old Frank is enthusiastic about girls who take the initiative at times in asking for dates. "It makes me feel good to know a girl is really interested in me," he says. "I like not having to screw up my courage to do all the asking all the time. It's a relief to be asked sometimes. It can also be great if a girl will offer to share expenses sometimes. I'm not that well off and a lot of girls have as much money as any of the guys I know."

The practice of sharing expenses for all dates, alternate dates, or occasionally is becoming quite common. The term for this at many high schools is "sharing." At other schools, "sharing" is simply called "splitting expenses" or "going Dutch."

How can you bring this subject up with a prospective date?

No matter what your sex or who does the asking, if you want to go 50-50 on expenses, you might say something like "I prefer sharing expenses. Is that OK with you?" at the time you're arranging the date. Never wait until the time of your date—when you're at dinner or the movie box office—to bring up the subject. Be open about your feelings well in advance so that the other person can express his or her beliefs in this regard (in case it would make a difference in where you go or whether you go out at all) and so the other person can be prepared to pay her (or his) own way. It's a good idea, too, to just express this as a preference, without a lot of comments about the other person's financial resources or lack of them (which could embarrass him or her).

Many young people contend that sharing responsibilities for making dates and paying for them helps them to be more equal and to get free of some hurtful games (such as the old feeling that a girl has to "pay" a guy back for all the money he has spent on her via sexual favors of some sort). Sharing power in this way can give each of you freedom of choice in many aspects of your relationship. You may even choose to treat each other to a special evening now and again—and that can be a joy, not an obligation!

GHOSTS OF PAST RELATIONSHIPS

I think my boyfriend is still in love with his old girlfriend. He talks about her a lot and says good things even though he swears up and down that he hates her and it's *all over. This talking about her so much hurts me. What can I do?*

Maura M.

Whenever we're feeling close and happy, my girlfriend will always bring up something about her old boyfriend. This really upsets me (even though she says she loves me and didn't love him). Why does she bring him up when things are going good for us?

Scott A.

Even though it's been over a year since John broke up with me, I haven't found someone else. What happens is, I like guys but as soon as one likes me, I stop liking him, and I've hurt some guys real bad. I wonder if I might be trying to get revenge on John by hurting other boys. I don't want to. How can I stop?

Tina G.

Memories of past loves and past hurts can linger for a long time, sometimes causing problems in new relationships.

Sometimes, unresolved grief can keep us talking on and on about a lost love (even when we claim to hate him or her) or can make us want to keep others away, avoiding further involvements that could also bring the risk of pain.

If you're struggling with such feelings, remember that this isn't at all unusual after a breakup. You're likely to feel a mixture of anger, grief, love, and longing for a while. If you become involved in another relationship before these feelings are worked out, you may find yourself bending your new date's ear too much. Be aware that this can hurt the other person. It can be interpreted as a sign that your past love was so wonderful and so cherished that he or she can't possibly measure up. You may also be saying—indirectly—to the new person in your life: "I can't be involved with you right now because my heart is still with my past love. . . ."

If you can, it's better to talk over your conflicting feelings with someone else—a friend, your family, or a counselor—instead of rambling on when you're on a date. This doesn't mean you shouldn't ever mention a previous love. At times, his or her name may come up naturally. But be aware that if you talk constantly about someone from your past, the new person in your life may feel rejected or pushed away.

If you find yourself avoiding or rejecting others in the wake of a breakup, your actions could be tied to a sort of revenge—trying to hurt your former love indirectly by hurting others of the same sex or by making him or her feel guilty by continuing to brood and refusing to go on with your life, telling him or her, in effect, "My life is ruined and it's all your fault!"

It's possible, too, that fear more than revenge could be your motivation. You may be so afraid of getting hurt again that you pull away from others when they show interest in you.

How do you stop this behavior?

Identify your feelings. Are you still feeling a lot of hurt? Anger? Bitterness? That keeps you tied to the past. Try talking about your feelings with someone you trust. Your grief will diminish with time, especially if you realize it's there and try to work it through rather than perpetuating it by avoiding or hurting others.

If you're being hurt by a person who seems tied to the past, it may help to understand your date's feelings and then act in an appropriate way. If your date talks a lot about an old boyfriend or girlfriend—especially during times when you're feeling very good about each other and particularly close—this could be a means of creating a little distance until he or she is better able to handle the growing closeness between you. This person may care very much for you, but still fear involvement a little.

Don't criticize your date, and, especially, don't try to put down his or her former love. Instead, simply report your feelings. Tell him or her that sometimes you feel hurt because you feel him or her pulling away from you and wonder if he or she can appreciate your good qualities. Instead of trying to get the person to say bad things about a past love, encourage him or her to say caring things to you.

WHEN YOU HATE THE PEOPLE YOU DATE

There's this horrible guy in my class that I absolutely hate. On a dare by a friend, I went to a dance with him because he asked me and no one else did. Now we're going steady and I still hate him! I thought it would be better than sitting at home on weekends, but I'm not sure because I can't stand anything about him!
Sorry Sophomore

I used to dream what it would be like to have a boyfriend. Now that I have one, I'm disappointed. I don't feel fantastic when I'm with him the way I thought I would, even though he's wonderful. Sometimes I like him and sometimes I don't so much. Does this mean I'm not ready to date yet?

Disappointed

This is a strange problem. I like a girl until she likes me and then I don't like her anymore. What's going on?
Randy C.

I'm overly critical of the girls I date. I want them to be perfect and look perfect all the time. If they aren't, I get turned off. What can I do about this?

Ryan T.

If you find yourself going with people you hate or discover yourself disliking people you date after a short time, perhaps as soon as they show a real interest in you, this pattern could have a number of causes.

The simplest, of course, is the situation described by "Sorry Sophomore"—going out with someone you dislike to begin with on a dare or because there's no one else available. As "Sophomore" is beginning to discover, there *are* worse things than sitting home on a Saturday night. Being with someone you dislike and playing games with that person (trying to pretend you like him or her when you really don't) doesn't do wonders for your disposition and self-esteem. You can get angry, frustrated, and upset at yourself for getting into such a situation. It's also cruel to mislead and use someone else in this way. Your actions can cause this person a lot of pain.

It's best, of course, to avoid getting into such a relationship at all. If you find yourself in one, get out. Breaking up with the person as soon as possible—instead of dragging the relationship on and on—will minimize the potential hurt somewhat and free you to feel better. Both of you will then be available once more to potential dates who are likely to be more suitable.

If, on the other hand, you find yourself disappointed with your dates because they don't match your fantasies of what a perfect date would be, keep in mind that fantasies are fun, but, in reality, no relationship and no person can be perfect. Even if you are fortunate enough to have a very loving relationship with someone, life will still have its usual ups and downs. The intensity of your love, your excitement, and your happiness with each other will be subject to the same ebb and flow as the rest of your feelings. You may love each other always, but have moments of special closeness and moments of loneliness. That's part of being human.

Give your boyfriend or girlfriend room to be human, too. There must be times when you don't look your best and times when you don't do or say the perfect thing. If you're overly critical of dates' imperfections, it could be that you aren't at peace with your own shortcomings. You may be afraid that if someone gets to know you too well and finds that you're less than perfect, you'll be rejected. That could happen. But you might hope that someone you like would care enough to give your good points extra weight and accept your limitations. Try giving others the same tolerance and understanding that you would like for yourself.

Low self-esteem can make you shy away from others, sometimes rejecting them as soon as they begin to like you. Maybe you have such a low opinion of yourself that you feel you don't deserve to be loved. Maybe you're afraid of involvements, unsure about your ability to deal with intimacy. If you can work on developing a higher opinion of yourself (look back to Chapter One for some ideas on this) you might grow to the point of learning to take affection as well as give it!

PARENTS VERSUS DATES

I don't think my girl's folks like me too good. I've hardly even met them, but I just have this feeling. They always want me to come into the house when I pick Dorie up, but it makes me uncomfortable so I just honk. How can I make a good impression?

Ken R.

My boyfriend's mom acts funny when I call and ask for him. She sounds irritated and she sighs a lot. I think this means she doesn't like me but I'm not sure. How can I get her to like me better?

Janice K.

Getting along with your boyfriend's or girlfriend's parents isn't always possible, but it is preferable. It can smooth the way for your dating relationship to continue, can make everyone concerned feel better, and can even be fun.

The key to getting along with a date's parents is consideration. Even a little from you can go a long way. Taking the time and trouble to meet and talk to a date's parents can make a big difference. Most parents feel somewhat protective and want to be reassured that you're a nice, reliable person who will not hurt or use their son or daughter. If you take the trouble to meet and talk with them, they're likely to feel that you're at least polite—which can get you off to a good start. Reassuring them may lead to fewer hassles and restrictions related to your dating their son or daughter. Everyone knows it isn't easy to strike up a fascinating conversation with someone's parents. Just a polite one will do, and when his or her parents see that you're trying, they'll be likely to give you a chance, too.

When you're phoning your friend, consideration again can help a lot. Avoid phoning constantly and tying up the phone for hours. Try not to call too early or late or during meal times. And if a parent answers, don't just ask abruptly for your friend. Instead, greet the parent by name, identify yourself, and then (or after a little more preliminary talk if you know the parent well) ask for your friend. Just taking the time to greet the parent personally—instead of treating him or her like a telephone answering machine—can make a big difference.

COMMUNICATION PROBLEMS

My girlfriend and I fight all the time. We can't talk about anything without fighting about it. What can we do?

Brad L.

I love this dude, but he's open about his feelings and I'm not. How can I change? I really want to be more open, but I'm not sure how to be. Help me, please!

Stacey E.

My boyfriend talks to me, but not about serious things like problems or feelings. I try to get him to let out his thoughts with me, but so far haven't had much success.

Connie N.

People have differing abilities to share feelings. Some are open and communicate easily. Others are good listeners, but find it hard to talk about themselves. Others are poor listeners, making assumptions, jumping to conclusions, and escalating an innocent discussion into a full-scale battle.

Some amount of disagreement is natural in a close relationship, but constant fights often mean poor communication—that you're not hearing each other and sharing feelings.

How can you communicate better?

Agree—during a peaceful, quiet time—that you and your partner will disagree at times. Make a promise to listen without jumping in to attack and to express how you each feel without leveling angry accusations at each other. Saying "I feel hurt and upset when you wait until the last minute to call and ask me out" instead of "You're really inconsiderate for waiting so late to make plans!" leaves room for discussion. Don't wait for a crisis to occur. Try communicating on little things. Express your feelings before they build up and erupt into a major argument. Learn to tell the other person what you would like to have happen as a result of your discussion and try to have a compromise in mind. Don't just expect the other to come up with a solution or to make all the concessions. If you each give a little—when possible—you may find yourselves fighting much less.

If your friend has trouble expressing his or her feelings, don't push. Just let the person know that you care very much about him or her and about his or her feelings, thoughts, and opinions. Ask his or her opinions on certain things. Share your own thoughts and feelings while reassuring your friend that you're there to listen to him or her, too.

If you have trouble being open and would like to share your feelings more readily, tell your friend that and ask for help. Start in small ways: express an opinion, tell about something you like, or recount a happy or sad past experience. As time goes on, your trust may grow and you can share even more of yourself. You may always be a more private person than most, but it can be a joy to be as open as you can with those you love.

BREAKING UP (HOW TO SURVIVE IT!)

How do you gracefully tell someone you want to break up without hurting that person? I need to know quick!
Trapped

My boyfriend of two years says we both need to meet and date others and he wants to break up, but remain friends if we can. Well, whenever he brings this up, I scream and cry and threaten to kill myself (which I wouldn't do—I just say it to scare him!) until he drops the subject. Even though we have a lot of fights now, I won't let him go! How can I keep him?
Patti P.

How do you know when a relationship has had it? I mean, when should you just give up and break up?
Jason H.

Breaking up is never easy and almost always involves hurt for everyone concerned.

There are times, however, when breaking up is a constructive move, something that must be done when there's nothing further that can be done to save a relationship. It can hurt—sometimes for a long time—but it can also clear the way for growth, new people, and new experiences.

For many couples, a breakdown in communication, a lack of willingness to keep trying, and constant hurt are symptoms of a dying relationship. There are other signs that your time with someone may be nearing the end.

- You avoid any talk of the future.
- You look for excuses to fight.
- Little habits and aggravations suddenly become a big deal.
- You start lying to each other.
- You constantly compare each other (unfavorably) with others.
- You shrug and say "It doesn't matter" instead of trying to resolve a difference.
- You feel like a hypocrite saying loving, affectionate things to him or her.
- You stop believing in each other.
- You start making unfair demands on the other (often prefaced by "If you *really* loved me, you'd . . .").

If you want to break up with someone, it's best to be honest yet gentle. Saying something like "You're a very good person, but I feel the need to date other people. I'm afraid I'm not the right person for you," may hurt less than saying "I want to break up with you because you're boring, not at all my type, and I've found someone better!" or just disappearing from that person's life with no warnings or explanations.

However kindly phrased, these words may be difficult to hear when you're on the receiving end. If you've done all that seems possible to work things out and the other person wants out, it will only perpetuate the pain for you if you scream, threaten, and beg to keep the other person from leaving you. As Patti's letter shows, keeping a boyfriend (or girlfriend) in this way is a dubious victory, practically guaranteeing a lot of anger and resentment and simply prolonging the agony of the breakup.

Grief is a natural reaction to a breakup and may come in several stages. It's important to let your feelings happen, even if they're very painful, instead of bottling them up or denying them.

"You must stay with your hurt until it heals," says Dr. Melba Colgrove, a psychologist and coauthor of the book *How to Survive the Loss of a Love*. "First, you may feel shock and denial. You don't believe this is happening. You don't *want* to believe it. Then there is anger and depression. It's OK to feel anger. It's *not* OK to hate yourself or hurt yourself. As you continue to heal, you'll move on to understanding and acceptance. Each of these phases is necessary and brings personal growth."

You may be tempted, in the wake of a breakup, to feel down on yourself, guilty, and completely unlovable. "When you lose a boyfriend or girlfriend, you may be afflicted with a bad case of the 'If only . . .'s,' saying things like 'If only I had done this (or not done that) he (she) would still love me,'" says Dr. Colgrove. "You may feel that if he or she doesn't love you, no one ever will. That's not true. If that one person doesn't love you, it means that he or she doesn't love you—period. Tearing yourself down is hurtful and will keep you from growing."

Give yourself time to grow past your hurt, to understand what you can give and what you want in a relationship, and to forgive the person you have lost.

"It's important to forgive," says Dr. Colgrove. "Whenever there is bitterness, there will be ties. Hatred is just as strong a tie as love. Forgiving is vital to your freedom."

When you have this freedom, you may be able to look back and realize the benefits you gained, the things you learned, the moments you enjoyed in that lost relationship—and to be happy for those good things. You will begin to see it not as a tragedy, but as a growth experience.

This new sense of freedom and joy will come gradually. Even then, there will be times, perhaps, when you miss the person you've lost, times when memories and tears will come flooding back. Be gentle with yourself during those times.

"Give yourself credit for having loved and for having given," says Dr. Colgrove. "Most of all, give yourself credit for being *able* to give and to love."

As you heal, you'll experience both pain and joy. You may begin to feel a sense of wholeness and power over your life when you see that you can lose a loved one and yet survive. You may come to appreciate joy in a new way once you have experienced deep pain. And you may develop new confidence and courage that will help you to make your own happiness by living as fully and joyfully as you can and by choosing, someday, to take the risk of loving again.

CHAPTER SEVEN

Love Relationships

Is it possible to be in love at 14? My parents say it's just "puppy love." My grandma calls it "infatuation." They make me mad because I think what I'm feeling about Cindy is love for sure!

Ron A.

My mom is on my back about my relationship with Kevin. The problem is, I love him and because of this, I've lost interest in school and in most of my friends. I can't stand to be away from him. Mom says we should spend less time together and more time studying. She also thinks I should spend more time with my girlfriends and the family. How can I make her understand that Kevin is more important to me than anyone? How can I get her off my back?

Shelley G.

How can you tell if you're really in love? I think I am, but I'm not sure. When does liking someone change into loving?

Lani N.

Even though many adults may smile condescendingly or shrug off your feelings with comments like "You're too young to know anything about love" or "It's just puppy love," the fact is that it's impossible to set an age limit on the ability to love. We love in different ways, according to the person and the situation, all our lives. You may love very intensely at 14, 40, or 100!

Feelings have no age limits. However, the character of your love may change, depending not so much on your chronological age—which is measured in years—as on your emotional maturity and your feelings about yourself.

Why do adults so often assume that what teenagers feel is not *real* love?

It may be due to the fact that, because of lack of experience and lack of complete emotional maturity, some (though certainly not *all!*) teenagers may not be in a position to give and share in a way that will build a lasting love with another person. When you're still doing a large amount of your emotional developing, just

learning to give, still trying to figure out who you are, and not yet independent, it can be difficult to form a mature, give-and-take love relationship. This doesn't mean, however, that the love you feel is not real. It can be very real and intense.

Our ways of loving change as we change throughout life. Chronological age doesn't always mean that you will—or won't—experience a mature and lasting love. Some people reach old age without developing the emotional capacity to experience a truly sharing love. On the other hand, some people can love in a mature, giving way at a very young age.

MATURE VERSUS IMMATURE LOVE

How can you distinguish infatuation—or immature love—from mature love?

- *Immature love* is focused on *you*. You're in love with the idea of being in love. The state of *being* is more important to you than loving or giving to someone.
Mature love is giving—with your partner's happiness high among your priorities. It means being in love with a *person*—not a fantasy!
- *Immature love* is clinging and possessive. You feel like two half-persons who must join to make a whole. You seek security in your need for each other. But this mutual neediness can keep you from finding lasting happiness because you both need too much and can't give enough to each other. You're both focused on getting, not giving. And you're fiercely jealous of anyone who has any claim to your partner's time, love, or attention.
Mature love means finding joy in your separateness as well as togetherness. You both take responsibility for yourselves, not expecting the other to give you security or happiness, but simply sharing the good and bad times with each other. You're independent people who could stand alone, but choose to be together. This doesn't mean that you never feel jealousy. But you see jealousy as a symptom of a fear, conflict, or problem to

be discussed and worked out instead of having it with you as a daily fact of life. You trust each other and feel committed in a special way. Friends, relatives, and others in your lives tend to add to—rather than diminish—your happiness together.

• *Immature love* means idealizing the other person. He or she must be perfect. If your loved one falls a bit short of this fantasy, you either lose interest immediately or try to transform him or her into your cherished image of what a mate should be. When he or she proves to be hopelessly human, you may feel bitter and disillusioned.

Mature love is accepting. You accept each other as you are and forgive each other for what you are not. Criticism, blame, and attempted transformations are not likely to be part of your relationship. Personal responsibility, tolerance, and mutual appreciation, however, are important to both of you.

• *Immature love* drains your energy. You're so caught up in the excitement of being in love that you neglect other aspects of your life—family, friends, schoolwork, hobbies, and sometimes even important personal goals.

Mature love is energizing. It means that you have more energy to give to all aspects of your life. Your good feelings enhance—rather than diminish—other areas of your life.

• *Immature love* tends to be heavily focused on physical attraction and excitement. Looks are a primary reason you like each other and sex may be crucial to your relationship. If you're in a situation where you can't make out or have sex, you don't really have a good time, and may even find it difficult to know what to say to each other.

Mature love means that there is more to your relationship than physical attraction. You may enjoy physical touching and sex very much, but can get excited, too, by talking and sharing feelings. You enjoy all kinds of activities together and value many different aspects of each other.

• *Immature love* can make you feel like a new person—instantly fulfilled or happily merged into the life of someone else. Your partner is your whole world, your whole life.

Mature love means that you have found fulfillment as a separate individual. Love doesn't mean instant fulfillment for you, nor does it diminish who you are. You feel that you—as well as your partner—are special. You know that, if your love should fade or die, *you* could survive.

• *Immature love* is fragile, dependent on living up to idealized images of each other and pleasing each other constantly. When disagreements or disillusionment happen, they can pose a serious threat to the relationship.

Mature love can survive joy and pain. You're strong enough—and trust each other enough—to be vulnerable, to cry together as well as laugh together. You can take the risk of being honest. You accept the fact that you will disagree and disappoint each other at times, but are willing to work through the hard times together, instead of losing interest or turning on each other.

• *Immature love* can happen—and vanish—in an instant. Often, it's like a race against time. You feel an urgent need to proclaim your love and to make promises and commitments to each other before your interest and excitement starts to fade.

Mature love is enhanced by time. You know that time will mean growth, that, in time, your love and understanding of each other will deepen, and you feel no need to rush into anything.

• *Immature love* makes a firm distinction between friends and lovers. Lovers are for excitement. Friends are for support. All too often, the two are mutually exclusive.

Mature love means that you're best friends and lovers as well. You like as well as love each other.

• *Immature love* hinges on illusions. You do and say only what fits your idea of what love is or should be. Things that you consider unromantic—like serious discussions about career goals, money, birth control, and conflicting or painful feelings—have no place in your conversations. You might also avoid revealing too much about your secret thoughts, feelings, and dreams, out of fear of ridicule or rejection. Or you may tell all early in the relationship, hoping to bind the other person to you forever by confiding in and needing him or her so much. You try to live the illusion of nonstop love, seeing anger and disagreements as betrayals of love.

Mature love means gradual, ever-growing intimacy. With time, you come to know each other very well—secrets, strong points, weaknesses, faults, and cherished dreams. You trust each other enough to share who you really are and you protect each other, never betraying a confidence or throwing it back in a hurtful way in moments of anger. Mature lovers know that intimate relationships have inevitable moments of anger, disappointment, distance, and loneliness. The intensity of your love will have high and low cycles. Whatever cycle you're experiencing, you'll still be there for each other, never losing your trust, your commitment, or your love.

WILL OUR LOVE LAST?

Curt and I are both 17 and plan to get engaged next Valentine's Day. We're not going to rush into marriage. We plan to wait at least until we both finish junior college and have jobs. We love each other very, very much. Sometimes I think about all the people who are hurt by love, all the breakups and the divorces that happen all the time, and I wonder what the future will hold for us. How can we make our love last?

Debbie Z.

Even though Neal and I love each other very much and plan to get married after we finish school, I'm getting scared because he's a year ahead of me in school and will go off (1,800 miles) to college a year before I can join him there. How can we keep our love alive when we're so far apart?

Lorri P.

Marcy and I really love each other. The only problem I have is with jealousy. I want our love to last so much that I get jealous and paranoid that someone will come between us. I know this isn't a good thing. How can I make sure our love does last without being so uptight all the time?

Mike S.

There are no 100 percent guaranteed ways to make your love last a lifetime. Lovers grow apart and drift away from each other for many reasons. But you and the person you love might have a better chance than most to keep your love growing if you keep in mind some of the characteristics that longtime lovers often share.

Your Love Is Mature Love Mature love, with a strong friendship component, tends to grow and strengthen with time.

You Give Each Other Space to Grow and Change People whose love lasts accept one another's differences and realize that time and people can't stand still. We grow and change all our lives. There is always the risk that you and your love will grow away from each other, but people whose love endures are usually willing to take such risks. The alternative—all too often—is stagnation, boredom, resentment, and constant jealousy. If you want your love to last, you will come to realize that you can't hold on to love by possessiveness and neediness. You do not—and cannot—own the person you love. You also can't really love someone you need desperately. If your love is to last, possessiveness and neediness must give way to trust, to being with each other, sharing with each other, and remaining together by choice, not necessity.

You Accept the Fact That There Are Many Ways to Show Love Many love relationships fade when a partner is unable to express love in exactly the way the other feels is right. Some people are able to talk freely about their love. Others express it more indirectly ("I'm so glad to see you!" or "I really missed you today!"). Still others have great difficulty saying words of love, but show their feelings in other ways—with a touch, a tender look, a tight, warm hug on a bad day, thoughtful surprises, or an obvious desire to share experiences and plan for the future.

It's important, if your love is to last, not to try to change your partner's love style to meet your expectations. If you talk about your loving feelings easily and long to hear "I love you!" from a lover who seems to prefer actions to words, you might express a need to hear these words every now and then. But don't expect this person to be able to express his or her feelings in words as easily as you do. It's vital to accept and appreciate each other's highly individual ways of expressing love.

You Know What Matters and What Doesn't in Your Relationship With some people, every disagreement or difficulty is a crisis. Some people pick at each other all the time—over big and little things alike. People who tend to stay in love are able to deal with issues that are important to them in an honest and caring way. They are willing to compromise. They are also willing to let less important things go. When you love someone for a long time, it's important to know what can be let go and what needs to be changed and worked out. Letting go of the unimportant annoyances can free you to have less resentment, fewer crises, and more fun together.

You Develop Your Communication Skills If your love is to last, you must keep in touch with each other. If you're separated by school, military or missionary service, or career demands, this means making an effort via letters, tapes, telephone calls, and occasional visits to share your feelings and experiences.

Communication takes effort, of course, even if you're not separated. It means sharing how you really feel with each other instead of assuming. It means listening when it's your turn instead of planning a response or interrupting with arguments and excuses. It means confronting issues and problems even when that's difficult, because you care enough to try to resolve your differences. People whose love lasts are *not* the ones who never argue. They're the ones who know how to compromise and to settle differences in a constructive way.

You Make a Mutual Commitment to Work to Help Your Love Last Love doesn't just happen. It not only takes time to develop, but it also takes hard work and constant nurturing to survive. It isn't always easy to think of another person's needs and feelings when you have needs and desires of your own. It isn't always easy to find and maintain a balance between your needs as a couple and your needs as individuals. Communication can be difficult at times, and changes—changes due to growth or to new lifestyles (marriage, working, parenthood) as well as changes in health, financial conditions, or your own dreams and goals—can put stress on your love relationship. It takes hard work and a willingness to compromise and grow to make your love survive—and thrive.

IS MARRIAGE FOR US?

I'm 16 and my boyfriend is 20. We want to get married, but my parents won't let me because they say I'm too young and this will ruin my life. I'm thinking about getting pregnant so they'll have to let me. What do you think?

Lisa L.

I'm engaged to a guy I love a lot. We're both 18 and plan to be married in November. I'm scared about getting married young, though. My mom did and she's had two divorces already. Do you think we should wait? We really love each other and I want our marriage to be happy.

Melanie K.

I'm fighting with my mother all the time over this one thing. I want to get married. I'm 15 and a freshman in high school. Joe is a junior. We both want to drop out of school because we know we could get good jobs. The only problem that could happen would be for me to get pregnant, but Joe said he won't let that happen. He says that if we only had sex every other day instead of every day, I wouldn't get pregnant, and he's willing to control himself. How can I get my mom to agree with us and give her consent?

Wendy in Washington

My boyfriend is 20 and I'm 18. We're engaged and hope to get married later this year. We have a fantastic relationship. We can talk about anything. We have a lot in common. We're hard workers (I'm a secretary and he's a carpenter-apprentice). We've gone together nearly three years and have been through a lot together. We feel ready for marriage, but how can we tell if we really ARE ready?

Gina T.

These letters show varying degrees of readiness for marriage—from ready to not at all ready!

If you found your own situation in any of these OR if you and your love are thinking about getting married, you might ask yourselves the following questions.

1. *Why do we want to get married right now?*

Love, a willingness to meet the challenges and responsibilities of marriage; a desire to share the good and the bad times with each other, to make a deeper commitment, and to become a family of two or more are all reasons people give for marrying. If these reasons are accompanied by a realistic sense of what the responsibilities of marriage are and how you as a couple can meet them and weather the rough times, these may be good reasons to marry.

But many people—often teens—have other, not-so-constructive reasons. Some of these include: marrying to get away from your parents; because most of your friends are marrying or you want to be the first in your crowd to marry; to have sex (if you're a firm believer in waiting until marriage); because your relationship is going downhill and you hope marriage will make everything better.

Marrying to keep up with the crowd or because you feel it's expected means your marriage is not strictly a free choice, and since it's such an important commitment, it *should* be. Using marriage—and each other—as a way of escaping parents, justifying sexual activity, or attempting to mend a troubled relationship is usually counterproductive. You may find that your sudden independence may be overwhelming and that you may be *less* free in many ways. You may find that sex alone can't make a loving, lasting marriage, and that if you had relationship problems before marriage, they're likely to intensify after marriage.

2. *Can we be economically independent?*

In today's competitive and inflationary economy—when many older couples find that both partners must work to make ends meet—two high school dropouts have a very slim chance of making it to economic independence. Even if you've completed high school, it's important to have job skills, career goals, and a sensible budget. Do you and your partner know what it costs to live in your area? Rent, utilities, food, medical and dental bills, car or other transportation expenses, insurance, clothing, Social Security, and taxes can take gigantic bites out of your paycheck, leaving you with very little—if any—savings or fun money, unless you can plan carefully, budget wisely, and control your spending urges. Can you both agree on budgeting?

Do you have the qualifications to get the kind of job

you'd like? If not, how can you acquire these or other marketable skills?

Why so much emphasis on mercenary concerns when we're talking about love? Because financial problems can create a great deal of stress in any marriage.

If your answer to financial uncertainty is to depend on your parents—living with them or depending on them for most of your income (perhaps while you finish school or job-hunt) be aware of what the trade-offs might be, of what lack of economic independence might mean to your marriage. First, it's very difficult, in most instances, to get your marriage off to a good start when you're still living at home, depending on your parents and more or less subject to their rules. When they make the rules and hold the purse strings, it can cause a lot of conflict in your marriage. Even if you're living away from home—at college, for example—being supported by your parents can also bring pressures and conflicts. It isn't always possible or practical to postpone marriage until you're completely independent financially, but the more economic autonomy you have, the more adult you can be, the better. That way, you can start marriage as two adults making your own choices and creating your own self-sufficient family. This doesn't mean that you and your parents should never help each other financially. Many parents and their children, too, get great pleasure from this. But it's best to start a marriage with as much financial independence as possible.

3. *Do we have independent living skills? Can we set and pursue goals in a realistic way?*

Can you draw up a budget and follow it? Balance a checkbook? Cook and clean? Apply for and get a job? Pay bills on time? Prevent an unplanned pregnancy by using a reliable form of birth control? Are you able to agree on and plan for long-range goals—like career advancement, starting a family, buying a house? Some goals will demand considerable sacrifice. Do you know what sacrifices you might have to make and are you both willing to make them?

4. *Do we have the emotional support of our families?*

Some happy and lasting marriages have started out with a storm of parental disapproval, but these tend to be exceptional. If your families strongly disapprove of your plans, it might be a valuable warning sign. Maybe they feel—and know—that you're not ready. They might be right. Especially if you're thinking of using pregnancy as a means of changing their minds, are in such a hurry that you don't want to finish high school, or feel if you don't get married, you'll break up, you may not be ready to make such a commitment or may not be emotionally mature enough to handle the responsibilities that marriage (let alone parenthood) will bring. Exam-

ine your own feelings. Could your strong desire to marry now—rather than later—be tied in any way to feelings of rebellion or a desire to escape an unhappy home environment? If so, there are more constructive ways to be your own person and to cope with conflicts—including seeking counseling.

Even if you decide that your parents' fears are unfounded, that your choice is a free, nonrebellious one, be aware of the fact that lack of emotional support and/or estrangement from one or both families can be shocking and stressful when you're newly on your own. You can't meet all of each other's needs. Do you have others—besides angry parents—to whom you could turn for help? It's a good idea, *especially* when your parents disapprove of your marriage, to seek premarital family counseling at your local Family Service Agency or from a clergyman or clergywoman. Getting help in sorting out all your feelings can help salvage family relationships and can either help you not to make a mistake or help you to get your marriage off to the best possible start.

5. *Can we marry legally with or without parental consent?*

States have differing laws about legal marriage ages. For example, Wendy in Washington and her boyfriend could not legally marry now, even with their parents' consent, since neither is 17, the minimum legal age for marriage in that state with parental consent. In most states, 18 is the minimum age for marriage without consent and, in some states such as Florida, New Mexico, Tennessee, and Wyoming, both partners must be over 21. In a few states—like Alabama and South Carolina—a girl may marry with consent at 14, but her boyfriend must be 16 or 17.

These laws may seem arbitrary and unfair, but they might help protect you from a premature and disastrous marriage. The divorce statistics for young couples are staggering: 90 percent of marriages in which one or both partners are under 18 end in divorce!

6. *If we had to wait a year or more to marry, how would that affect our relationship?*

If you love each other, are willing to keep working to grow and to build your relationship, and plan realistically for your future together, time can be your friend. It can make your love for each other even stronger. On the other hand, if waiting time diminishes your love, your commitment to each other might not have been strong enough to sustain and nurture a marriage.

7. *Do we enjoy many aspects of each other and share many interests?*

Opposites may attract, but the more you have in common and the more you enjoy about each other, the better your chances of having a lasting marriage. Companionship, caring, shared interests, a sense of humor, and liking as well as loving each other all mean much more—in the long run—than physical attraction.

8. *If we had to, could either of us live alone and do fine?*

Marriage is, ideally, a union of two competent, strong, independent people who can make decisions, work, and function as adults both alone and together. If you can't make it on your own, this could be a danger sign, a signal to wait until you've developed a stronger self-image and sense of separateness. Then you'll be two people *choosing* to share your lives and your chances for happiness will be greater.

9. *Do we have realistic expectations of marriage and of each other?*

If you think that marriage is a panacea for loneliness, boredom, low self-esteem, and other feelings that are part of the human condition, you could be in for a shock! Marriage brings demands, responsibilities, and complications as well as joys. It can intensify existing conflicts and can curtail freedom in some ways while offering you freedom in others. Your mate can be loving and hateful, giving and stubborn, strong and weak. You can't meet all of each other's needs, be in a constant state of bliss, or be otherwise perfect. Making the decision to struggle together, to compromise, and to share whatever may come your way—whether painful or joyful—reflects more realistic expectations.

So does the decision to seek professional counseling help—either before or after marriage—if you can't resolve some important problems. This isn't a sign of failure. Many happily married couples get counseling in an effort to make their marriages even better. Seeking counseling in time for it to be of real help to you can be a way of showing your commitment and your caring for each other. It is often a sign of strength—not weakness—in a relationship.

SHOULD WE LIVE TOGETHER FIRST?

My boyfriend and I—we're both 19 and working—are thinking of living together before we decide whether or not to get married. We thought it might be a good way to test our relationship. We feel OK about it and our families, even though we know they'd rather we got married, don't have any strong objections to this. Is living together a good way to prepare for marriage?

Bonnie Y.

Living together before marriage is a controversial but increasingly common choice of lifestyle.

For those who find it morally and socially acceptable (these are usually young working people in their late teens or older), living together *can* be a way to get to know each other under more intimate circumstances than dating. Living together may give you clues—rather quickly—if you're obviously mismatched, incompatible, or not ready for such closeness.

But is living together a realistic test—and preview—of marriage prospects?

The matter is questionable. Some recent studies have found that the divorce rate for couples who lived together before marriage is about the same as the rate for those who didn't live together first.

These surprising findings might be due, at least in part, to the fact that some couples treat living together as an idealized extension of courtship.

"Many live-in couples tend not to face their problems before marriage, or else they nurture the hope that getting married—making that additional commitment—will solve any existing problems," says Dr. Craig Messersmith, a psychologist and marriage/family counselor at the Washington (D.C.) Psychological Center. "But marriage doesn't fix everything. When you take away the option of leaving easily—as you can when living together—and mix it with the intensity of living together on a daily basis, pre-existing problems may be escalated."

There may also be some significant differences between living together and marriage.

Marriage implies permanence, and your reactions to this may vary. You may feel more emotional security and freedom to be yourself. Or you may feel trapped and disappointed and find yourself reacting more strongly to little habits and irritations that you suddenly realize could be part of your life for years.

Marriage can also bring new expectations. Sometimes, when you marry, dreams and expectations you didn't know you had suddenly surface. Maybe you hope deep down for a fairy tale, happily-ever-after marriage. Maybe you expect your partner to change now that you're married. Working through these expectations can cause some conflicts and upsets—ones you may not have if you're living together.

Your family relationships may be different, too, when you're married. When you're living with a loved one, your parents' reactions may range from supportive to strongly disapproving, with many parents feeling embarrassed and uncertain how to relate to—and what to call—your lover. When a roommate becomes a spouse, the guidelines are clearer and parental approval is usually forthcoming. On the other hand, if your parents *still* disapprove, the hurt and anger can intensify.

Your feelings of love may grow and change with marriage, too. Ideally, you will grow past an idealized view of what love means to establish a loving friendship—a more flexible, tolerant love that thrives with a solid commitment and can withstand more pressures than a living-together relationship might. This, of course, doesn't happen as soon as you say "I do!" but can be part of your adjustment and growth during your years of marriage.

In the final analysis, living together first *may* be helpful if it isn't contrary to your moral beliefs, if it keeps you from making a marital mistake, and/or if you use it as a time of learning to be more honest and to compromise and tolerate each other on a daily basis. But you may find—through firsthand experience—that while marriage and living together may seem superficially similar, they are never quite the same.

GETTING OFF TO A GOOD START

My husband and I are both 18. We've been married for just two weeks. So far, it's great. But we want to keep our love for each other strong all our lives. We expect fights and troubles, but how can we keep our love all through this?

Andrea W.

What advice would you give an engaged couple planning to be married in three months? How can we have a really good marriage?

Kelly-Ann M.

Building a strong, loving, and lasting marriage may be the most difficult and joyous challenge you'll ever face. Keeping some of the following suggestions—all from licensed marriage counselors—in mind may help you get off to a good start.

Be a Complete Person Before You Marry   "You need strong self-esteem, interests, goals, and values," says Elizabeth K. Ryser, a marriage counselor in Salt Lake City. "That way, you can see your marriage with the concept 'I'm fortunate to meet someone who is *equal* to me. We've both worked hard to become who we are.' Then you'll be able to be supportive of each other. If, on the other hand, you lack self-esteem and a sense of completeness as a person, you may go into marriage with unrealistic expectations, feeling that marriage—or your partner—is going to make you into the person you want to be. *You* must be in charge of being the person you want to be. Ask yourself 'What can I bring to this marriage?' As a complete person, you'll enjoy a special sense of togetherness with your partner. Some people mistakenly believe that marriage means two halves meeting and forming a whole person. But an enduring, growing marriage relationship requires two whole people who have much to share."

Expect Some Disillusionment—and Don't Be Scared by It When It Happens   "Typically, there is a period of blissful idealism just before and just after marriage," says Dr. Milo Benningfield, a psychologist and marriage counselor in Dallas. "It can take about a year for most couples to begin to look objectively at their relationship and to see aspects of it that may be interfering with mutual satisfaction. This can be a real problem time, but you might also see this time as an opportunity—a chance to work out conflicts and learn how to compromise. Remember that marriage is a partnership requiring many hours of effort in compromising, dealing with conflicts, and developing clear communication."

Listen to and Try to Understand Each Other's Perspectives   "Try to understand the way your partner sees the world," suggests Dr. Alan Wabrek, a physician and codirector of the Sex Therapy Program at Hartford Hospital in Hartford, Connecticut. "It's easy to assume that everyone sees the world as you do, but that's not so. It's also easy to get into major arguments about who's right and who's wrong—when you may both be right. This can happen, for instance, in matters like varying needs for closeness. One partner may need more privacy and time alone. The other wants more hugging, touching, and togetherness. In this case, you would need to find a compromise, a way to change enough individually to meet each other halfway. You can gain perspective about each other by active listening. Sit down and take turns listening to each other for five minutes at a time without interrupting or planning a defense. Listen to discover how you both feel and why you feel this way. If you start really listening to each other, you'll begin to discover how your life perspectives differ and how they are the same. This can lead to new understanding and closeness."

Make Communication a Daily Habit   "The most common problem I see in married couples is lack of communication," says Doris Lion. "Sometimes this happens when you suppress your feelings because you don't want to hurt your mate's feelings or you want to protect yourself from rejection, or you feel he or she wouldn't be interested in what you have to say. Also, quite often, couples will tell each other only negative things, never expressing praise and appreciation. Sharing both positive and negative feelings can bring you closer together. Communication can be risky and it needs to be practiced constantly. Sit down and talk over your feelings—talking and listening without blaming. Talk about what's going right, what you love and value in each other. Take time for yourselves, time to share all your feelings. You're going to be in this marriage—hopefully—for a long time, so take some moments out of your busy daily life to improve your communication skills and nurture your relationship."

Be Willing to Work   "It's easy to get caught up in the excitement and joy of being in love and to ignore certain realities that marriage will bring," says Dr. Joyce Vesper, a psychologist in Scottsdale, Arizona. "Some of the realities you need to consider and work out—preferably before marriage—include: financial plans and budgeting, career objectives, educational goals, household responsibilities (especially if you both work outside the home), whether or not you'll have children, and if so, when, your feelings about sex and about birth control. Be willing to work your problems out to create a feeling of honesty and trust between you."

Make Time for Each Other and for Fun   "You need to make time for each other, especially if you're both working and after you have children," says Craig Mes-sersmith. "Organize your life to include precious moments alone. Go away for a weekend—just the two of you—occasionally. Go out for the night. Talk about your relationship. Marriage is work, but it can also be fun. Make time for both work and fun in your lives. If you don't, you can lose each other emotionally. If you're willing to put time, effort, and fun into your marriage, it has a good chance for survival."

Have Realistic Expectations   "Couples who are in growing, lasting relationships tend to have realistic expectations," says Dr. Lloyd Mendelson, a marriage and family therapist in Atlanta. "They don't expect their mates to give them everything. They accept each other's differences. They don't expect to be happy all the time. They accept the fact that no marriage is ideal and that every relationship has its growing pains. They see the painful times, though, as an opportunity to learn. They communicate well. They know that marriage is a search, not an answer. Marriage means learning to live nonviolently with another person. Such learning can bring you pain and joy and wisdom as you share feelings of love, sorrow, growth, tears, and laughter every day of your life together."

CHAPTER EIGHT

Sexual Choices

It's so hard to know what's right anymore when it comes to sex. My Church says that any sex, except married sex, is wrong. My friends say sex is OK if you love the other person. My parents can't talk about sex at all and, even inside, I'm confused. It's like my body says "Yes!!!" and my mind says "No!" So how do I know what's right for me?

Wondering

Choices, especially when they relate to sexuality, can be confusing. TV and movies may give us one view of what is right and our religious upbringings quite another. Messages from our peers may differ a great deal from those we get from our parents. And many of us experience internal conflicts—where our values and beliefs may clash with physical desires.

It is in this atmosphere of conflict that we make our sexual choices. Some of these choices may relate to feelings and fantasies—whether you enjoy them or try to push them out of your mind—while others relate to actions, what kind of sexual relating you do, with whom, and under what circumstances.

WHAT INFLUENCES OUR SEXUAL CHOICES?

There are a number of factors that influence our sexual choices.

Basic Feelings About Sexuality Do you feel that all aspects of sexuality—from fantasies to relating with others according to your own values—are good and natural? Do you feel that *some* aspects are all right, given certain circumstances? Or do you feel that sex is, basically, dirty—whether you're thinking about it or doing it—or that it's mostly a duty in marriage or just for having kids?

How you feel about various aspects of sexuality can determine some choices you will make. This doesn't mean that if you have positive feelings about sex in general you'll spend all your time fantasizing or rushing out and having lots of sexual relationships. It does mean that you feel good about your sexuality, that you enjoy and don't feel guilty about the choices you make, which at this time may be fantasizing, masturbation, and/or sexual intercourse. You may or may not choose to have premarital sex. For example, a sex-positive person who is *not* sexually active may value sex as a beautiful expression of love to be shared only by people who are married and so might choose to remain a virgin until marriage.

A sex-negative person—who feels that sex is dirty or simply a duty or a means to a particular nonsexual, nonsharing goal—also may or may not be sexually active. Some avoid all aspects of sex as much as possible, even when married. Others, who don't feel good about themselves, may engage in sex as a way of getting something—like keeping or gaining another person's interest—or perhaps to punish themselves with feelings of guilt.

Some people, too, have conflicting feelings—thinking that, in theory at least, sexuality-related choices are good, yet feeling twinges of guilt about certain choices. If these feelings sound familiar to you, they could mean that you're acting in a way that may not be a wise choice at the moment. Or such guilt feelings could simply be a carry-over from early impressions about sexuality.

Early Impressions and Experiences If you grew up in a home where your parents expressed positive feelings about sexuality—either by what they said or by the warmth they showed for each other, in the ways they helped you feel good about your body and your sexual feelings—this can have a huge impact on your present feelings and choices. If, on the other hand, sex was a taboo subject in your home and/or viewed in a very negative way, this, too, could influence your choices. (For example, you might find yourself either agreeing with or rebelling strongly against parental attitudes.)

If you've had some painful experiences—such as molestation, rape, or incest incidents while growing up (see Chapter Eleven for more suggestions about coping with these experiences and feelings)—these, too, can influence choices you make right now.

There are some theories, too, that early childhood experiences and impressions may have some influence on your sexual orientation—that is, whether you're heterosexual or homosexual. Some studies have attempted to link domineering or retiring mothers or retiring, domineering, or absentee fathers with people who are primarily homosexual.

However, Dr. Evelyn Hooker of UCLA, a noted researcher in the area of homosexuality, says that it's impossible to generalize about the family relationships of young people who grow up to prefer those of their own sex. She has noted, though, that in some cases, early experiences *may* influence sexual preferences, that unpleasant experiences with the opposite sex or puritanical parents who put too heavy an emphasis on the evils of heterosexual behavior *may* make a young person feel guilty and anxious just thinking about the opposite sex—and that homosexuality might be the lesser of two evils.

At this time, however, there has been no conclusive evidence about the origins of sexual preferences. We still don't know for sure whether these preferences are due to a genetic predisposition or whether they are learned behavior—and if they are learned, how and at what age.

Values Values influence our choices in many ways. You may feel very positive about your sexuality and choose to limit expression of this to ways that coincide with your own values. This may mean that although you find many people physically attractive, you choose not to have sex with just anyone attractive who comes along—because you don't believe in premarital sex, or you believe in developing a total one-to-one relationship based on many factors besides physical attraction, *or* you believe in being faithful to the one you love. You may also basically have good feelings about your body, yet choose not to masturbate because this would be against the teachings of your religion. Or perhaps your values include relating honestly with others—never playing games or trying to mislead them in any way. All of these values—among many others—can influence your sexual choices.

Feelings About Others When you love someone very much, this can have a great impact on your choices about how you will express yourself sexually. If you value your friends and their opinions a lot, what they think and say about sex can influence you. So can feelings of rebellion against your parents, feelings of pain and desperation (such as in the wake of a parental di-

vorce or desertion), *or* feelings that you would do anything to avoid hurting or disappointing your parents.

Feelings About Yourself These, too, can exert a big influence on your sexual choices. For example, you may feel that you don't have much to offer as a person and that others won't like you unless you come on strong sexually or are sexually compliant. Or you may value yourself a great deal and feel free to say "Yes" or "No" depending on what seems right for you. And these are just two examples of the many ways your self-image can influence your sexual choices!

COMMUNICATION AND SEXUAL CHOICES

I have a problem: I can't talk with my parents about sex! My parents are intelligent, good people, but are uptight about the subject of sex. I'd like to talk about it with them and get some information I need, but I feel embarrassed to bring the subject up.

Bryan B.

My friends talk about sex a lot and some pretty weird and confusing things are mentioned. I'm not sure what's true and what isn't. I'm afraid if I mentioned anything like this to my parents, they'd just think my friends were horrible and dirty-minded (they're not!) and wouldn't let me be with them. Or they'd think I was talking dirty or being dumb. How can I clear up some facts I've heard?

Gillian C.

My boyfriend wants to have sex. I'm tempted because I love him so much, but I'm afraid of being used. I'm scared that it wouldn't mean as much to him as it would to me and that he'd look down on me afterwards or tell everyone in school. How can I decide what to do?

Katie O.

Another important factor in sexual choice-making is communication: communication with sources of sex information (like parents, peers, doctors, and others), with your present or potential partner, and with yourself!

Communicating With Parents and Other Information Sources

Communicating with your parents about sex can be a beautiful sharing experience, an excruciatingly embarrassing exchange, *or* a nonevent, an exercise in frustrating noncommunication.

Trying to see and understand your parents' perspective about sexuality—yours in particular—may help you to start communicating more effectively with them.

While a minority of parents have very negative feelings about sex in general, many are simply concerned and sometimes bewildered by the fact that you're now at an age where real sexual choices are possible. They may love you deeply and fear for you in many ways. They may be afraid that you'll be hurt, that you'll fail to see the value of beliefs they cherish, and that your future may be jeopardized by unwise choices you might make now. They may fear that you'll become sexually active before you're emotionally ready or mature enough to handle the responsibilities that sexual involvements bring. They may express this fear by more rules and restrictions, by lectures, or by terse replies like "Why do you want to know about THAT?" in answer to any specific questions you may ask about sex.

Understanding that these communication problems can be caused, at least in part, by parental concern and by the fact that your parents' generation did not grow up talking as openly about sex as you and your friends do might help you to have more patience with your parents instead of labeling them sex-negative or really out-of-it. (If your parents *are* extremely negative about sex in general, realizing your separateness and having compassion for their point of view—while quietly holding on to your own opinions—may help.)

Why is it important to try to communicate with your parents? The fact that they care so much for you and usually have your best interests at heart is one reason. Many sex educators believe that the best possible sex education is centered at home. Many of your feelings about yourself and your sexuality have been learned—often in subtle ways—at home. For this reason, it can be helpful to talk over feelings, values, and views with your family.

Of course, this is often easier said than done. Embarrassment, fear of being misunderstood, and denial of one another's sexuality can all get in the way of communication.

It may be best to start cautiously—perhaps asking your parents' opinions about a specific matter, discussing some sexual information you've heard (without being too specific about the source, if you choose) and asking your parents what they know about it, feel, or think about it.

Sometimes, your parents can't give you the information you need because they don't know (e.g., many new discoveries about VD and birth control are being made all the time) or because they're uncomfortable sharing such feelings and ideas with you. In this instance, other people—your physician, a nurse practitioner, a sex education teacher or counselor at a youth clinic or organization such as Planned Parenthood, or other relatives—may be able to help you.

It's important to seek such help and to make sexual choices with as much correct factual information as possible. That way you can begin to make informed choices—knowing all the pros and cons and possible consequences of what you're choosing.

Communicating with Your Partner

Communicating with your partner is also vital.

"If you and the other person see sexual involvement—anything from kissing and petting to actual intercourse—as meaning very different things, this can be potentially hurtful," says Dr. Charles Wibbelsman, an adolescent medicine specialist and coauthor of *The Teenage Body Book*. "Maybe one person sees physical involvement as a sign of love and the other sees it as a way of proving himself or herself. The latter may like his or her partner a lot, but may not be ready for a total, sharing relationship. It's important to be able to share your feelings about what sexual involvement means to you right now. And, if your feelings about this meaning differ, can *both* of you live with such differences? Communication is very important in a caring relationship of any kind. There is so much more to loving and caring than sex. Being together, sharing experiences, and talking are important, too. Being able to talk openly about feelings, fears, and preferences is very important."

Honest Questions to Ask Yourself

It's important, too, to be honest with *yourself*. Try asking yourself the following questions when you're faced with a sexual choice.

What do I really want? What would be the advantages and disadvantages of acting on my wishes right now? Are my expectations about sexual involvements realistic?

Do you want warmth and love? Do you want reassurance that you're a worthwhile, desirable person? Do you want to share who you are with someone special? Sexual involvement may—or may not—meet these needs.

Some people, for example, expect that being sexually involved with another in some way will bind them forever in love. Others expect that sex will make them instantly mature, wise, or happy. All may be disappointed. Sexual relating of all kinds—from kissing to intercourse—can be pleasurable, an expression of love and a way of sharing yourself with another, but it can't bring love, wisdom, relationship security, or self-esteem where none existed before.

Am I really ready for sexual involvement?

How can you tell if you're ready or not ready? To start, you might read through some of the following general observations and compare them with your feelings and your own life.

You may NOT be ready for sexual involvement if:

• You expect sex to make you mature, happy, and wise or to make your love last forever.

• You're using sex to hold on to another or are misleading the other person to get what you want.

• You see the other person as a conquest or a challenge or just as someone to be with, nobody special.

• You can't communicate with the other person and are unable or unwilling to discuss sexual preferences, feelings, or responsibilities (like birth control).

• You'd rather take a chance on pregnancy than deal with anything as "unromantic" or "premeditated" as an effective method of birth control.

• You need to pretend (even to yourself) that each sexual encounter is an accident, that you simply got carried away by passion or were under the influence of alcohol or drugs.

• You haven't weighed all the possible consequences —both good and bad—of your actions. It's true that, as you share sexually in addition to other ways, your love, commitment, and closeness may grow. But consequences such as VD, pregnancy, or pain caused by disappointment or violation of your own values must not be discounted. Part of caring and sharing with each other is taking responsibilities to prevent or minimize such negative consequences.

• You're violating your own feelings, beliefs, and values by your actions, having sex because someone else expects it or because everyone else seems to be doing it. If you have a need, for example, to feel that sex was an accident or that any kind of preplanning (such as use of birth control) is wrong, this can be an important clue that your values and your actions might be at odds and you may not be ready for sex right now.

People who ARE ready for sexual involvement:

• Usually do so within the framework of a caring relationship and have realistic expectations of sex and of each other.

• See each other as people with feelings who are valuable quite apart from sexual sharing. They like and often love each other. They can be vulnerable and real with each other.

• Try to communicate openly with each other about feelings, expectations, preferences, and fears.

• Have correct information about sex—not only about lovemaking techniques and how to give each other pleasure, but also how to prevent unwanted pregnancy or avoid spreading venereal diseases.

• Freely choose to relate with each other sexually, *not* out of fear of losing each other or because everyone else seems to be having sex.

• Take responsibility for their actions—not only in the sense of preventing unwanted pregnancy or the spread of VD, but also trying to be honest with each other, not hurting or exploiting each other.

How will I express my sexuality right now?

We express our sexuality in many ways—by feelings and fantasies as well as by actions, either alone or with others.

It's important to realize that all fantasies and feelings are OK. Feelings just *are,* they cannot be judged—as actions are. Fantasies can be a safe way to channel your sexual feelings when you're not ready or able to be sexually active. Fantasies can sometimes, too, add excitement and variety to sexual relationships.

Masturbation is also a natural expression of sexuality for people of all ages and both sexes. It isn't harmful unless it violates your own values or religious beliefs and causes extreme guilt, or unless it begins to take the place of other important activities in your life, such as getting to know others and facing problems, for example. It is also a good idea not to masturbate with objects that may be irritating. However, masturbation does not make you strange or unusual. Neither does deciding *not* to masturbate. Either way, it's simply a matter of personal choice.

Relating to others can take a number of forms. It may mean just being together, enjoying one another's company. It may mean kissing and fondling each other. Or it may mean heavy petting or actual intercourse.

It may also take the form of masturbation or sexual experimentation with a friend of the same sex. This can occur in a number of situations—most often in early adolescence. It can be a way of comparing sexual development, feelings, and reactions in a way that seems safe (during a time when relating to the opposite sex may be a bit threatening). The majority of people who participate in these activities are not—and don't ever become—homosexuals.

In any event, putting labels on yourself as a result of some choices you may make now isn't very useful. Although each of us may be *primarily* heterosexual (preferring people of the opposite sex as sex partners) or homosexual (preferring to relate sexually to those of the same sex), very few people are 100 percent one way or the other. In fact, the Kinsey Institute has devised a sexual orientation scale with numbers ranging from 0 to 6. Extreme heterosexuals, who have *never responded emotionally or physically* to someone of the same sex, would rate a "0", while an exclusive homosexual would be a "6". Most people would fall somewhere in between the two—since it's quite common and normal to feel love and caring for someone of the same (or opposite) sex with or without actual sexual involvement, and to respond physically (to some extent) to either sex, depending on what choices we happen to make.

Sex educator and psychologist Sol Gordon echoes a number of experts' sentiments when he defines a homosexual as "someone who—*as an adult*—has a *constant, definite* sexual preference for those of the same sex."

There is considerable controversy over whether sexual preferences are primarily learned—and therefore can be unlearned. Some therapists feel that if someone is highly motivated to change his or her sexual preference, this can be done with supportive therapy. However, it's difficult to tell in these instances whether such changes are in one's actual sexual orientation—that is, one's feelings—or merely in one's sexual behavior. Many psychologists and counselors are beginning to feel that it is often most constructive to help a gay person learn to accept and understand his or her feelings instead of trying to deny or change them.

If you are troubled about feelings that you are—or may be—gay, it might help to talk with a trained professional counselor at your local youth clinic, Family Service Agency, or gay community service group. For information about the latter, you can call The Gay Switchboard (215-978-5700) for the phone number and/or address of the service closest to your area. If you feel that you are gay and have shared these feelings with your parents (or would like to) all of you may find some help and support from a local Parents of Gays group. There are fifty-four of these groups in twenty-seven states, and five in Canada and England. For information about them, you can write to: Betty Fairchild, 1435 Vine Street, No. 6, Denver, Co. 80206; or to Nancy Hayward, P.O. Box 823, Baltimore, Md. 21203. Ms. Fairchild and Ms. Hayward—both parents of gays—have also written an excellent book that both you and your parents may find very helpful. It's called *Now That You Know: What Every Parent Should Know About Homosexuality,* was published in 1979, and should be available in your local library or bookstore.

A number of counseling professionals (including a growing number of clergymen and clergywomen) are beginning to feel that the ability and capacity to love and share—not the gender of your lovers—is most important.

Growing in self-acceptance and your capacity to share with others is an important goal to keep in mind whatever your sexual orientation or choices may be. And when you're faced with a sexual choice, it might be helpful to learn to ask yourself, "Will this choice be hurtful to me or to the other person? Does it involve real sharing? Is it something we can *both* feel good about?"

Do I feel as free to say "No" as I do to say "Yes"?

Choosing *not* to have sex with another can be a very positive choice. especially when you're acting according to your own values or your own feelings that the person and/or circumstances are not right for you. In the long run, it can be far better to risk disappointing someone else (as gently as you possibly can, of course) rather than risk disappointing yourself and losing your own self-respect.

Feeling the freedom to say "No" may help to calm a lot of fears. If you fear being used sexually, you can keep from being used if you feel free to say "No" in circumstances where your instincts tell you that this could be a distinct possibility. You may also be less fearful of others when you realize that you have the power to refuse any suggestion or request that's not acceptable to you. Whether you are approached by someone of the opposite sex or the same sex, all you usually have to say is "No, thanks. I'd rather not."

Am I willing and able to be sexually responsible?

Sexual responsibility has a number of aspects.

It means preventing unplanned, unwanted pregnancies by either abstaining from sex OR by taking adequate birth control measures.

This can mean doing some research and learning about what works and what doesn't instead of guessing, assuming, or taking your chances.

Reading *The Teenage Body Book* (which has detailed information about each method of birth control available today) or similar health publications can be a good start. Consulting your physician or your local Planned Parenthood clinic can be a logical next step.

A majority of the most effective methods of birth control—including oral contraceptives (the Pill), IUDs, and diaphragms—must be prescribed by a physician—either your private doctor or a doctor at a birth control clinic like Planned Parenthood. A physician, sexuality counselor, or nurse practitioner at one of these facilities can help you to decide which method of birth control would work best for you. There are some health risks involved in using birth control pills or IUDs (just as there are serious risks for some very young teens who become pregnant!) and there are special directions for use of a diaphragm that a health professional will need to explain and discuss with you if that is your contraceptive choice.

There is one quite reliable nonprescription method of birth control that you can obtain and use without going to a doctor or clinic: a condom (used by the male) in combination with contraceptive foam (used by the female). This method is only as reliable as you and your partner are, however. To be effective, it must be used carefully and every time you have sex, not just some of the time. Using foam alone and using a condom alone are somewhat less effective methods (with the condom being the more effective of the two). Either condom or foam used alone, however, is better than taking a chance or using a highly risky method like guessing "safe" days based on the woman's menstrual cycle. (Preventing pregnancy is NOT a matter with room for guesswork! Couples who use the "safe days" method—called the *rhythm* method—with some success are usually older, highly motivated, and able to keep elaborate charts and records of possible fertile or nonfertile times.) Another risky, not-recommended method is withdrawal—where the man withdraws (or tries to withdraw) his penis from the woman's vagina before he ejaculates (comes). The problem is, sperm can be in the lubricating fluid that appears on the tip of the penis during sexual excitement, often well before climax. Also, it can be difficult for a young man to withdraw in time. A lot of teen pregnancies have resulted from use of this nonmethod.

All *effective* birth control methods do require some planning ahead and, obviously, the admission that you are sexually active. Taking responsibility for your choice, however, is a vital part of being a mature individual. And using a reliable form of birth control can also heighten your sexual enjoyment, by decreasing your fear of the possibility of pregnancy.

Preventing the spread of venereal diseases—or sexually transmitted diseases (STD), as these are now usually called—is another aspect of sexual responsibility. These diseases afflict people of all ages and lifestyles. Nice people get STD. People who don't have sex that much get STD. You could, too. Since many forms of STD can cause discomfort at best and serious, even life-threatening health problems at worst—especially if undetected—prevention is vital.

What preventive measures can you take to keep from spreading VD/STD?

First, know the signs and symptoms of sexually transmitted diseases. *The Teenage Body Book*—among others—gives an in-depth listing of symptoms, descriptions, and treatments of many types of STD. Suffice it to say here that *any* unusual discharge (particularly if it's irritating and foul-smelling), itching, burning or pain with urination, painless OR painful sores, blisters or warts on or near the genitals, pelvic discomfort, or parasites (like lice) in the pubic area require immediate medical attention. With proper medical treatment, many forms of STD can be cured quickly. With the possible exception of pubic lice, which might be treated effectively with the over-the-counter medication A-200, sexually transmitted diseases do *not* lend themselves to self-cure measures. So prompt medical treatment—and notification of your partner or partners so that he, she, or they can also get tested and treated—is an important step toward responsible sexual behavior.

Regular medical checkups—even when you don't have symptoms—are a good idea if you're very sexually active. Many people with STD (for example, an estimated 80 percent of women with gonorrhea) have no early symptoms. Some undetected venereal diseases can cause serious health complications and damage future fertility. Getting a checkup at least twice a year might help detect such diseases early and prevent serious complications in you *and* your partner or partners.

Other preventive measures include good hygiene (like washing the genitals before and after sex), use of condoms, and knowing your contacts. The latter may seem rather elementary, but if your lifestyle includes casual sex with people you don't know well, take the responsibility of getting a partner's phone number or some other way to get in touch with him or her in case you should develop any symptoms of a sexually transmitted disease, so he or she can get treatment, too. This can be a major way of controlling the spread of these diseases, which has reached virtually epidemic proportions today.

Not exploiting others is another aspect of responsible sex. This can mean seeing others as people with feelings—not objects to be used. It can mean putting an emphasis on sharing, not scoring. It can mean being a friend as well as a lover. A friend will never try to force someone to act against his or her best interests. A friend will not ridicule, reject, or abandon another in a crisis. A friend will respect another's choices, privacy, and confidences—never bragging or laughing to others about a partner's most private or vulnerable moments, feelings, and choices. A friend will enjoy another as a total person who has much to share *besides* sex.

Another important part of sexual responsibility is being true to yourself—and making choices that are right for you instead of allowing yourself to be prodded, bullied, talked, or shamed into making choices that are contrary to your values.

"Your sexuality is as much a part of you as your personality, your interests, your talents, or the color of your hair and eyes," says Dr. Wibbelsman. "People have all these qualities in a unique combination. How you express your sexuality—the choices you make either right now or in the future—is very much up to you. It can't really be based on what others do or try to urge you to do."

A large part of responsibility—and maturity—is realizing that you don't have to prove yourself to anybody. What might seem right for everybody else may or may not be right for you. Having the courage to be your own person and the maturity to appreciate—even rejoice in—your uniqueness can make you better able to share who you are with others—in whatever ways you choose.

CHAPTER NINE

Sex Roles: Coping With a Changing World

I hate women's lib! I don't want to be equal. I like it when boys treat me good and pay my way places. I've never wanted to be anything but a wife and mother when I grow up, but now that's not considered cool or even normal. It's not fair!

Disgusted

Why is it that the more I grow up, the more I'm expected, as a female, to act like a child? My friends think I'm really warped because I don't believe that a guy should have to pay for me all the time or open doors or help me on with my coat. Since I'm not an invalid and have money from a part-time job, I can take care of myself. I don't like being treated like a child. At the same time, I don't want to embarrass a guy or make him feel stupid. I just feel that all the little gestures and customs say a lot about the fact that society thinks women are inferior and very little about how much people like or love each other. Is there ANYONE out there who agrees with me?

Ellen S.

What bugs me about women's liberation is that some women think that they're superior to men and act like they hate all men. It's like they're mad at the world. Why are women so upset when most men treat them OK?

Rick G.

I believe in equal pay for equal work, but that's it. How come these women are so down on men and hollering and protesting and messing things up for normal people like me?

Sandi W.

I like the idea of changing roles for men and women. I just wish some of the changes would happen faster where I live! I'd love it if a girl would offer to pay her way once in a while, or if she would ask me out. The whole dating process is very expensive and nerve-racking for guys. I'd be flattered if a girl called me or asked me out. I'm very attracted to strong women who know what they want, women who have minds and lives of their own!

Joe T.

As these letters show, changing times and changing ways can inspire many conflicting feelings. As the barriers between men's and women's worlds begin to break down; as traditional roles and concepts of masculinity and femininity are being questioned, re-evaluated, and challenged in a number of ways, many people feel confusion, fear, and anger.

Some young people who have looked forward to assuming traditional roles as adults feel betrayed when old ways of living become only one of several alternatives. Others feel fear and uncertainty over where all the changes in male-female relationships will take us, wondering whether they will still have the choice of living in a traditional way, fearing that changing expectations about what it means to be a man or a woman will somehow diminish who they are.

Others see the beginnings of change—women starting to make progress in business and the professions, more men making a commitment to share themselves emotionally with their families—and feel angry that these changes have been so long in coming and that they are still new and uncommon enough to be news events.

But social changes take time—and can bring pain.

In the wake of changes that affect how men and women see themselves and each other, it's natural to feel uncertainty, fear, and anger at times—no matter how you stand on the issues.

Sometimes you may wonder how and why all this came to be. Why all the fuss about roles? Why all the talk about sexism? Why are some old ways of being not working for everyone today? Understanding where we've been—as men and women—can help you understand what's happening now.

SEX ROLES—WHAT ARE THEY?

Roles in life—much like roles actors play on the stage or screen—tend to dictate certain ways of being, acting, or reacting in specific situations. If you choose a role for yourself and if performing this role brings you pleasure and satisfaction, that's fine. It's not a problem for you.

If, however, you're assigned a role simply because of your sex, age, or race, it can be quite another matter.

Ageism, for example, may classify you as a wild, unruly, rebellious teenager who doesn't know the first thing about love. That can really hurt if you're a loving and adventurous, but sensible person.

Racism tries to link color of skin with the presence or absence of characteristics such as intelligence, certain interests, or behavior patterns, regardless of the fact that scientific studies have not found any evidence to prove that one race is more intelligent than another. If you're a black person who is ambitious, intelligent, and self-respecting, and who doesn't necessarily have rhythm, the old racial stereotypes can be especially hurtful and upsetting.

The same can be true of sex-linked roles and stereotypes. Sexism—a way of thinking that insists that men and women have very different roles and ways of thinking and acting—dictates that *all* women are basically passive, less intelligent than men, illogical, and natural homebodies and nurturers, while all *real* men are, of course, strong, aggressive, good providers and protectors, natural sportsmen, and logical, nonemotional thinkers.

The problem with rigid roles and stereotypes is that while some people fit comfortably and happily within these confines, many people don't. A man who isn't a sports hero, superaggressive, or ambitious may be berated as a sissy or a milquetoast. A woman who is intelligent, ambitious, and sports-minded may be put down as pushy and distinctly unfeminine. Both may be made to feel anxious and guilty about not fitting neatly into predetermined "masculine" and "feminine" categories. They may also feel frustrated, trying to reconcile their feelings about how society says they *should* be with how they really are.

Rigid roles have hurt both sexes, denying both men and women equal access not only to opportunities, but also to feelings.

Women, for example, have not always had the option to develop their capabilities to the fullest extent. They've been counseled to play dumb, to deny their competence in "masculine" areas such as math and science, and to live for and through others—as somebody's wife, somebody's mother—instead of with others and for themselves. Their roles and their worlds have been strictly defined: woman's domain was the home, man's was the world outside . . . and there was little question about which was more important and interesting. Women themselves, all too often, have put each other down as dull, and have sought the company of men. Until quite recently, most women have been brought up with one goal: to attract a man, get married, and settle into homemaking—regardless of their individual talents and inclinations.

Because "catching" a man has been the top priority, many women have traditionally been unable to get past competitiveness and become close to each other. Looks have been overrated and beauty of spirit, intelligence, generosity, strength, and achievements in other areas have been underrated. Women who are not physically beautiful and/or married have, all too often, been considered "dogs" or "old maids." In contrast, men in similar positions are valued more for what they do and are therefore seen as "rugged" and as "dashing bachelors."

Even women who are fulfilling their traditional roles as homemakers have been minimized by society as "just housewives" or as "the little woman" and have been denied equal protection under the law in many ways.

Women who work outside the home have been plagued, until quite recently, by a lack of growth opportunities and by low pay. Even today, women earn, on the average, 59 cents for every dollar earned by a man. And a man with an eighth-grade education may earn the same as or more than a female college graduate—despite the fact that most women aren't working for extra money, but because they must. Many thousands of women in this country are sole providers and heads of households. Many more are keeping their families out of poverty by adding their income to their husbands'. The concept of "equal pay for equal work" doesn't go far enough or solve the situation, many experts insist, since women have traditionally been denied access to jobs held by men and men have rarely taken jobs in so-called "women's fields"—such as elementary or primary school teaching, nursing, or secretarial jobs. The pay for these "women's jobs" has usually been considerably lower than the pay for most men's jobs, despite the fact that the women—and men—who fill them often work as hard or harder, need a great deal of education and/or training, and take considerable responsibility. It's another sign that women's time and women's skills have not been equally valued.

Men have suffered, too. The old stereotypes have been just as hurtful—in some instances, maybe more so—for them. For the old macho stereotype seems to demand that a guy meet superhuman standards: always strong, tough, and in charge; a ruler at home who must take all financial and decision-making responsibilities; an achiever, a provider, and a tireless lover.

Men as well as women have been channeled into narrowly defined ways of being—into a role that seems to demand unrelenting ambition and drive, a role that values a man primarily as a provider and diminishes him as a feeling human being.

Men traditionally have been hit with total financial

responsibility, from paying for dates to supporting a family—often working a second job to keep the family living well in suburbia or, in these times, simply eating well. Men have been disinclined to learn—and sometimes discouraged from learning—vital living skills like cooking, cleaning, or ironing because these activities were considered feminine. Lacking these skills, men have often been helpless and dependent in some important areas of their lives.

Men have also had to contend with being perpetual strangers: to their children, who see them only for a short time every day; to their male friends, with whom they must seem tough, confident achievers; to their wives, whom they feel they must protect and who can't always hear their admissions of uncertainty or cries for help; and to themselves, unable to feel comfortable with, and to express, their less macho, more tender emotions. Men have all too often been denied the freedom to admit fear and uncertainty, to cry, to show their love and affection openly, to share responsibilities, joys, and sorrows, to nurture and get to know their children, to have choices and options about the way they will live their lives.

Questioning sexism and its stereotypes is nothing new—even though women's (and men's) liberation received a new impetus from the atmosphere of social change in the sixties and seventies.

Actually, as early as 215 B.C. women in Rome demonstrated against restrictive laws that kept women off the streets and economically dependent. In the late 1700s and mid-1800s, feminist pioneers like Mary Wollstonecraft and Lucy Stone challenged the social order with their writings and speeches. The Seneca Falls Conference of 1848 is considered to be the real beginning of the feminist movement in this country. At that time, a few women were living their lives in ways that might still be somewhat newsworthy today. For example, Lucy Stone—like a growing number of women today—kept her own name when she married Henry Blackwell. And she became related by that marriage to two other amazing women: Elizabeth Blackwell, who overcame incredible odds to become this country's first female physician; and Antoinette Brown Blackwell, the first woman to be ordained a minister.

Despite these promising beginnings well over a century ago, women did not win the right to vote in this country until 1920, and are still denied equal access to the law in many ways today. For example, 300 state laws had to be rewritten in order to put women on an equal footing with men legally when the Pennsylvania State Legislature passed the Equal Rights Amendment!

Equal rights is often seen as a feminist issue, but it's really a human issue. More equality for women will also mean more freedom—and equality—for men. When people oppose this equality, they're often expressing fear that changing roles will spell disaster for the family, the end of masculinity and femininity, and the beginning of new and equally restrictive roles—which would require all women to work outside the home, for example.

The fact is, changing roles and growing equality could mean *more* options—including the option to live in a traditional way if that's your choice—and *more* freedom—freedom to live in a way that fits your individual personality, talents, and needs. Flexible roles, for example, would allow for two breadwinners in a family, or allow partners to alternate breadwinning tasks, and could thus help some families to survive in an era of soaring inflation and growing unemployment. Businesses are already becoming more flexible about working hours in many areas, allowing parents of both sexes to spend more time with their children. Children could gain a lot, too, by having two parents fully participate in their care. Women could gain a great deal by getting in touch with their strengths, and men could gain by feeling free to experience the full range of their feelings and interests. In time, more men and women may find that "masculine" and "feminine" are descriptions of gender, not accurate descriptions of the activities, interests, and feelings of a total person.

CHANGING ROLES AND YOU

My boyfriend says I shouldn't be too independent and I should always agree with him because he's the man and the boss. I don't like this. He says I'm wrong to feel this way. Am I?

Maggie G.

I like the idea of sharing expenses on dates because my girlfriend has as much or more money than I have and it means we could do more together. But how do I bring it up in a way that she wouldn't be hurt or insulted?

Steve M.

I have a male teacher who goes on about women's rights until I could barf! I don't want to hear about that because I want to get married. I don't want to be forced to go out and work at a boring, horrible job! Lots of my friends feel the same way. How can we get him to stop?

Debbie B.

I can't believe my adviser. She's still in the dark ages! She's on my case because I want to be a doctor eventually. She says this won't go well with marriage and a family.

How come no one ever says this to guys interested in medicine? I think I should be able to do whatever I want and not be held back because I'm a woman!

Cassie L.

Changing roles and expectations can cause some awkward times for you right now, but they can also bring advantages. For example:

• If you and your boyfriend/girlfriend can begin to see each other as *people* not locked into roles, you can become even closer. If a woman has the power to have her own opinions and a man has the freedom *not* to initiate everything, they may have a more sharing relationship.

• As more girls begin to share expenses and responsibilities for asking for and initiating dates, it can change the dating scene in some very positive ways. Girls won't be stuck waiting for a guy to call. Guys won't be stuck with doing all the calling, asking, risking, and paying. And when girls share expenses, they'll feel more free to ask guys out (since it's really hard to call and ask someone to spend money on you!). It can also mean, as Steve points out, that young couples will be able to do more together. If you're trying to introduce "sharing" into a dating relationship, accent the positive ("I feel that this would allow us to do more things together") and ask how the other feels about it—well in advance of a planned date!

Some teens are puzzled about changing customs and courtesies. Some guys are afraid girls will take offense if they offer to open a door or light a cigarette for them. Some will. And some will be offended if these little courtesies aren't offered. So what do you do?

You might ask your date what she prefers and/or do what makes sense. You might hold a door for her (without making a huge production out of it) going into a building, but let her open her own car door when you arrive at a destination—unless she's sitting there obviously waiting for you to open it. Ask her if she needs help with her coat or a light for her cigarette (if she smokes) before springing into action. And, if you're a woman, you might consider extending these same courtesies to the men you date. If you get to a door first or he's having a struggle getting into his overcoat, open the door or help him with his coat—again, without making a big deal about it. And if a guy extends a traditional courtesy, don't put him down angrily. You might explain later—in private—how you feel.

• The growing number of options for both men and women can give new power and joy to your choices. What teachers, counselors, or others say about changing roles can be interesting to hear, but it doesn't have to dictate your choices. If you choose traditional roles and ways of being—either as a homemaker or as a sole provider—these roles will represent happy, active, positive choices—instead of being roles you fall into without much thought.

Or you might be inclined to try new options. Many young people, for example, are establishing themselves in careers and are becoming self-sufficient individuals before marrying. Some are choosing not to marry at all. And some who marry are remaining voluntarily childless. Some brides are keeping their own names after marriage, thereby retaining the lifelong identity that men have always taken for granted. Women are finding new joy and challenge in achievement as doors are beginning to open to them and as the trend to ostracize and pity them as old maids if they're not married at a certain age (or ever) continues to diminish. And men, too, are living in new ways. Some are seeing parenthood as a joyous and important priority in their lives. Some are getting in touch with long-buried feelings—feeling as free with their tears as they do with their laughter, as accepting of their limitations as they are of their strengths. And men and women are beginning to discover each other as friends and to get in touch with their diversity as human beings.

These positive changes are quite evident to some teenagers who have grown up during this time of change.

"Changing expectations about what men's and women's roles should be—I call it *people's* liberation—have allowed me to be the person I am," says Mike, an 18-year-old college freshman. "I like sports of all kinds, but I also like to keep my room neat and cook. Now I can enjoy all parts of myself without worrying about whether or not I'm masculine."

Zachary, 17, adds that "the changes in sex roles are great not only for girls, but also for guys because they take away the pressure of proving I'm a MAN! If I don't have to have the biggest biceps, drink the most beers, or conquer every woman I meet, I can get on with the task of becoming a mature adult."

Robyn, 16, feels that changing roles are giving her more power over her life. "That doesn't mean I'm never scared," she says. "Asking a guy out isn't easy, but now I know what guys go through. We have more to share. It isn't easy to plan and work toward a career in a traditionally male field—engineering. But I'm doing it and I feel good about myself for trying and doing what's right for me."

Kevin, 17, sees changing roles vastly improving male-female relationships. "Eliminating the game playing and stereotypes will help relationships to be more open and trusting," he says. "Maybe marriages of the future will last longer, too, if the people in them don't expect each other to fit a particular mold, but know and respect each other's abilities, disabilities, virtues, vices, likes, and dislikes, and are willing to encourage, compromise, and share. . . ."

Having a full range of choices and feeling free to be assertive, sensitive, loving, ambitious, vulnerable, strong, and silly—whatever your sex—can do more than allow you to make active choices or to have loving, honest, and sharing relationships with others. Having a full range of options—from traditional roles to new ways of being—can also free you to be yourself at last.

CHAPTER TEN

A Crash Course in Etiquette

My parents gave me an etiquette book for my 15th birthday last week. It's really a weird trip, I'll tell you. You could go crazy remembering all the picky little rules and customs. You couldn't breathe without doing something wrong! How important is it to know all that stuff?

Carleen C.

If you're like many teens, you may cringe at the mere mention of the word "etiquette," conjuring up visions of stuffy Victorian types who are hung up on minute details and outdated social rules. If you've tried to wade through a huge etiquette guide with its thousands of rules, large and small, or if you've come up against some strict etiquette training at home or in school, it's easy to get the impression that the smallest mistake can spell social disaster.

I remember being a 14-year-old freshman at a straight-laced girls' boarding school and receiving a booklet containing the school's 211 rules. This booklet left a lasting impression, for toward the end, one rule screamed out in larger type than all the others. Sandwiched in between dire warnings about smoking on campus and wearing strapless formals to the prom was Rule No. 143: "NEVER, NEVER BUTTER A WHOLE PIECE OF BREAD!!" The implication seemed to be that lightning—or at the least the wrath of the dining room monitor—would strike anyone who dared commit such a gross and terrible social error.

Many social rules have become more flexible in the past decade. You can be polite and correct these days without being stuffy or becoming preoccupied with tiny details and strange rituals. A lot of etiquette today simply means consideration and common sense. Social skills can save you from a lot of embarrassing, uncomfortable situations, whether they're everyday occurrences or rare happenings. Not knowing what to do in certain situations can be agonizing. For example, have you ever:

• Been immobilized with uncertainty in a nice restaurant (like on prom night) because you didn't know how to order, what fork to use, or how much to tip?

• Shuddered under the steely gaze of a taxi driver or hairdresser you unwittingly undertipped?

• Been asked to leave or been given big hints to leave a friend's party or house after a visit because you overstayed your welcome?

• Stammered while introducing people?

• Been trapped on the telephone by a long-winded caller or *been* a long-winded caller because you didn't know how to end the conversation?

• Been at somebody's house for dinner and been horrified to discover that the main entree was something you couldn't stand?

• Had trouble choosing the right gift for someone?

• Put off writing thank-you notes for gifts or for weekend visits because you had no idea what to say?

• Had trouble getting along with your doctor?

• Bombed out on a job interview?

• Said something in a wedding reception line that somebody told you later was DUMB?

If any of the above have happened to you, you're far from alone. Everyone makes mistakes. You can't expect to be a social star all the time. But you can keep absolutely mortifying things from happening to you and worry much less if you know how to cope with some common situations.

SOCIAL GATHERINGS

Handling Invitations

If I'm going to ask someone out or have a party, how far in advance should I do the asking? I've heard it's rude to ask too far in advance AND with too little notice. Help! How do I know what's right?

Confused

If I get a party invitation with R.S.V.P. on it, do I have to reply even if I'm not going? Also, how do I know if I'm invited alone or whether I can bring a date?

Julie N.

I had a really embarrassing experience last night. This guy asked me out for Friday and after I hung up, my mom goes "Where are you going? Who's driving? What time will you be home?" and what's worse, she made me CALL this guy up and find out or else she wouldn't let me go out at all! I felt like a total nerd!

Mortified

I have a question that comes up a lot, I'm sure: What do you do when someone invites you somewhere and you're not sure you want to go or you'd rather go with someone else (who may not ask you at all!) What if you accept a date for the prom and someone better asks you? Is it really rude to break the date if you give the first guy advance notice of a week or so so that he'll be able to get another date?

Kerry M.

When you're doing the inviting, timing can be important. If you ask someone to a party or to the prom months ahead of time or for a date weeks ahead, it can be awkward for both of you if that person declines. Few people are socially booked up months ahead of time, so a refusal here would carry a more personal message of rejection.

On the other hand, if you ask someone out the week of the prom or the day before (or day of) a date, it may give the person the impression that he or she is your last choice—even if that's not true.

The best approach, perhaps, is to ask someone for a special date (like a prom) about three to four weeks ahead of time, to a less formal dance two weeks in advance, and for a date a week to three days beforehand.

It's never a good idea to preface an invitation with "What are you doing Saturday night?" That could be awkward if the other person is *not* busy but doesn't want to do what you want to do, or if the person has claimed to be busy, anticipating an unexciting invitation, only to discover that he or she really *would* like to go out. To eliminate such game playing and noncommunication, it's best to be specific right away, saying something like "Would you like to see *The Empire Strikes Back* with me Friday night?" or "I've been invited to a party at Jane's a week from Saturday and if you're not busy, I'd really like it if you could go with me."

It's also thoughtful to give the other person as many details as you can (to avoid a situation like "Mortified's"). Tell the other, if possible, specifically when you will arrive or when and where you should meet, what you'll be doing, what kind of dress is appropriate,

how you're getting there, and when you're likely to return.

If you're being invited somewhere you don't want to go and/or by someone you really don't want to go out with, give a tactful but definite "No." Don't string him or her along with "I'll let you know later" as you wait for a more promising invitation. The worst possible breach of dating etiquette is to accept a date for security, breaking it when someone you like better asks you out. If you don't really like someone, it's better not to accept a date at all, even if it means sitting home alone on Saturday night. If you're waiting for someone to ask you to a prom, you might summon all your courage, take the initiative, and do the asking. That can be a lot better than waiting and wondering *or* going out with someone you can't stand—or even worse, hurting or using another person.

Under most circumstances, "I'll let you know" or "Let me think about it" are not polite answers to an invitation. However, this can be OK if you need to check with your parents for permission first, if you need to check the availability of a steady date's time, or if you have a possible time conflict that can be worked out. In such an event, you might say something like "That sounds like fun, but I do need to check with (name) first. May I call you right back?" Then do it!

If you get a written invitation to a party and it has R.S.V.P. on it, call or write to the host whether you're planning to attend or not. Especially when a meal is involved, the host will need an accurate count of guests.

Usually invitations—verbal or written—indicate whether or not you should bring a date (and if you're going steady or engaged, it is often understood that your date is included in the invitation). If it isn't clear to you, *ask* when giving your answer to the R.S.V.P.

The Prom—Who Pays for What?

I go to a girls' school and have to ask a guy to my senior prom. I plan to ask a boy I like and have dated a few times before. What I need to know is what should I pay for. Do I buy the tickets or do we go half and half? Should I pay for dinner before or snacks after or what? Should I expect to buy my own corsage? Help!

Phyllis A.

In a number of co-ed schools, individuals buy their own tickets and may split expenses for the entire evening—depending on their feelings about sharing expenses. If you go to a one-sex school and have to ask someone who goes to a different school to go to your prom, it's reasonable for you to pay for the tickets (after all, this person is your guest). In any event, the man will usually pay for a corsage. Dinner could be handled any number of ways. It could be the treat of the man who has been asked to the prom (in a case like Phyllis's). Or the woman might choose to treat the man to dinner, either at a restaurant or at a special home-cooked feast with her family. (The latter may not be the best idea unless your date knows your family and is comfortable with them.) The couple might also eat dinner separately before meeting, then one or the other could pick up (lower) expenses for a late night post-prom snack. Whatever you choose to do, it's important to discuss all the options—and who pays for what—well in advance of prom night.

Handling Introductions

What do you do when you have people over for a get-together and some of them don't know each other? How do you introduce people without sounding weird or phoney?

Don W.

My mom had some friends over the other day. She introduced them to me as Maggie Todd and Anne Walker. They're both in their thirties, I guess, and I'm 15. I didn't know whether to call them "Mrs. Todd" and "Mrs. Walker" or by their first names so I didn't call them anything. What would have been right?

Tracy E.

Is it OK to introduce yourself at a party or something where you don't know a lot of people? How do you talk to someone after that? I don't get in this spot often, but when I do, I HATE it!!!

Speechless

There are some basic rules of etiquette about introductions, stating that a young person is always introduced *to* an older person, a man to a woman, such as: "Aunt Martha, this is my boyfriend Jerry Smith."

However, what's *most* important is to say the names clearly so that the people being introduced can hear them. It's also thoughtful to give the people some sort of further identification or conversational hook so they don't stand there staring at each other and smiling uncomfortably after they say "Hello." For example, instead of saying "Kim, this is Joanne Culver. Joanne, this is Kim Barnes," you might help your friends out by saying something like "Kim, this is Joanne Culver. She's just moved here from Chicago. Joanne, this is Kim Barnes. She shares your interest in tennis." Now

they know enough about each other to at least *start* a conversation.

You can use the same tactic when you're introducing yourself to someone at a social gathering. Introduce yourself and mention a friend you may have in common (the host?) or an interest you guess you might share.

Never approach someone with a line like "You don't remember me, do you?" or a bright "Hi, I'm Sue. Remember me?" if there is the slightest chance that the other person *won't* remember. That can be embarrassing for both of you. Be gracious and refresh a person's memory by introducing yourself and adding an identifying line like "We met at the church beach party last June. I remember that you told a funny story about. . ." or something similar to give the other person an instant frame of reference.

If you're alone and unknown at a social gathering and feel funny about going up to groups of people, look for someone else standing alone. Go up and introduce yourself with an identifying line that may start a conversation (e.g., "I just moved here. . ." or "I'm a classmate of Judy's. . ."). The conversation won't always be fascinating or even get rolling at all, but most people will be grateful to be approached and many will be friendly and fairly easy to talk with. If you get someone who is impossibly grim, silent, or clannish, just remember that this can happen to anybody and is no real reflection on your social skills. If you're friendly and polite, most people you meet will react in a similar way to you.

What do you call someone you've just met? If it's another teen, first names are usually in order. If it's an older person (anyone past adolescence) it's a good idea to start off calling that person by title and last name—Mr. Black, Mrs. Randall, Dr. Greenberg—unless he or she says "Oh, please call me Joe (or Mary or whatever)."

Table Manners

I've been invited to a friend's house for a formal dinner (her parents are into those) and I'm really nervous! What if there's more than one fork and I don't know which to use for what? What if I do something awful and don't know it? What if they serve something I don't like? I'm kind of a picky eater and I can't stand spinach or asparagus or anything with yogurt or mayonnaise on it. What if they serve something like that?

Dreading Dinner in Des Moines

Dinner at a friend's house can be as informal as barbecued hamburgers in the backyard or as formal as a candlelit sit-down dinner. In any case, your best table manners are in order. Talking with your mouth full, picking your teeth, reaching across someone else to get a food item (instead of asking "Please pass the——") or making negative editorial comments about the food ("EEEUUUWWW. . . it's practically raw! What IS this stuff?" or "How come there's buttermilk in the salad dressing? I think buttermilk is gross!") are all *obviously* not cool.

Obvious don'ts aside, there's one more to remember: don't panic. If you're worried about grabbing the wrong fork, just remember to use your eating utensils from the outside in. That is, the fork that is nearest to your hand is the one you use first, probably for the salad. If a fruit or fruit salad is served as an appetizer, you would use a spoon if the fruit is served in a cup or bowl and a fork if it's served on a plate. If you're still in doubt, look around and see what everyone else is doing!

Remember, too, to look around before digging in. Some families say grace before eating. In others, it's considered polite to wait until everyone is served before you start eating.

What if the meal includes something really fattening, bizarre, or otherwise repulsive to you? If you're among people you don't know too well, you might try taking a little of everything. Eat what you like (or can tolerate) and leave the rest. You might try a bite or two of the food you're sure you don't like (you may be pleasantly surprised!). Fewer people these days are hung up on absolutely clean plates and it's likely no one will comment if you leave some food on yours. If someone does, you can just say that you're full (and that your eyes were bigger than your stomach when you filled your plate). If someone is urging something on you that you can't tolerate at all, you might try saying you're allergic to it. While people will, many times, try to argue you out of a food dislike or off a diet, most don't want to fool around with a possible allergic reaction. (And you're not lying, really. If you dislike something that much, you *are* allergic to it in a way!)

If you're on a strict diet and will be eating at a good friend's house, you might say something to your friend beforehand like "I don't expect you or your mom to plan the menu around my diet. I just hope you don't mind if I take small portions or don't eat some things. . . ." A forewarning, in private, can save embarrassment or hurt feelings at the dinner table.

Knowing When to Leave

I don't seem to know when to leave! People are always having to push me out the door practically. How do I know when to leave after a party or visit so it doesn't have to be so obvious? I know it isn't polite to leave too early either. What do I do?

Pete D.

Knowing when to leave can be a real social art. Ideally, you should leave while everyone is still enjoying you—not so soon that it looks like you didn't have a good time and not so late that people are staring at you with glazed, half-closed cobra eyes and wondering if you'll *ever* leave.

Be sensitive to signs from yourself and others that things are beginning to wind down. If you're starting to feel tired, it may be time to tell everyone that you're having a great time and would love to do this again soon, but need to get home now. If others are leaving (and getting no arguments or only feeble protestations from the host) this could be a tip-off that it may be time for you to start gathering yourself together to leave, too.

Body language can also be a clue. Look at your hosts. When people begin to tire and withdraw more into themselves, they may lean back from you, arms folded. They may show signs of fatigue (rubbing eyes, yawning). They may not make eye contact as often or hold it as long.

Food—or more precisely, lack of it—can be another clue. Some people stop serving food or refilling drinks about half an hour or so before they hope their guests will start to leave. So if the soft drink supply seems to have run dry or your coffee is low and getting colder by the minute, start making a gracious exit. Your friends will love you for it!

OVERNIGHT AND WEEKEND VISITS

I've been invited to spend a weekend at my boyfriend's parents' summer place at the beach. How can I make a good impression?

Janine G.

My pen pal, who lives over 1,000 miles away, and her parents have invited me to come spend a week with them this summer. I've never met any of them in person. How should I act? Should I offer to help around the house? Should I take a gift? If so, WHAT? I'm looking forward to going and want to be a good guest. Any advice?

Polly J.

I have a friend who's really gung ho on the etiquette thing and she says you ought to write a thank-you note to the host or hostess whenever you stay over anyplace. Does this mean I've been rude not to send a thank-you note to my best friend Shari's mother every time I stay over there (about once or twice a month!)? If so, I'm really embarrassed! But Shari's mom never acts like she thinks I'm rude. What should I do?

Upset

If you want to be a popular (and asked-back) overnight guest, you might keep the following suggestions in mind:

• Be flexible, adaptable, and nonintrusive. Follow the host family's schedule—rising, eating, and going to bed when they do. If they've planned a picnic or a hike in the woods or are crazy about miniature golf, go along happily—even if you're sure you'll hate it. If they love card games and you don't, be a good sport and play a game or two anyway. (You may vow never to return, but be gracious while there!) If a number of people are sharing a bathroom, don't monopolize it when it's your turn. If the family has annoying little kids, be as patient as you can with them, and if there's a family fight, step back and don't get involved in the hassles.

• Pick up after yourself. This means clothes and towels off the floors and onto hangers and into hampers. Make your own bed and offer to help with the dishes, meal preparations, and other chores. Clean the tub after you've finished using it. Your hosts will appreciate your help—and your offers to help (even if they don't take you up on all of them).

• Bring a gift. Flowers and candy have been traditional offerings. However, many families are cutting down on sweets these days and might enjoy a more permanent gift than cut flowers. A potted plant or terrarium, a photo album for family pictures, or a basket of fresh fruit might be welcome and useful house gifts. These are not necessary if you're just staying overnight with a close friend or relative you visit often. (However, in these instances an *occasional* gift might be a nice surprise. It might be something homemade, like jam or cookies or a macrame holder for hanging plants.)

• Leave on schedule. Overstaying your planned visit time might interfere with family plans or give your hosts time to get tired of having company. It's better to leave with the family wanting you to come back soon than to stay around until they start wondering if you'll *ever* go home!

• Send a thank-you note promptly. It should be addressed to the hostess (if you're visiting a friend's family, this would probably be your friend's mother) and should be sent within two to three days after you return home. (Although a verbal thank-you as you leave a close friend's home after one of many overnights will do, an occasional thank-you letter or card can be a nice gesture.) If you send a thank-you card instead of a full letter, *still* take time to add a few lines to personalize it.

Do you have problems knowing what to say? "Thank you" is a good beginning. Some samples:

Dear Mrs. Smith:

Thank you so much for a very special weekend. I enjoyed sharing your family's activities, especially the picnic on Saturday. And I'm still laughing over Mr. Smith's great stories about his college days. The company, the food, and everything else about the weekend were just perfect and I'll remember it for a long time. Thanks again and best wishes to you, Kelly, and the rest of your family!

Sincerely,
Jenny Black

Dear Mrs. Smith:

I want to thank you and your family for a wonderful weekend. From beginning to end, from the company to the food to all the fun activities you planned, my visit was a great experience, something I'll remember for a long time. Thanks again for your warm hospitality.

Sincerely,
Jerry Clark

GIFT GIVING AND GETTING

I don't know what to get my girlfriend for her birthday. I was thinking of a T-shirt, but my mom says it's in bad taste to buy clothes for someone you're dating. When I ask my girl what she'd like, she just says "Oh, anything you gave me I'd like." I'm still stuck and have no idea what to get.

Jason R.

When choosing a gift, it's important to keep a person's interests in mind. If you're having trouble deciding on a gift, sit down and write out the person's interests and likes. If Jason were to do this, he might remember—let's imagine—that his girlfriend likes the beach, cooking, anything with butterflies or owls on it, the Bee Gees, romance novels, and anything that looks old or antique.

Given such interests, possible gifts might be: a thick

beach towel in her favorite colors, a photographic wall poster of the surf, a recipe file or new cookbook, a box of stationery with butterflies printed on it, a little ceramic owl, the newest Bee Gees album, a romance novel, a jar of potpourri, lace sachets, or an old-fashioned-looking tea cup and saucer (which can be bought very inexpensively at a thrift shop or discount store or even a small antique shop).

While intimate clothing items (e.g., underwear, nightgowns, or very expensive outer garments) are not usually exchanged between dating couples, a *tasteful* T-shirt may be a much appreciated gift. Use common sense in choosing one. A T-shirt with pictures of marijuana plants or slogans like "How Do You Spell Relief? S-E-X!" is not likely to endear you to your friend's parents (and might even turn off or embarrass your friend). If your friend likes such T-shirts, let her (or him) buy them for herself (or himself)—and take the parental heat!

Flowers—either real or silk—or a plant can also be a cherished gift.

What do you get for a guy who has everything? My boyfriend's folks are very rich and they bought him an MG, an electric typewriter, and lots of clothes for his graduation (and for going away to college in the fall). I want to get him a nice graduation gift too, but I can't afford anything really expensive. I'm afraid my gift will look dumb next to all this!

Peggy A.

The sentiments of the sender, not the price of the gift, matter most. If you give someone a well-chosen gift with a message of love and best wishes, it will be cherished. Even if someone close to you seems to have everything, you can find some gift-giving clues by taking stock of what he or she already has and choosing a gift that may be related to these things. For example, Peggy might get her boyfriend an "MG" key chain or key case; an auto emergency first aid kit; an auto care kit with polish, soft cloths, and buffers; a desk diary for keeping track of college assignments; a large wall calendar for his dorm room; some good stationery with a booklet of postage stamps tucked inside (a gentle hint to keep in touch!); a terrarium or plant to brighten his room; or a good pen and pencil set.

My best friend is going away to college in a month. I want to give her a goodbye gift that she can really use. What could that be?

Marcia K.

There are many survival items that a college student might appreciate.

For example, you might make up a basic survival kit in a pretty box or tote bag and include: aspirin, sewing needles and several spools of thread, safety pins, packets of instant coffee and soup, a ballpoint pen, some pretty post cards, and maybe even a few postage stamps.

Eye shades and ear plugs (for someone who likes to go to bed early or who has trouble sleeping with any noise) might ease your friend's adjustment to the realities of life in the dorm.

Again, a desk diary, stationery, a good pen, plants, or a wall calendar can be a thoughtful gift.

If your gift budget is a little larger, check with your friend (or her parents) to discover what electrical appliances—if any—are allowed in the dorm. Depending on dorm rules, a heating coil for coffee or soup, a small coffee maker, a crockery slow-cooker, or travel iron might come in handy.

Another special gift: lots of postcards, cards, and letters to your friend, especially in his or her first few months at college. Those can be exciting but lonely times. A letter from you could really brighten your friend's day!

How do you buy a Christmas gift for a mother who says "Don't you guys dare get an expensive gift for me this year! Forget the nightgowns and the dusting powder and the slippers. I have enough already. No more knickknacks or kitchen gadgets. They're taking over the house! And no more plants because I'm sick of taking care of them all!" What's left?

Exasperated

Maybe your mother wants a gift of time. You might type or print a lot of coupons and make them into a booklet. What can the coupons offer? They might make offerings like "Good For . . . One Saturday Night Gourmet Dinner (Planned and Cooked by Me!)," "One Thorough Lawn-Mowing," "Breakfast in Bed," and "Babysitting Services—One Evening," to be redeemed whenever the recipient chooses.

Offering your services (with a written pledge on a card) for a major chore like putting all family photos in an album and labeling them, clearing a jungle-like backyard, or cleaning the garage can also be a great gift!

My great-grandma is 84 and living on Social Security so she's not exactly rolling in money. But she keeps asking what I want for my birthday. She used to do nice needlepoint things for me until her eyes got bad two years ago. What can I ask for that won't cost her much or anything at all?

Melissa F.

If you're in a situation like Melissa's, you might ask for a unique gift that only an elderly relative can provide: a link with your roots.

You might, for example, ask for an old photo from his or her collection, to keep as part of an ongoing family history scrapbook. It might be a picture of your mother or father as a child, or your grandparents in their youth or childhood.

Or you might ask your elderly relative for the gift of his or her time and memories for an oral history of the family. You could take notes or tape-record the old family stories and tales about life in another era. Some of the memories may be long and rambling and not exactly spell-binding. Some may be fascinating and touching. An oral family history or tapes of a grandparent's memories can be a unique treasure, especially as you get older. And it can be a joy to your elderly relative, too, to feel valued and useful and to have someone really listen with interest to those old stories!

My cousin is getting married and I'm a bridesmaid. I want to get her a nice gift that she won't have to return. (It seems like everybody gets two or three blenders, toasters, or crockery pots!) What can I get that would be different and useful? When I asked her what she really wanted, she said "Just your love and emotional support." Now what?

Julie O.

Love and emotional support can mean a lot! Being available to run last-minute errands and help the last few days before the wedding could be a great gift!

If you want to give a material gift as well, you might think about linens—towels, sheets, and/or pillowcases. These can always be useful. (But check out preferred colors and bed size first, maybe with the bride's parents.)

Other not-so-usual, but nice, gifts—a pretty picture frame (to hold a wedding picture later); a framed wedding invitation; a picnic basket; or decorating items like candles, figurines, or even a lovely polished stone or large seashell—can add a special touch to a newlywed couple's home.

If you're a good photographer, you might think about taking candid pictures of before-wedding activities and of guests at the reception. Most couples have formal wedding pictures taken by a professional. These can be beautiful, but are often very obviously posed and only include a few people. Some candid pictures can complement professional albums wonderfully. One of my bridesmaids surprised Bob and me with candid portraits of each guest at the reception and some fun pictures of our own preparations, too. Jeanne gave us an album of memories that our formal portraits never captured—and it's one of our most cherished gifts.

Do you always have to write thank-you notes for a gift? I just hate doing this but my parents say I have to. If I have to, what do I say besides "Thank you?"

Wade W.

Thank-you notes are in order for just about any gift—even if you've already thanked the giver in person. "Thank you" is a good way to start. Then you can mention the gift and how you're using and enjoying it. Some examples:

Dear Aunt Molly:

Thank you so much for the little music box! It's so beautiful and unusual. I reach over and turn it on whenever I'm feeling bogged down with homework or a little sad—and lots of other times, too—and it really brightens my day. Thanks so much for a lovely (and very treasured) birthday gift!

Love,
Jane

Dear Grampa:

Your Christmas check was a wonderful surprise! Thanks to you, I was finally able to buy that electronic baseball game I've wanted for so long. I've had so many hours of fun with it and am getting good enough so that the machine only beats me half the time! I can hardly wait to show it to you when you visit.

Thanks again for making it all possible and for thinking of me!

Best,
Curt

TELEPHONE MANNERS

How should I answer the telephone at home or when I'm babysitting someplace? I get scared when I'm alone that some crazy person might find out I'm alone. How can I avoid sounding alone when I AM alone?

Scared

"Hello" is still the most generally accepted way of answering the phone at home. If the caller asks for a parent or the resident of a home where you're babysitting (without identifying himself or herself), you might say "He (she) is not available to come to the phone right now. May I take a message and ask him (her) to call you back?"

I'm spooked by the telephone and I'm not good at it. I talk fine in person, but get awkward on the phone. I don't know how to ask for someone without getting nervous or how to end a conversation right or introduce myself. How can I get better?

Bill T.

Developing a good phone manner takes time, confidence, and lots of practice!

The following are some points to remember

• When you call someone, identify yourself immediately. For example:

"Hello, this is Bill Thompson. Is Mark there, please?"
"Hello, Mr. McIntyre. This is Bill Thompson. Could I speak with Mark, please?"
"Hi, Mark? This is Bill Thompson. . . ."

Never play guessing games like asking "Guess who this is . . ." or launch into jokes or conversation without identifying yourself. Some people's voices sound different over the phone and you can save both you and your friend some uncomfortable moments if you just say who you are and get on with your conversation.

• If you get a wrong number, don't just hang up or say "Who's this?" or "What number is this?" Instead say, "I'm sorry. Is this (the number you're calling)?" When you discover it's the wrong number for sure, apologize and then hang up.
• Let the phone ring at least six times before you hang up—in order to give your friend time to reach the phone from a distant part of the house.
• If your conversation is likely to go on longer than two or three minutes, make sure that your timing is convenient for the person you're calling. For example, you could say: "Hi, Mary! This is Sue Smith. Do you have a few minutes to talk?" (or: "Is this a good time for me to be calling you?"). If it *isn't*, get off the phone as soon as possible, saying you'll call another time.
• Usually the person who makes the call ends the call, but the rules are flexible. If you're holding up one

end of a conversation that's starting to drag or if you need to get off the phone right away, you might say something like "Well, I'd better let you go, but it's been nice talking to you" or "I've got to run, but I'm so glad you called" or "I'll see you Saturday then. I'm really looking forward to it!"

I work part-time in an office after school. People are always giving me grief about answering the phones wrong. I can't understand it because I say the name of the company and ask who's calling like I'm supposed to. I don't disconnect people. What could I be doing wrong?

Worried

Tone of voice and one or two extra words can mean a lot. Do you answer the phone pleasantly—or grudgingly? If you're feeling tired, angry, or upset, does that show in your voice? Since your voice represents the company to callers, it's important to sound your best even at the worst of times! Smile as you speak (even if you don't feel like it!). What you say can make a difference, too. If the person asked for is present and wants his or her calls screened, a curt "Who's calling?" can sound rude, even if it isn't meant to be. A softened version would be: "May I tell him who's calling?" or "May I ask who's calling, please?" This sounds friendly, yet is efficient, too.

If the person being called can't or won't come to the phone, telling the caller "I'm sorry, but Mr. Jones is not available at the moment. May he return your call?" sounds better than "He's not here" or "He's in conference," with no offer to take a message. Give the person on the other end of the line the impression that you really want to help him or her. An important part of being professional is learning to work pleasantly and efficiently despite bad moods, rude people, and phones that seem to ring off the hook. If you're pleasant to callers, they're likely to return the kindness. By making a little extra effort to be professional and polite, you can make things much easier for yourself in the long run!

JOB-HUNTING DOS AND DON'TS

Everyone has a summer job but me. I interviewed for some, but didn't get any. What could I be doing wrong? What makes someone want to hire you?

Ray L.

I'd like to get a part-time office job and I hear that there may be an opening at an insurance company close by, but I haven't seen any ads in the paper. Do I call or go by there or what? I'm 16 and have good typing skills. Do you think I'd have a chance?

Mary-Ellen S.

The competition for summer and part-time jobs can be stiff, with most jobs going to those who not only have good skills, but also have good attitudes and know how to apply for a job, communicating enthusiasm and willingness to work to a prospective employer.

Finding a job may be as simple as asking around among friends, getting an offer from someone you know, or spotting an ad in the local paper. If you're answering an ad, pay close attention to the instructions. If it asks that you apply in person at a certain day or time, don't call, don't write—be there. If the ad asks that you call for an appointment or apply by letter, do that. The ability to follow directions may be a quality the employer is seeking!

Many jobs are never advertised and are found by word of mouth (i.e., knowing someone who works there) or by luck. To increase your chances for luck, send letters to companies that interest you. If you know someone who works there, ask who should receive your job-inquiry letter. Or you could call the company and simply ask the receptionist for the name of the personnel director (or the person who does the hiring). A letter sent to an individual—rather than to a company or department—may get swifter attention.

Your letter of application should be typed on plain stationery (or handwritten neatly) and should follow the business format, telling the person what you have to offer and how you may be reached. It is also a good idea to offer to call for an appointment instead of asking that the person call you. This puts you in a better position to take action. A sample letter:

Mary-Ellen Schaeffer
5545 Whitsett Avenue
North Hollywood, CA 91607
(213) 995-8454

February 10, 1981

Ms. Mary Bevington, Director of Personnel
Allright Insurance Company
5000 Laurel Canyon Blvd.
North Hollywood, CA 91607

Dear Ms. Bevington:

I am a sixteen-year-old junior at North Hollywood High School, have a "B" average, and type 60 words per minute. I am preparing for a career in business and am most interested in working with your company as a part-time clerk-typist or general office assistant.

I would like very much to meet with you to talk about job possibilities and will give you a call regarding this early next week. I would be available for an interview any weekday after 2:30 P.M.

Thank you for your consideration.

Sincerely,
(Signature in ink)
Mary-Ellen Schaeffer (typed)

When you go for a job interview, there are some important points to keep in mind.

• Arrive a little early and alone. Don't bring friends along for moral support and don't rush in late. Be organized; bring a pen and pencil as well as some paper with you. Arrive a few minutes early so you'll have time to catch your breath and to fill out any necessary application forms.

• Dress neatly and conservatively.

• Show enthusiasm and an interest in the company. Know as much as you can about the company and its objectives before going for the interview. And even if the job isn't exactly fascinating, even if it doesn't utilize all your skills, it can be a good learning experience in working with others and disciplining yourself to work hard under less than ideal circumstances. If you don't have much to offer yet in the way of specific skills or experience, a willingness to work hard and to learn can go a long way.

So instead of answering your interviewer in sullen monosyllables or with long rambling stories, give polite, enthusiastic, and specific replies to his or her questions. Make eye contact. Let the interviewer know that you're really interested in the job and the company.

• Don't smoke or chew gum during the interview.

• Ask about the duties and requirements of the job if they aren't clear to you.

• Know when to leave. If the interviewer stands up and/or tells you he (or she) will be in touch, stand up, thank him (or her) and take the cue to leave. Don't expect an on-the-spot job offer. That might happen, but more likely the interviewer will say something like "We'll be in touch with you." Say "Thank you" and leave.

This is also the right procedure if you're turned down for a job on the spot. Don't argue or react angrily or otherwise burn your bridges. A gracious "Thanks for considering me" will leave a better impression and help you to feel better about yourself, too.

If you get the job, you may face a new challenge. Many people believe that young people these days don't know how to work. You can prove them wrong if you remember to take responsibility and be a real professional on the job. This means being on time. It means being pleasant. Remember that—although working can be fun and the people with whom you work can become friends—your place of employment is *not* generally the place to air personal problems, have temper outbursts, chat by phone or in person with personal friends and relatives, or make a game out of seeing how little you can do and get by with. Even if the work is tedious and boring, remember that you're earning money AND you can learn a lot about discipline and self-control and can take a giant step toward maturity if you try your best.

COPING WITH SPECIAL SITUATIONS

At the Doctor's Office

My doctor is a really cute young guy and I've been seeing a lot of him because I have problems with my skin. We got along great until recently. I don't know whether it upset him when I called him by his first name ('cause I feel like we're friends) or whether it's because he felt I was pushy for asking him if he wanted to go sailing with me (he didn't). I sent him a Christmas card, too. All I know is, he's much more businesslike and not as friendly. Did I do something wrong?

Lisa N.

I don't like my doctor because she gets impatient if I don't remember symptoms or am late for an appointment. She's nosy, too, asking me questions instead of just figuring out what's wrong and doing something about it. How can I make her change (since my folks won't let me go to another doctor!)?

Annoyed

Ideally, your relationship with your doctor should be one of mutual respect. It can also be a complicated one. Your doctor may know intimate details about your body and your life. He or she may care a great deal about you and you may feel comfortable telling him or her about your problems, symptoms, and feelings. You may admire your doctor, may even have sexual fantasies about him or her and feel very close in a way. And yet . . .

the relationship is not quite a friendship. It can be confusing.

To eliminate confusion, embarrassment, and annoyances on both sides, it may help to keep the following suggestions in mind.

Don't Confuse Professional Concern With Friendship or Sexual Interest Your doctor may, in some ways, be a special friend to you—helping you to cope with your changing body and to make decisions about your health care. However, he or she must be able to see you objectively in order to properly evaluate your symptoms, diagnose, and treat you. It is for this reason that most doctors do *not* treat close personal friends or family members, preferring to make a distinction between personal friends and patients. Most doctors lead busy lives and have little enough free time as it is without socializing with patients outside the office. Also, professional ethics dictate not becoming sexually involved with a patient. "Ideally, the doctor-patient relationship is a delicate balance of honesty, caring, and mutual respect," says Dr. Charles Wibbelsman.

Dr. Wibbelsman, who is young and attractive and who relates warmly with his patients, has definite opinions about what he considers appropriate behavior for himself and his patients. "I'm careful not to embarrass a patient and try not to hurt anyone unnecessarily either," he says. "I care very much about all my patients. I listen to them and advise and treat them the best way I know how. But I expect some consideration, too. I'm their doctor, not a pal, and I don't like it when a patient breezes in calling me 'Chuck.' Some doctors might disagree, but I feel that calling me 'Dr. Wibbelsman' keeps things very clear about what function I serve in the patient's life. I also dislike it when a patient is seductive and flirts. (It's OK to have sexual fantasies about someone like a doctor or teacher, but don't *act* seductive with that older person!) I get upset when this happens because I feel that flirting with a doctor is not only inappropriate, but also rude. It's showing disrespect for his or her professionalism. You can be friendly without being seductive."

What about giving a doctor gifts or sending Christmas cards?

"That can be fine if it's done in the right spirit," says Dr. Wibbelsman. "For example, last Christmas I got a Christmas card from three young brothers I see quite often as patients. It had a little handwritten note on it thanking me for caring for them that year. That made me feel really good and appreciated. But the best way you can show your appreciation for your doctor is to come back to him or her and to seek help promptly if you have a problem or if a prescribed treatment isn't working."

Make the Most of Your Time With Your Doctor Be on time for your appointment. Know, or try to find out, details about family medical history, your past illnesses or hospitalizations, and if you are a girl, your menstrual history (including the date of the first day of your last period). Be prepared to give detailed descriptions of any symptoms, and you might write down any questions you have before you visit the doctor so you won't forget to ask them when you're in his or her office. Most doctors are busy, but want to give you the best possible medical care. You can help a lot by being prepared and organized.

Don't Play Games With Your Doctor "Some patients spend a lot of time trying to shock me with how bad or tough they are," says Dr. Wibbelsman. "But I've seen thousands of patients and I can't think of anything or anyone likely to shock me—or most doctors I know. So it's a waste of time. Also, don't expect your doctor to be a mind reader. Maybe there's something you need to talk about but you don't know how to begin. Instead of waiting for the doctor to guess that you may have something on your mind (which may or may not happen) you might say something like 'I need to talk about something, but I'm not sure how to start or how to say it.' Then the doctor may be able to help."

Show Consideration in Little Ways "You'd be amazed how many patients come in beautifully dressed or perfectly made up, but who haven't bathed in who knows how long," says Dr. Wibbelsman. "I don't care what patients wear to my office, but I *do* appreciate a reasonably clean body when I'm doing an examination. Also, if you're not going to be able to keep an appointment, call and cancel, preferably at least a day before but even that day if you must. If you just don't show up, you may be denying another patient—who is hoping to be worked into the doctor's schedule—a chance to come in sooner. If you needed to be worked in, wouldn't you want someone to show the same consideration for you?"

Doctor's office etiquette is a two-way exchange. You have a right to be treated with respect and consideration. If you're not, you should complain and/or change doctors.

Receiving Lines

I went to a wedding reception last week and when I was in the receiving line, I congratulated the bride and groom.

They seemed to think it was OK, but my mom had a fit at me later because she said one should NEVER congratulate the bride—just the groom. Is that true? Is it terrible what I did?

Stephanie G.

My parents and I went to the funeral of a family friend a few days ago. It was really a memorial service. Anyway, afterwards the family of the lady stood outside the church and we were supposed to file by and say something. I didn't know what to say! What do you say in a situation like that?

Stuart F.

Receiving lines aren't so intimidating if you remember that:

1. The people standing in them aren't hearing half of what you say anyway. Your gracious manner, warmth, and sincerity matter most.
2. Whatever you say, it's best to be brief.

In wedding receiving lines, you might briefly introduce yourself to those you don't know and say how nice it is to meet them and how you've enjoyed the wedding. Use a variation of this with those you *do* know. A past superstition or rule of etiquette has dictated that you congratulate the groom and offer best wishes to the bride. In this era, however, most couples won't be likely to take offense if you congratulate them both. In lieu of congratulations, you might smile and say something like "I hope you have a very happy life together," or "Thanks for sharing your wedding day with me. It's a lovely wedding and I wish you many years of happiness." It's the spirit of your good wishes, not the exact wording that's important.

Funeral or memorial service receiving lines seem to be more common these days. If you find yourself in this situation, be brief, respectful, and warm. If you know the family—or a family member—a warm squeeze of the hand and a soft "I'm so sorry. We'll miss——very much," or something like "You have my love, sympathy, and prayers" can mean a lot. Don't break down and cry or go on and on about how you can't believe the deceased has gone or ask for vivid details about the death. (I recently heard ALL this done in a funeral receiving line. The family was most gracious, but it was an obvious extra strain for them.) If a dear friend of yours loses a loved one, do your crying together in private where you can share as much time, as many details, and as much vulnerability as you both choose.

Tipping

I have a problem with tipping. I never know how much to leave. How much do you tip a hairdresser? What about taxi drivers? Do you need to tip in a coffee shop or just in a nice restaurant? If you leave your coat with a check-room person, should you tip him or her? What about those strange ladies that sit in ladies rooms some places just to hand you paper towels?? Help!! I don't want to look like a stupid person all my life!

Beverly N.

If you're confused about tipping, too, you have lots of company! The following guidelines might help, but keep in mind that considerably larger tips may be expected in major cities. These are the average *minimum* tips you should expect to leave.

- *Hairdressers* 20 percent of the bill.
- *Barbers* usually about 50 cents.
- *Taxi drivers* 15 to 20 percent of the total fare. However, for short rides, tip 20 cents if the fare is less than 50 cents or 25 cents if the fare is between 50 cents and $1.50.
- *Waiters or waitresses* in an elegant restaurant and/or for excellent service, 20 percent. Otherwise leave 15 percent of the bill (excluding taxes). If you eat in a family restaurant where you order and pick up your food and the waitress serves coffee and drinks and removes the plates, tip 15 percent. If the waiter or waitress simply removes plates, leave 10 percent. If you're eating at a lunch counter, tip 15 percent of the bill (or 15 cents—whichever is more). If you just have a soft drink or cup of coffee at the counter, no tip is really necessary.
- *Restroom attendants* 25 cents (usually put in a dish on the counter) if the attendant hands you a towel. You're not obligated to tip otherwise.
- *Coatroom attendants* 25 cents per coat (may vary from place to place).
- *Valet parking attendants* 25 cents when the car is brought to you (may be higher in some cities).

Special Dinners Out

On prom night, I'm taking my girlfriend to a very nice restaurant first. We don't usually go to such places. Actually, we've NEVER been. I don't know what to do or how to act. How do I make a reservation? When we get there, do I walk first to the table or does she? Am I supposed to tip the person who shows us to our table? Should I order for both of us or let my date order for herself? What's "a la carte"? How do I know how much to tip and do I hand it to the waiter or just leave it on the table? As you can guess, I'm new at this and need all the advice I can get!

Rick H.

Even though a prom night meal at an elegant restaurant can be quite a different experience from a usual dinner date at your local Burger King or pizza place, you can survive the evening without embarrassing yourself—and even have a wonderful time—if you know at least a little about what to do and what to expect.

- When calling to make reservations, you might say "I would like to make a dinner reservation for 6 P.M. tomorrow for a party of two. My name is. . . ." (Also check with your parents or other people who might be familiar with the restaurant to see how far in advance you should make the reservation. At some restaurants, the same day is fine. However, some very popular, exclusive restaurants book reservations far in advance.)
- When the hostess or maître d' escorts you to your table, it's customary for the woman to go first, following him or her.
- You don't need to tip the hostess or maître d' if all he or she does is seat you. If he or she has taken great pains to prepare a special table, prepare a food item for you, or fulfill a special request, tip him or her $2 to $5.
- Although, in the past, men always ordered for their dates, this custom seems to be changing. Now, many waiters and waitresses ask the woman directly what she would like to order. If the man gives the order and the waiter asks the woman a specific question—about what kind of soup or what type of salad dressing she would prefer, for example—she should answer the waiter back directly instead of relaying the order through her date. And when you're ordering separately, the woman usually orders first.
- Although most menus are quite clear and specific about what the restaurant has to offer, it may help to know that "a la carte" means that you pay separately for each item. This can add up to quite a bill. You might save money—and have a wonderful meal—if you order a dinner with a set price that includes soup or salad and vegetables, maybe even a beverage as well. These are sometimes called "Table d' hôte dinners" or "Complete Dinners."
- If the waiter or waitress will be tossing a salad or cooking a flaming entree or dessert at your table, he or she may show you the ingredients first. Don't panic. Just smile, look at the ingredients, and nod.

• If the waiter or waitress appears at your elbow with an open breadbasket, don't try to take the basket, just take a roll.

• Leave the tip—at least 15 percent of the bill, but 20 percent if the restaurant is an exceptional one and if the service was excellent—on the little tray presented to you with the bill. Don't hand it to the waiter (or waitress).

• If you're feeling intimidated by a waiter or waitress, if he or she seems overbearing, remember that he or she is there to serve *you*.

ONE LAST WORD

The last word in etiquette—for any situation—is consideration. You don't have to memorize etiquette rulebooks. Even if you're not up on all the many little social rules and rituals described in these guidebooks (and most people aren't!), you'll always be a welcome guest and a treasured friend, client, patient, or customer if you use thoughtfulness, tact, and a lot of common sense!

CHAPTER ELEVEN

Coping With Crisis

Please help me. Since my dad died five months ago, I haven't been the same. I think about dying a lot. I'm scared to do anything, even to go to school half the time. My mom is about ready to give up on me. She thinks I'm crazy. I'm just desperate!! How can I get back to being the me I used to be?

Sharon L.

I have a horrible problem: I was raped when hitchhiking a couple of days ago and I'm scared to tell anyone. If I tell my parents, they'll yell at me for hitchhiking and maybe call the police who'll think I was asking for it. And the guy who did it said he'd kill me if I went to the police. Every time I think of what happened, I get sick to my stomach and start crying. I'm 17 and wasn't a virgin, but still it was so awful! I need help! Where can I go?

Melanie C.

I've been having a lot of problems this year. Things aren't too great at home, especially since I got caught shoplifting at a store near here. I don't know why I did it. It was the first and only time! I've been drinking a lot, too, and me and my best friend have been thinking about running away, but we haven't figured out where to go. Can you tell me where I can get some help because I'm pretty messed up already.

Falling Apart

These letters are all from young people in crisis situations—and they illustrate the different kinds of crises that can occur.

There are crises related to feelings. Maybe your fears and phobias keep you from living a normal life. Maybe the death of a parent, relative, or friend seems to be more than you can stand and you're not sure you can go on. Maybe you have frightening feelings or fantasies of ending it all.

There are crises related to others' actions. We touched on some of these in Chapter Two—parental alcoholism and physical or mental abuse, for example. But there are some other-caused crises that will be treated in more

detail here: incest and rape. You may find yourself the victim of sexual abuse (or some other crime) and experience a second crisis as you try to cope with your feelings about the experience.

And there are crises that are tied to your own actions: shoplifting and other illegal behavior, compulsive behavior (like overeating and self-imposed starvation, called *anorexia nervosa)*, drug or alcohol abuse, and running away from home. In some cases, this behavior is an effort to cope with problem feelings—to anesthetize feelings of pain, to get away from unbearable home situations, or to draw attention to your unmet needs.

A crisis can happen to anyone. While there are steps you can take to cut your chances of becoming a crime victim or of dealing with feelings in nonconstructive ways, you can't eliminate the possibility that you will face some crises in your life. So it's important to know how to cope and when and where to seek help. That's what this chapter is all about.

CRISES OF FEELINGS

Fears and Phobias

You're probably going to think I'm crazy, but here goes: I'm scared to get in an elevator! I feel real shaky and sweaty and sick, like I'm trapped and can't get out. I'm too embarrassed to tell anyone about this. I take stairs everywhere, but at my sister's 18th-floor apartment—which she just moved into—it isn't going to be easy. I can't handle the elevator at all and I don't think I can fool her with my usual physical fitness line. She thinks I'm an exercise nut now. If she knew the truth, she'd think I was a real nut. What can I do about this?

No Name, Please!

I'm 18 but it's like I'm 8. Something is really wrong and I don't know where to turn. I get panicky at the thought of going anywhere. It started last summer and I can't even go to business school like I'd planned or get a job. I just stay in the house and my parents are getting really upset with me and want to take me to a psychiatrist. I'm really scared. Help!

Linda B.

Fear is part of all our lives. There are times when you are quite naturally and reasonably afraid. If someone were pointing a gun at you or if a truck were bearing down on you, it would be very unusual if you didn't feel some fear. It's also understandable to feel a bit of fear in a new situation—like getting up to give a class report, walking into a room full of people you don't know, or waiting in the wings for your first entrance in the school play. These little bouts of stage fright have happened to just about everyone in one way or another.

Sometimes, though, fear goes beyond its realistic limits. You may irrationally fear things that aren't normally dangerous—like going shopping or being in the same room with a cat or enjoying the view from a third-story window. That's when fear becomes a *phobia*—and some phobias can interfere a great deal with a victim's life.

Sometimes a phobia can develop after a traumatic event—like the death of a loved one, a serious illness, a drastic change in life circumstances, or a bad experience with a feared animal or person. Sometimes there is no discernible cause, but the symptoms can be annoying, even disabling.

For example, a fairly common phobia—seen mostly in females—is *agoraphobia,* which is fear of open or public places (often, anyplace besides home). The agoraphobic may become a prisoner in her own home, fearing not only public places but also the feeling of fear itself.

That's true of many phobias. The feelings of fear are so intense (the victim may hyperventilate, feel nauseated, break into a sweat, shake, and feel his or her heart pounding) that this fear reaction becomes as threatening as the object or situation feared . . . and reinforces the original terror. So elevators may become more and more menacing to "No Name" and Linda may become increasingly immobilized at home.

There are a number of other common phobias: fear of water, fear of heights, fear of germs, fear of cats or dogs or insects or snakes, fear of blood, fear of the dark, fear of flying, fear of being alone, and fear of the rain.

Experts estimate that at least 14 million Americans suffer from irrational fears. Many function fairly well day-to-day. If you have a snake phobia or faint at the sight of blood, you can often avoid being in situations where this phobia might be a problem without seriously disrupting your life.

However, if you can't use an elevator, get dizzy if you look out a window higher than the ground floor, can't face flying, become hysterical at the sight of a cat or dog, or can't leave your home, this could limit your life in crucial ways.

How can you cope if you have a phobia that's threatening to become a major problem?

Some people cope successfully via self-help measures—sometimes with the aid of friends. For example, if you fear having dental work done, you might sit with your eyes closed for a few minutes before your appointment or before the dentist begins to work. You might imagine a pleasant, peaceful scene, someplace you can feel totally relaxed. Feel the calmness, the sense of peace wash over your body. . . . This mental imagery can work for some people who are confronted with stressful situations.

Others may be able to confront their phobias with the help of friends. If, for example, you're afraid of elevators or other closed spaces, or of going into a crowded store, going there with a loving, supportive friend or relative who can offer you constant reassurance may defuse some of the fear. Then you'll have the memory of mild rather than intense fear—and gradually decreasing fear—in connection with the situation. And you may be able to build your courage and confidence to cope.

But not all phobias lend themselves to self-help measures. Many times, the best way to conquer a phobia is to face it with the help of a trained professional counselor. There are psychologists, psychiatrists, and marriage/family counselors who might be able to help you. There are also special treatment programs for those with phobias.

How can a professional help you to overcome a phobia?

In the past, many therapists tried to help by getting to the root of the phobia, trying to find its causes. This didn't always help much, though, since the causes are often elusive.

Today, treatment quite often centers around alleviating symptoms of the phobia—via hypnosis or by a gradual step-by-step process often called "contextual therapy," which helps the phobic person to confront the situation he or she fears most with the support of the therapist.

In therapy, you take each step to the point of mild discomfort, then stop, then proceed a little farther the next time. This way, you build memories of positive (or at least not extremely negative) feelings in the feared situation.

If, for example, you're afraid of riding in elevators, a therapist might have you approach the situation in your imagination first: approaching the elevator, pushing the button, and—if your anxiety level stays down below the alarm stage—actually getting inside. You might next imagine yourself riding in the elevator with comfort and ease. When you've learned to imagine such a sequence without extreme fear, you may retrace your steps in reality. Some therapists (who generally accompany their clients through such routines) advise bringing a favorite snack or other item that you like with you on the elevator to make the ride even more memorable as a pleasant experience.

If you're scared of cats, a therapist might take you through similarly pleasant imaginary encounters, going on to pictures, and finally progressing to the point where you can be in the same room with or even hold a live cat without fear taking over.

With an agoraphobic who is afraid to leave home, the therapist may make house calls at first, helping the client to imagine leaving home and then do it step-by-step. The therapy—taken gently, step-by-step—may last for weeks or even for months.

Any one of a number of counselors or psychotherapists in your area may be able to help. Calling your Family Service Association for referral to a counselor may be a valuable first step. Some therapists may help you to deal with your fear and its symptoms and may also help you to explore any personal problems that might be contributing factors.

If you want to concentrate on alleviating your phobia, you might opt for the highly specialized help available at a phobia clinic. Treatment at one of these may range from two to five months in duration and cost from $400 to $1,000. If you'd like information about the phobia clinic nearest you, send a self-addressed, stamped envelope to: Dr. Alan Goldstein, Temple University, Health Sciences Center, Department of Psychiatry, 3400 North Broad Street, Philadelphia, PA 19140. (Dr. Goldstein runs a national clearinghouse for phobia clinics.)

If you suffer from agoraphobia, you may be able to get help from a Terrap Center. There are 22 of these across the nation and costs at each center vary. For more information about this (including a list of all the centers), write to: TERRAP—Menlo Park, 1010 Doyle St., Menlo Park, CA 94025.

If you're afraid of flying, you might overcome your phobia in a Fearful Flyers seminar (which is held at selected cities and costs $100). For information on this, write to: Fearful Flyers, Pan American Airways, Inc., 30 South Michigan Avenue, Chicago, IL 60603.

Coping with the Death of a Loved One

You've got to help me. I'm falling apart. My dad died of a heart attack two weeks ago. It was quick and he died at work so we didn't get to say goodbye to him. It hurts so much. When I think of all the times I mouthed off to him or made him worry, I start crying. I also cry when I think of the fact that I didn't get a chance to tell him I loved him. I really did, even though we fought a lot in the last year, and now he'll never know. I just feel nothing matters much any more. I don't think I'll ever get over this.

Full of Regrets

My 7-year-old brother died earlier this year and, even though I loved him very much, I couldn't cry. I can't yet. I'm walking around with this big, hurting lump inside me. I tried hitting myself to pound the hurt out, but it didn't work. Since Tommy died, my parents have been fighting a lot and sometimes I think they wish I had died instead of Tommy. I hurt so bad I can hardly stand it. Tell me what to do!

Jean N.

My best friend was killed in a car wreck almost a month ago. I still can't stop shaking and crying whenever I think about it even after all this time. I can't believe I'll never see Dee again. She was the best friend I ever had and she truly loved life. I can't believe I'll ever feel good again either. I can't think of anything else or concentrate on homework. My grades have gone way down and nobody seems to understand how bad I feel. They think I should be over it by now! Help!

Shawna C.

Losing someone you love by death can bring many deeply painful feelings and conflicts.

When a loved one dies, you may feel disbelief and fear. In our society—which tends to be death-denying—we have very little actual contact with death or the dying. Often, we don't accept the fact that it can—and will—touch our lives, claim our loved ones. When death happens to someone close, it can be a devastating experience for you. You may find yourself struggling to believe that this has really happened, that your parent, sibling, relative, or friend is really gone. You may half expect to see him or her any minute or you may dream that he or she will wake up and be fine. You may wish it could all be just a temporary situation, a mistake.

You may be angry—angry at the deceased for leaving you. When Terri's father died, she felt angry at the world for a long time. Finally, she decided to talk with a counselor recommended by a friend. In the course of their session, Terri mentioned that her father had died some months before. She and the counselor then explored her feelings about his death and what she might like to say to him if they could meet again. Finally, the grief she had held inside began to burst out in a torrent of anger and tears and love: "Oh, Daddy, Daddy, how could you leave me when I love you and need you so much? Why did you have to die?"

Terri's feelings are far from unusual. When a loved one dies, you may feel anger at the person and also anger at being left out if the person was a sibling whose fatal illness, perhaps, demanded the lion's share of parental attention for a long time. Before the person's death, you might have felt like saying "Hey, how about me? I count, too!" After the death—when the focus may be on parental grief—you might feel like saying "What about me?? I hurt, too!" And both times, you may hate yourself and feel very guilty for your anger. But these feelings, too, are very common and understandable.

You might also feel a lot of guilt when someone close to you dies. You may feel guilty about past arguments or feelings of rivalry or about the fact that you couldn't prevent the death. (Feeling that you might have prevented the death "if only . . ." can be a way of denying your helplessness in the face of death.) This feeling can be especially strong if someone you love dies in an accident or commits suicide—and you feel that if only you had been able to do this or that, it wouldn't have happened. This is a very painful situation and it may take a long time before you stop blaming yourself and accept the fact that what happened *happened* and, even if you had taken all the steps you imagine, you might not have been able to prevent it. But the hurt may take a long time to heal.

You may also feel guilty about surviving. This can be especially true when a sibling dies. In their grief, your parents may give you the impression that they wish you had died instead. This impression is usually a mistaken one, often born of your own guilt feelings over surviving. If a parent says something like this to you, it may help a bit to remember that people sometimes say things in moments of stress and grief that they don't really mean.

Facing the death of a loved one may take all your energy for a while and you may have little left over for school work, social life, or hobbies. You may feel so helpless, so alone, and so exhausted by your grief that you can't imagine life ever getting back to normal.

You may also be frightened by the fact that someone close to you has died. Confronting this death can also mean realizing your own mortality—the fact that you will die, too. So you may find yourself grieving not only for the death that has happened, but also for the death that will someday be your own.

How can you help yourself through this maze of feelings?

Let Your Feelings Happen   You may feel like crying a lot—or not at all just now. There is no *right* way to grieve, only your way. Some people need more time than others to get past the initial shock. Some people need to be alone. Some need to be with others more than ever as they work through their grief. At some point, if you let your feelings happen, grief will hit and the tears may come. Tears are a wordless expression of your grief, a way of healing, *not* a sign of weakness. They are as appropriate for men as for women.

Talk and Share Your Feelings with Others   Sometimes this takes effort. You may not be able to talk as much as you might want with usual confidants (e.g., with parents if they are also involved with the grieving process), and others may have trouble hearing your cry for help. You may need to be a bit assertive in expressing your needs.

Joyce, whose mother died of cancer not long ago, remembers how it was for her just after her mother's death. "I was in a state of shock and wanted to talk to someone about the whole thing," she says. "I got on the phone and called several friends, who were very sympathetic, but scared. They also assumed I didn't feel like talking. They'd say 'Oh, Joyce, that's terrible. Oh, let me know if there's anything I can do to help. I know you don't feel like talking now!' Only I *did!* Finally, I said to one girlfriend, 'But I *do* feel like talking. I need to talk. Do you have time?' We were on the phone for over an hour and I told her all kinds of details and memories about my mother's illness and death. I needed to share it because it was not only terrible, but also awesome. We both cried several times during the conversation and felt that it helped us both in many ways. But the sharing wouldn't have happened, maybe, if I hadn't asserted myself a little."

You might also find it helpful to share your feelings with other teens who are experiencing similar losses. Some counseling organizations, such as the Family Service Association, offer group counseling rap sessions in some areas for teenagers experiencing significant losses. You can check the availability of such a group in your area by calling your local Family Service branch office.

Give Yourself Time   Accept the fact that it takes time to heal. Some counseling experts believe that it can take about two years to work through your grief over a parent's death, for example. The fact that it may take a long time to recover fully from your loss may make you wonder at times if you'll ever be happy again—or cause you to feel guilty for some moments of joy in the midst of your pain.

"The pain as you cope with loss and change is much like the pain involved in giving birth," says psychologist Dr. Randi Gunther. "The pain may be intense at times, but it isn't constant. There may be moments—even days—when you feel pretty good, yet you may be afraid to let people know that you feel good because then they may not take your pain seriously when it comes back. But what you're feeling is okay. It's okay to feel your pain and yet to laugh during the times in between. That will help you to be stronger when the next pain comes. Giving yourself permission to laugh between your pain will help you to grow as you experience this loss."

Accept the Death Part of the work of grieving is accepting the fact that death has occurred, that this can't be changed, that you can't bring your loved one back. If you're religious, your faith may give you a great deal of help in accepting another's—and ultimately your own—death. But even if you're not particularly religious, it's vital to face the fact of death, grieve, and then gently let go—let go of the wish that death could be reversed and that life could be as it once was, and then go on with your life as it *is*. Accepting the death and then going on does not mean forgetting. Your loving memories of the person you lost may bring you joy all your life. Your sorrow over the loss of this special person may also be with you for a long time. There will be moments when you suddenly miss your loved one, wishing he or she could come back for a moment, just to share it with you. And sharing another's death may give you a new appreciation for the precious moments of your own life. When you know—with new finality—that life as you know it can't go on forever, you may learn to savor life's pleasures and challenges all the more.

Suicidal Feelings

I've been so depressed it scares me, because thoughts of killing myself have crossed my mind. I almost took sleeping pills once, but I chickened out. I'm scared of dying, but living isn't so hot either. Please help me QUICK!!!!!
Mixed Up

When you're in the middle of a deep depression, it may seem that you've never felt happy and you never will. The fact that most depression is cyclical and will pass with time tends to elude you. You may feel helpless and hopeless.

It is this feeling of hopelessness that can drive people to suicide or suicide attempts. This is a very real danger for young people, who may be especially prone to feeling "Life can *never* be any different."

It's estimated that suicide is the number-two cause of

death—after accidents—for adolescents. And some accidents (especially involving automobiles) may, in fact, be disguised suicides.

There are many more suicide attempts than completed suicides. These attempts are often ways of saying, "I don't want to die, but I do want life to be different. Yet I feel powerless to change anything. Help me!"

Suicidal feelings are not particularly unusual, but they *are* danger signals, signs that you need help in dealing with your feelings. A suicide attempt is a definite cry for help.

Help is available all around you. Your parents, family, and friends may all care much more than you think they do. They may be happy to help you—if you'll let them.

Special professional help may be necessary, too, to enable you to gain more effective coping skills and a better self-image and, most important right now, a renewed sense of hope that things *will* get better.

For immediate help—if you have suicidal feelings—call your local Suicide Prevention Hotline (there are over 200 of these nationwide), a crisis hotline, or your local community mental health center. If you're feeling too frightened, confused, and desperate to look up the number of a crisis line, pick up the phone and dial the operator. Ask for help. He or she will connect you to a source of help. There are people all around you who care and who can help you to change your life for the better. All you have to do is reach out.

When and How to Seek Professional Help

I've been having problems because my parents are getting a divorce and I've been real depressed about this and some other things in my life. When I was talking to my best friend yesterday, she said I ought to go to a professional counselor! Well, I was really hurt and mad when she said that because I'm not crazy, I'm just upset. Since then I've been thinking and see, the thing is, I've been feeling like I should be able to handle my own problems or get advice from friends, but it isn't exactly working out. So I'm thinking that maybe getting some kind of help might not be so terrible. I always thought it was a sort of cop-out before or just for crazy people. If I did decide to get professional help, where could I get it? How much would it cost? (I don't have much money and neither do my parents just now.) Who ARE these people and how do I know if they're any good?

Leslie P.

There are some old myths still around about seeking help in dealing with your feelings. Some of these include the old notion that you have to be crazy to seek professional help or that it's a sign of giving up on taking responsibility for your own life.

Nothing could be further from the truth. People who go to a counselor or therapist *before* they have a mental health crisis may profit the most from such help, as they learn to get in touch with their feelings, and can often prevent a mental health crisis. And seeking help in understanding yourself can be a way of taking responsibility for your life, of learning ways to cope more effectively with your problems instead of feeling helpless.

When Is It a Good Idea to Seek Professional Help?

In any of the following circumstances, you may want to see a professional:

- When you've been feeling upset and depressed for a long time—as weeks go by, you feel more depressed, helpless, and alone.
- When you're facing a stressful life change. This might be a parental divorce, the death of a loved one, or even a happy change like getting married.
- When you feel you can't handle your problems alone—when all self-help measures have not been enough and when friends and family haven't been able to help much either.
- When you've lost control over some aspect of your life—like starving yourself or eating compulsively, drinking, or using drugs—and this is interfering with and complicating your life.
- When you feel you need someone who can help you to understand yourself better.

What Kind of Help Is Available?

Depending on your personal preferences and financial resources, you may decide to go to a psychiatrist, a psychologist in private practice, a mental health clinic, a family counselor, or a youth counselor at a special teen facility, or to your clergyman or clergywoman.

It's possible to find skilled, empathetic therapists among all these categories of helpers. A psychiatrist is a physician (an M.D.) who has special training in psychology and who is also able to prescribe drugs, if needed, in conjunction with therapy. A psychologist usually has a Ph.D. degree in clinical psychology. A licensed family counselor/therapist may have an M.S. or M.A. degree in psychology or marriage/family/child counseling. A psychiatric social worker has an M.S.W. (Master of Social Work) degree. There are a lot of counselors, too, especially at special help centers, who may not have a lot of impressive degrees, but who do have empathy, understanding, and skill in helping people cope with their feelings.

While a person's academic credentials can give you some idea of that person's training and experience, this does not mean that he or she is automatically competent or right for you. A lot depends on the chemistry between you—whether you really trust the person, whether you can communicate, whether you can work together in a constructive way. Be wary of a helper who wants to lecture you nonstop, who claims to be able to solve all your problems instantly, or who tries to push a particular set of beliefs or lifestyle on you.

The best therapists are those who know how to listen actively, who help you to face your feelings, to cope with them, and to find ways—yourself—to make constructive changes. A counselor may make some suggestions now and again that can be helpful, but usually he or she will not feed you answers or solutions—but may help you search for your own.

There are many different kinds of counseling help—just as there are a variety of helpers. You can get individual counseling—just you and the therapist. You can be part of a therapy or rap group, where you get together with peers and a therapist to share feelings and ideas. (This approach might help you feel less alone in some of your conflicts, and the constant give-and-take of a group may be good for you. On the other hand, if you are a very private person, are shy, or need intensive help, a group might be frustrating.) Some people opt for both individual and group counseling.

Family therapy can also be a good way to go if your parents agree to it. This can be especially helpful if you've been having problems at home, because everyone (ideally) learns to share feelings, ideas, and growth in a safe setting with an objective party (the therapist) present. It is possible to confront issues and learn to communicate in much more constructive ways with the help of a counselor, and with family therapy, you have a chance to work together actively as a family in changing the home environment as you grow as individuals.

If you find yourself feeling alone, desperate, and too upset to face a counselor right now, you can get immediate help by calling a hotline. This is a sort of emotional first aid, not a long-term alternative. A hotline counselor may refer you to longer-term sources of help and/or help you examine your alternatives.

How Much Does Therapy Cost?

It depends. Spending years in psychoanalysis with a psychiatrist, for example, could cost thousands of dollars.

On the other hand, there are some special centers—especially youth crisis and runaway centers—that don't charge at all for their services.

Some counseling organizations—such as Family Service Associations—charge according to ability to pay—which can range from *nothing* to $40 a visit.

There are some services that will treat you without parental consent and others that do require parental consent. Your parents may be a bit dubious about your getting therapy. They may feel that they've failed if you're having a problem that you feel requires outside help. They may have negative views of therapy based on the old notion that it's for crazies. They may wonder, too, if you're not in an obvious crisis, why you would want to seek such help. (If you're in the middle of a serious crisis, they'll probably be more likely to see the need for it.) Your parents may have more positive feelings about your getting therapy if you explain that you're interested in learning to cope with your feelings *before* you have a crisis, that with the world as complex as it is today, you want and need extra help in making choices, that you want to increase your ability to communicate with them and get to know yourself better. Their apprehensions and negative feelings may not change magically all at once, but they may agree to give you a chance to try some sort of counseling.

Professional help, of course, has its limitations. A therapist can't transform you, take away all your pain, or offer instant solutions. If you stop to think about it, you wouldn't want any of that. You need to make your own choices, live your own life, and find your own solutions. That's what independence is all about. If you're committed to work hard, a good therapist can help you to develop the skills, the confidence, and the courage to take charge of your own life.

CRISES CAUSED BY THE ACTIONS OF OTHERS

Incest

I don't know how you can help me, but please try. This all started when I was about 8 and my father would come in my room at night (usually drunk) and put his hands all over me. He said he'd hurt me if I didn't lie still and be quiet or if I told anyone. I was so scared, I didn't tell even after he started doing worse things. Now I'm 13 and he doesn't bother me as much except he won't let me date or even talk to guys on the phone and I think he's starting in on my little sister who's only 6. I want to tell Mom or somebody but I'm scared about what this would do to our family and also what might happen to me, especially if no one believed me. What should I do?

Anonymous

I really feel scared. I read something about incest today where it said it could ruin your life. It got to me because my brother and me did a few things with each other last year before we started dating others a lot. Could we be messed up because of that? I wasn't scared about that until today.

Worried

I'm writing this about my boyfriend. He told me something today that I don't know how to deal with and neither does he. His father died four years ago and his mom remarried last summer. Dave told me that his stepfather tries to get funny with him, touching him in certain places whenever he gets a chance. Two nights ago, he came in Dave's room and tried to go down on him only Dave wouldn't let him. Dave thinks that this guy married his mom just to get closer to him. (The guy is a lot younger than Dave's mom—only 27. Dave is 15.) He's thinking of running away except he is only 15, a good student, and it seems unfair to get his life all messed up because this jerk his mom married is a fag. He doesn't know whether to tell his mom or not but Dave can't stand to live with that guy. What can he do?

Melissa B.

Incest—which means sexual contact of some sort with a close blood relative or someone related to you by marriage (such as a stepparent) has been taboo in nearly every civilization throughout history.

Because of this taboo, incest has been reported only rarely, and even today, organizations compiling statistics on this problem guess that only about 40,000 of the estimated one million cases in the United States are reported.

But reported cases *are* increasing. A spokesman for the National Center for Child Abuse and Neglect says that between 1975 and 1978, they saw a 200 percent increase in the number of reported incest cases. And when the Sexual Abuse Hotline started in Knoxville, Tennessee, there was a *one thousand percent* increase in reports of incest in that area! There are more than 40 clinics nationwide that offer help and therapy for families with incest-related problems. (The first of these clinics, the Child Abuse Unit of Santa Clara County, California, opened in 1971, and its caseload has increased tenfold in the intervening years.)

While incest can occur in many forms—including sexual contact with siblings, parents, stepparents, grandparents, aunts, or uncles—the most common form of incest is brother-sister sexual experimentation. Experts contend that this form of incest is less likely to cause problems because it's often an outgrowth of sexual curiosity and exploration, is usually of short duration, and also does not usually include dominance or force. As a result, fewer *problem* cases of incest seem to involve siblings.

Most incest-related problems coming to the attention of experts and authorities involve men and their daughters or stepdaughters between the ages of 2 and 15. It is estimated that 1 to 2 percent of all adult women have had sex with their fathers or stepfathers. In a survey of families where a parent was the sexual offender, 97 percent of such parents were male and only 3 percent female.

Such liaisons can create special problems for the invividuals involved *and* the family because they can and often do involve a parent's using his power over the child to get his way. This may not always be simply physical power; it can also be the power to give love, special privileges, or closeness that the child may crave. Such a relationship can put a daughter into direct competition with her mother (even though some mothers know about and tacitly endorse such activities in order to avoid sex with their husbands or to keep the financial support of the husband and the family intact). The daughter may also feel she has to bear the responsibility of keeping the family together. Incest is often accompanied by other family problems, such as physical abuse, alcoholism, lack of communication between the parents, and emotional problems of a parent who may have been abused as a child, too, and who is now perpetuating the cycle.

If you are the victim, an incestuous relationship can cause many conflicting feelings.

You may feel angry, frightened, and used. You may also feel special—special that you were singled out for this attention and glad that you're not being abused in other ways (as other family members might be). You may even enjoy some of the activities and, at the same time, feel guilty and ashamed. You may want help, but may be afraid to tell anyone for fear you will be blamed or not believed or your family life torn apart.

If you're an incest victim, it's important to remember that you're far from alone. There are more people than you'd ever imagine—maybe in your own community—who have experienced some of the same things. Such cases are more common than most people suspect.

It's also important to realize that you're not to blame. Even if you've had sexual fantasies about family members (this is quite common; what's NOT advisable is acting on these feelings) or flirted a bit with the family member in question, it's the adult's responsibility to use his or her power in a positive way and to steer your relationship clear of overt sexual activities. So incest is really a sign of a problem with the *adult*.

What can you do if you're in an incestuous relationship that is a problem to you?

Some experts advise telling the other parent—who may or may not be responsive to your plea for help (most seem to be). Many families, however, hesitate to seek help from authorities because they fear that the adult offender will be jailed and the family (and its livelihood) jeopardized.

Increasingly, however, special counseling centers are taking a less punitive approach, noting that in the past, jailing a father or putting the children in foster homes could be as traumatic as the incest and other family problems. Now—more and more—intensive family counseling and therapy are used to try to help the family solve its problems together.

You may be able to find special help by looking in your phone book for the "Social Services" sublisting that will probably appear under your city or state government listing. You might also call your local crisis hotline for instant help and a quick referral. You may find some comfort, too, in talking with your physician, clergyman or clergywoman, teacher, or school nurse. Telling others about your problem will not mean that your relative will be arrested. It could mean that your family will begin to get the help it needs. Remaining silent will not help you—or your family.

Sexual Molestation and Rape

I need help badly. You see, when I was younger, I was sexually molested and now I'm really scared of things like that. I have lots of trouble talking with boys and such. It's really going to affect my future. What's your advice?
Scared of Boys

I was raped several weeks ago and I still can't get over it. I was working late one afternoon at school on the yearbook and was alone when a guy I never saw before came in the room. He had a knife and said he'd kill me if I screamed. So I let him rape me. I told my parents and they got mad and blamed ME because I was at school alone and they said I should have fought him off and screamed for help. They said it's no use going to the police, but we did go to the emergency room, but since I had taken a bath (I felt so DIRTY), they didn't find much. I didn't have any cuts or bruises and a policeman I saw later took a report but said I shouldn't have bathed first and that I didn't have signs of a struggle. Should I have fought, even if the guy had a knife? Everyone is making me feel so guilty like I asked for it and wanted it to happen! Plus I feel so scared and nervous. I can't eat and can't go out without getting all shaky and I feel like I can't do anything anymore. Is this a sign of craziness? Who can I talk to who could help me??

Val N.

If you're female and a teenager, you're in a high-risk group for rape and other sexual assault.

The latest figures show that over 50 percent of rape victims are between the ages of 10 and 19. And rape—a crime of *violence* rather than passion—is the fastest-rising crime in the United States, with the FBI Crime Reports for the first three months of 1979 showing an 11 percent increase over the same time period for 1978.

Most rapists, studies show, are males between the ages of 15 and 22 who have a need to control and dominate another person. They often have low self-esteem, a history of family problems, and poor relationships with women. A survey of sex offenders in California revealed recently that these factors—*not* sexual feelings—were major reasons for rape and other sexual assault.

Because sexual assaults involve sexual organs and/or gestures, there is a lot of guilt and shame associated with being a victim. The victim may be blamed for leading the rapist on with provocative clothing, but since rape is not usually in response to sexual feelings, this is not an accurate (let alone *fair!*) judgment. Toddlers, nuns, and elderly women as well as young girls have been raped. Some young boys and men are also raped homosexually or molested, but the data on these is sparse and the incidence is estimated to be lower.

You can be victimized sexually in several ways. There is *molestation,* which can mean someone fondling your breasts or genitalia or kissing you against your will. There is *sexual assault,* which is a general term covering any forced actions that include oral or genital sexual contact. *Rape* is sexual assault involving *penetration* of the vagina or anus with the penis.

About half of all rapes and assaults take place in the victim's home (or a home where the victim may be visiting or babysitting).

If you're faced with the possibility of sexual assault, what can you do?

It depends on where you are, what you feel capable of doing, and whether the would-be assailant is armed.

If you're in an area where help is nearby and the assailant seems to be unarmed, some rape counselors suggest dropping everything and running, while screaming "Fire!" Others advise attacking the would-be rapist—kneeing him in the groin, punching him in the nose and/or the pit of the stomach, and gouging his eyes. Some feel that if you don't fit the mold of the passive rape victim, the rapist may leave you alone. However, it's important to know what you're doing—to be able to really injure the man instead of just make him mad. A

self-defense course would be an excellent investment—since most women are not brought up knowing how to fight, throw a punch, and not hold back.

It's important to remember that the man who is attempting rape is a highly disturbed person who may match any violence on your part with more violence—particularly if he is armed. If you're faced with an armed attacker, especially, some psychology on your part may be your only hope of avoiding rape. Some potential victims have protected themselves by telling the attacker that they have their period, cancer, or VD. Some talk soothingly to the rapist, showing concern for the problems that would cause him to rape and encouraging him to talk about himself. Others, using their fear to advantage, may pretend to faint or actually urinate or vomit and thereby frighten, surprise, or repel the rapist.

These tactics don't always work, however. Experts advise that if the assailant is armed, your first priority must be to avoid serious injury or death. In such an instance—especially if help is not nearby—it could be a fatal mistake to antagonize the assailant. Rape, in this case, may not be preventable. Don't antagonize the rapist. Reassure him that you won't tell anyone about it. One victim who lived to tell her story asked the *rapist* not to tell anyone "because my boyfriend might break up with me over this."

As soon as the assailant has gone, of course, it's vital to seek help. One of the best sources of help is a rape crisis center (listed in your phone book, or ask your telephone operator for assistance). There are a number of these nationwide and they perform a crucial service, offering immediate help and support to rape victims.

For example, at the Ventura, California Rape Crisis Center—which is typical of many such services—volunteers (many of whom have been rape or assault victims in the past) will come to the victim and take her to the hospital, offering hand-holding, compassionate support all the time. (It's vital to get a medical examination immediately—before bathing or changing your clothes—for your own good as well as for physical evidence should you decide to prosecute your attacker.) The physician will examine the victim's vagina for evidence of semen (a necessary bit of legal evidence for prosecution) and signs of external or internal injuries, and may give the victim special treatment to avoid VD or possible pregnancy. The rape crisis counselor will stay by the victim's side all through this as well as through police questioning should the victim decide to press charges. (Many women do not, but experts strongly urge women to do so, because most rapists are multiple offenders and will rape again if not caught. In some states, to successfully prosecute, the victim must show proof of resistance, but there is a movement now to change this requirement, since studies show that victims who resist are more likely to be seriously injured or even killed than those who do not. Also, many police departments have become more sensitive to the feelings and needs of rape victims and have female officers to do postrape questioning. This can also be less traumatic if you have a rape crisis counselor by your side.)

The rape crisis counselor is usually also available to you on a continuing basis as long as you need her for further help and follow-up counseling while you deal with your feelings after the fact.

Feelings can include anger, guilt (especially if you keep thinking you should have resisted more), depression, and fear of sex.

Rape or other sexual assault is a traumatic experience and it can take a long time to begin to feel better and resume your normal routines. You may be turned off by men and sex for some time. (It may help to remember, though, that the man who raped you was emotionally disturbed and not representative of ALL men!) Your recovery can be helped a great deal if you can talk with someone who can understand your feelings and help you to sort them out. This can help a lot even if the assault took place a long time ago, especially if you haven't had a chance to talk about it and your feelings. You might talk with a rape crisis counselor, a psychotherapist, a family counselor, or a physician. Your friends and family may be able to help, too, although studies show that in many instances they are so shocked and angry about your assault that they may not be able to help you or listen to you as much as they might like to.

It's important to repeat to yourself—over and over—that you are not to blame for your attack and that, since you survived, you chose the right way to handle the attack. Give yourself credit for surviving instead of rebuking yourself for not resisting or fighting more. You did the only thing—and the best thing you possibly could—and that was to survive.

How to Avoid Being a Crime Victim

My friends say I'm paranoid, but the more I hear about teenagers getting mugged and raped and murdered, the more scared I get to go places and do things. How can I keep from being a crime victim without staying home all the time?

Penny S.

How can you avoid being a victim of rape or other violent crime? No one is 100 percent safe, but there are ways you can keep the odds in your favor. Among them are the following:

- At your home, encourage your parents to install deadbolt locks on all outside doors, a phone in at least one bedroom, locks on all windows, possibly a burglar alarm, and a one-way peephole in the front door or an intercom device so you can screen callers before opening the door. Don't open the door—under any circumstances—to someone you don't know when you're at home alone.

- If you're babysitting, make sure all doors and windows are locked and don't open the door to anyone.

- If you're alone in a house or apartment, don't let a phone caller or anyone speaking to you through the door know that. Say the man of the house is not available at the moment.

- If you awake to find a burglar in your room, pretend you're asleep and don't alarm him. (Many of those who steal do so to support drug habits and may be armed and dangerous.) If he attacks you, scream to attract the attention of others. If you hear a burglar in another part of the house, lock yourself in your room and quietly call the police (if you have a lock and a phone) or slip out a window and run for help.

- If you're driving alone at night, make sure that all doors of the car are locked and keep the windows rolled up. Make sure you have plenty of gas and stay on well-lit main streets. If you have car trouble, wait for help from police or the Highway Patrol. If another motorist stops, ask the person to summon the police or AAA, but don't let him or her into your car.

- If you're walking alone at night, avoid dark streets or known crime areas. If you're dubious about a person or area, walk in the street, not on the sidewalk, avoiding dark doorways and bushes. (Of course, it's best not to be out alone late at night anyway, unless it's absolutely necessary.)

- If you're taking a subway or bus late at night, sit close to the driver or conductor, and if someone approaches you as you wait on the platform, scream and run to safety. (It's better to feel foolish in the event of a false alarm than to be assaulted!)

- Don't hitchhike and don't pick up hitchhikers. This is the way many young teens fall victim to violent crimes. Many young people do hitchhike and especially in cities with poor public transportation it can be a big temptation, but DON'T if you can possibly avoid it. In Los Angeles, crime statistics have linked hitchhiking to a high percentage of the area's rapes, robberies, kidnappings, and murders.

As a reporter for a national magazine a few years ago, I covered three hitchhiking-related murders and, at the same time, spoke with young hitchhikers about the safety precautions they used. Some girls told me that they hitchhiked only if a friend was along; some hitchhiked only if the driver was female or was accompanied by a female; and some girls said they hitchhiked only when their boyfriends were with them. Many others said they hitched only occasionally; and one girl said that she knew self-defense and judo and so felt safe with anyone.

Precautions, however, were not enough for the three murder victims whose lives and deaths I studied and whose families I interviewed. The first victim had been hitchhiking with a girlfriend and had been picked up by three men and two women who then proceeded to sexually assault, beat, and stab their two victims to death. The second victim had been hitchhiking with her boyfriend when she was killed. The third young woman, whose mother told me she was an expert in judo and could throw a man twice her size, was murdered the second time she ever hitchhiked. So the risks are always there, even though it's hard to imagine that anything like that could happen to you. In fact, the father of the first murder victim told me sadly that young relatives—including his surviving daughter—still felt that hitchhiking was OK, that lightning couldn't strike twice. Maybe not. But why take the chance? You can greatly decrease your chances of becoming a crime victim if you avoid putting yourself in such a vulnerable position.

YOUR OWN CRISIS-CAUSING ACTIONS

Trouble with the Law

I got caught shoplifting the very first and only time I tried it not too long ago. Boy, was it a shock to see the trouble it caused! My friend, who was with me, talked me into taking some earrings. She dared me and said if I didn't, she'd tell everyone at school I was a baby and a priss. So I did and got caught by a store security guard. Right away, my EX-friend started screaming and crying and saying how she tried to talk me out of it and everyone believed her! Now I've been arrested; have a juvenile record; and have lost a lot of friends, the trust of my parents, and my own self-respect. What I'd like to say to other teens is this: DON'T!!!

Sorry

I got busted last weekend because I happened to be at a party at a friend's house (his folks weren't home) where people were drinking and smoking all kinds of stuff and one person had cocaine. When the cops came (after neighbors complained of the noise), they arrested everybody, even those of us who weren't doing anything illegal! My

parents won't believe I'm innocent, but I am! What can I do?

Unjustly Accused

Things are really bad at home. My dad drinks too much and my parents fight all the time. I can't sleep at night, things are so terrible. I was thinking of running away because anyplace almost would be better, but my friend said I could get arrested and thrown in jail for that. Is that true? What can I do? I can't stand it here much longer!

Jana G.

Crises that can cause you legal problems may stem from a number of causes.

• You may be in the wrong place at the wrong time. It's important to know that if you're with someone who commits a crime—from shoplifting to murder—*you* can be arrested, too. So if you smell trouble, stay away. If a party you're attending is getting out of hand, leave. It's generally better to be called a chicken than to get arrested.

• You may feel like challenging the Establishment. That's a natural tendency—especially when you're young and particularly in an age of rising inflation and depersonalization. It can be a temptation to rip off items to get back at business for ripping off consumers, or to vandalize to vent your anger and protest in a way. Unfortunately, though, the losses caused by these acts are *not* absorbed by the government or big business, but fall back on *people*—on taxpayers and consumers. For example, in New York City, it's estimated that shoplifting costs consumers $600 million a year. On a personal level, the pantyhose you buy may cost 15 percent more just to cover losses from shoplifting. So one person's method of trying to beat the system can mean a real rip-off for many others. It might be more constructive and effective to join a consumer protection or political action group where you could protest more effectively (without risking higher prices, higher taxes, or an arrest record for yourself!).

• You may have feelings and problems that cause you to act impulsively. Maybe you feel ready to explode from stress. Maybe you're angry and upset about something. Maybe you feel unloved at home or unpopular at school and would do anything to get accepted or to get away from a bad situation. So you may strike out at a stranger, vandalize property, steal, drive recklessly, or run away as a means of expressing some of your tumultuous feelings.

The problem is, expressing your feelings in this way

can bring even more problems and trouble into your life. Besides obvious violent crimes, common offenses like shoplifting (over 50 percent of those arrested for this crime are teenagers) or status offenses like running away or truancy can get you arrested and even jailed in some instances—which can be a lot worse than you've ever imagined!

Getting into legal hassles can get you ostracized (even more) at school, can cause more trouble at home, and can even affect your life for years to come—since an arrest record (even as a juvenile) can jeopardize your chances of getting certain jobs (with the government or anytime a job application asks if you've ever been arrested), certain professional licenses (e.g., real estate or stockbroker), and admission to the bar as a lawyer. It may even keep you from getting into the college of your choice.

What if you *are* arrested? Remember that you have the right to remain silent. You need only give police your name and address and the names of your parents. That's all. Since anything you say—even in a moment of joking or stress—can be used against you in court, wait until you see your lawyer before you talk. You also have a right to see a lawyer—even if you're told your offense is minor. You're allowed one phone call. Use it to call a lawyer, if you know one, or your parents, asking them to call a lawyer. If you have little or no money, you can get free legal representation from the Public Defender's Office or Legal Aid.

Preventive measures are always best, of course. If you're feeling angry and upset, talk with someone. If there's no one in your life you feel you can trust, call a hotline. Talking on the phone to a crisis counselor or requesting a referral for face-to-face counseling can help you to deal with your feelings in constructive ways.

If you feel that if you don't do certain things, your peers will think you're a baby, a chicken, a priss, or a goody-two-shoes, keep in mind that if you do something illegal, especially if you get caught, you can't count on your "friends" to be supportive—as "Sorry" told us in her letter, or as a teen named Leslie discovered after *her* arrest for shoplifting. "I had to shoplift to get into an exclusive club at school," she remembers. "But when I was caught in the act, the girls just laughed, called me stupid for getting caught—and don't want to have anything to do with me!"

It's far better for your own self-esteem to do things that are legal (and kind) to cultivate the sort of friendships that can weather good times and bad, even if it means you're not fated to win any popularity contests. How *you* feel about yourself is most important!

If you're too upset to go to school or are thinking of running away because of trouble at home, there are some constructive alternatives. You and your parents may get help from your local chapter of Families Anonymous, an organization dedicated to helping troubled families. For the address and phone number of the group nearest you, write to: Families Anonymous, P.O. Box 344, Torrance, CA 90501.

Another excellent—and fast—source of help is The National Runaway Switchboard in Chicago. You don't have to be a Chicago resident—or even a runaway—to get help and referrals from the Switchboard's hotline counselors. (The toll-free number to call if you're calling from out of state is 800-621-4000; Illinois residents should call 800-972-6004.)

A Switchboard counselor may be able to direct you to good counseling services or even to a special residential shelter in your area where you can stay while you and your parents try to work out your problems through counseling.

So if your feelings and problems are threatening to get you into legal hassles, stop and keep in mind that you have alternatives and that people who care and will help are all around you.

Compulsive Overeating

I'm 15 and I really hate myself right now because I blew my diet. I lost 6 pounds and had another 30 to go when I started eating everything in sight this afternoon. Now I feel terrible and I know my parents will yell at me when they get home from work. My mother especially nags me about my weight. I just lose control and can't stop eating sometimes. I think I did it today because I'm nervous about finals coming up. But if things are real good, I have trouble controlling myself, too. How can I keep from making myself feel so bad? I can't understand why I do it!

Patsy D.

Eating disorders can cause a health crisis and a family crisis and, at the same time, can be *symptomatic* of emotional or family problems.

Patsy, for example, seems fairly typical of many compulsive overeaters. A compulsive eater may eat in response to *emotional* rather than physical hunger cues. He or she may eat to soothe feelings of anxiety, tension, and anger. Fear of new situations may cause eating binges. Some overweight teens may try to mask their developing sexuality with their fat and may go on binges when they are starting to show progress on a diet because change is so scary. Rebellion against a weight-conscious parent can figure into compulsive eating, too, as the teen fights the parent with his or her body.

But while food can act as a tranquilizer of sorts (a throwback to the old days when you got a cookie for being a good girl or boy or to stop your crying), and while it can be a way of expressing anger and rebellion, using eating in this way can cause a lot of problems. It can inhibit your communication with others because you don't express your feelings to them directly. It can reinforce your own poor self-image as you struggle along, a fat person in a thin world, seeing yourself as unattractive at a time in your life when physical attractiveness can mean so much. It can also be unhealthy for you and be the beginning of a lifetime of yo-yoing between dieting and binging.

How can you help yourself if you're a compulsive overeater?

Joining a self-help group like Weight Watchers, Overeaters Anonymous, TOPS, or the Diet Center counseling program can be a good start. All of these groups are available nationwide and are listed in your phone directory. They can help you by letting you know that you're not alone, that there are ways to modify your behavior and that you must take responsibility for your own life in order to control and change your eating habits.

This can mean making note of trouble times in your days (or nights) when you're likely to overeat, then making a list of alternate activities you can substitute for eating. Maybe you come home from school tense or bored and head for the kitchen. Try jogging, dancing to music, or swimming instead. Exercise is a much better tension reliever than food—and it's definitely nonfattening!

Taking charge can also mean identifying your feelings—like anger or fear—and learning not to channel them inward so that you do hurtful things to yourself like overeating. It may mean becoming more assertive with your family and others, and being nicer to yourself. You can find new ways to cope with stress and express your feelings—including your need for independence—without hurting yourself in the process. Some counseling—group or individual—may help you to get in touch with your feelings and express them in a more constructive way.

Anorexia Nervosa

I'm a 13-year-old girl with a big problem: I can't eat hardly at all. At first, I didn't want to eat because I wanted to lose weight, but now I can't eat, even when my family begs me. They think I'm too skinny. I'm 85 pounds and 5'6", but my stomach still pooches out so I'm not as skinny as they think. But I can't eat. What scares me is feeling tired all the time and I'm losing some hair. But I'm also nervous and upset and exercise helps that a lot, even when I'm tired. How can I feel better and stop getting my family so upset?

Chris R.

Anorexia nervosa, the eating disorder that Chris seems to be describing, is a psychosomatic disorder of the gastrointestinal system which may cause the victim (usually female) to literally starve herself. It is a puzzling and complicated problem.

Anorexia nervosa seems to be particularly common among middle-class teenage girls who are perfectionists and achievers and who come from somewhat rigid families. Some experts see anorexia as a body-image disturbance and a possible sign of difficulty in identifying one's wants and needs, as well as a struggle for autonomy. Some experts, too, feel that anorexia can be tied to a girl's discomfort with and need to deny her sexual development. Some think that anorexia can be tied, at least indirectly, to impossible standards of beauty presented in advertising and fashion publications that feature abnormally thin models.

Whatever the causes, the course of anorexia nervosa can be alarming. The teenager—who may be of normal weight or slightly overweight at the beginning of her ordeal—may start a diet and be unable to stop. She may become obsessed with food, but unable to eat. She may binge, then make herself throw up. She may be tired, moody, withdrawn, *and* hyperactive—exercising compulsively. She usually has a distorted body image, seeing herself as fat even when everyone else is aghast at her emaciation. Anorexia victims may lose nearly half their body weight, stop menstruating, and even die without medical treatment.

Treatment for anorexia victims may include a period of hospitalization in conjunction with individual and family therapy. Since anorexia is often a sign of underlying family problems, treatment for the whole family is often seen as a necessity.

At Children's Hospital of Los Angeles, for example, the anorexia victim is hospitalized for about a month in an effort to remove her from the home situation and pressures, stabilize and boost her weight, and modify her behavior. Weight gain, not eating, is emphasized. Rap groups—where the teens can share feelings and fears—as well as family therapy are an integral part of this program, which is similar to a number of others available throughout the country.

If you're suffering from anorexia or know someone who is, it's important to seek prompt medical help. No physician will encourage you to become overweight, but it's vital to your health to control and contain your weight loss before it becomes life-threatening. Getting medical help and psychological counseling may ease whatever feelings and conflicts triggered this disorder. Recovery, of course, isn't an overnight matter. It will take a lot of effort and commitment on your part, but it's possible to stabilize your feelings, your self-image, and your weight at healthy levels. Seeking help isn't a sign of failure. It's a sign of strength. The sooner you get help—via your physician or local hospital adolescent unit—the better!

Substance Abuse

I have a bad problem with drinking because I can't stop even when I'm at school. Everyone is upset with me, but I can't help it. It's like I'm an alcoholic except I'm only 14. What can I do?

Clark Y.

We had a talk on substance abuse in health class today and someone mentioned caffeine can be an abused substance. I wonder if I abuse it because I drink about two six-packs of cola a day, more if I can get it, starting first thing when I get up. Could this hurt me?

Jim M.

Like a lot of people my age (14), I smoke pot sometimes. That's no problem. The problem is my parents, who nag me and wave all kinds of new findings in my face like I was a real doper or something! In The Teenage Body Book, you didn't mention all these dumb studies. Are they for real? Could pot be a problem for me if I only smoke it once in a while—like at a party every couple of months?

Brianna S.

People of all ages use drugs like alcohol, caffeine, nicotine, and marijuana (to name some of the most common ones!).

With some of these substances, abuse is a matter of quantity. If you drink so much coffee or cola that your hands shake, you feel jumpy or depressed, and you can't get along without caffeine, it could be a problem for you. If you need to smoke marijuana on a daily basis or several times a week in order to cope with your life, it could signal an abuse situation. If you've lost control over your drinking and alcohol is beginning to affect your life adversely, this, too, is a clue that you have a substance abuse problem.

Some substances, however, are so dangerous that their use at all means abuse to your body. (Among these are drugs like PCP or cocaine.)

How can you tell—if it isn't immediately evident—that you might have a problem with substance abuse? We discussed problem habits extensively in *The Teenage Body Book,* and the short quiz on determining such habits seems worth reviewing briefly here.

Think about the habits you have—whether you drink alcohol (including beer or wine); smoke cigarettes or joints; or drink caffeine-containing beverages like coffee, tea, or colas; and then consider the following questions. Answering "Yes" to any *one* of these can indicate a possible abuse problem.

1. *Does your habit influence—for the worse—your relationships with others?*

Does it trigger hassles with your parents? Cause you to withdraw from friends? Say things you later regret?

2. *Does your habit require you to break a law, even sometimes?*

A number of drugs—including marijuana—are illegal in most areas. Some, like prescription barbiturates, are legal, but may be acquired illegally. In most states, high-school-age teens can't legally buy alcohol or cigarettes, although people do it all the time. And sometimes people shoplift or steal from family and friends the alcohol or cigarettes they need or the money required to support a habit.

3. *Does your habit expose you to medical hazards?*

Many substances carry medical hazards, and it's a good idea to know what they are when you're choosing whether or not to use a particular substance. Medical reports may or may not change your mind, but at least you'll know what risks you may be taking. For example:

Caffeine in moderate doses can make you more alert. Used to excess (i.e., six cups of coffee a day or 12 to 15 colas), it can cause headaches, irritability, gastrointestinal problems, anxiety, depression, and possibly, irregular heartbeats. There are also some studies—still fairly inconclusive—linking caffeine to complications of pregnancy, including miscarriage and premature birth, and with benign breast tumors.

Cigarette smoking has been linked conclusively with cancer. Heavy smokers are 24 times more likely than nonsmokers to get lung cancer as well as oral, stomach, and bladder cancer. They also have a higher risk of strokes, heart disease, emphysema, and peptic ulcers. Some studies, too, are exploring possible links between women's smoking habits and their risk of having miscarriages, stillbirths, and low-birth-weight babies.

Marijuana's adverse side effects are still controversial, but a number of new studies have come out since *The*

Teenage Body Book was written and they seem to urge caution.

Much of the concern over marijuana these days is that it is often more potent now than it was in the past—containing 5 percent THC (the principal chemical of pot) instead of the 1 percent more typical only a few years ago. Unlike alcohol, which is passed out of the body within hours, THC settles in fatty tissues, including the brain and certain internal reproductive organs (like the ovaries), and it leaves the body so gradually that even if you smoke pot only once a week, your body may *never* be free of the substance.

Recent studies have shown that this lingering THC *may* cause some brain cell damage, lower the body's ability to fight infections, and cause possible fertility problems in men and women alike. Researchers have also found that pot, which is smoked in unfiltered form and inhaled deeply, may cause the same problems in terms of health that heavy smoking does. Smoking only five joints *a week* may eventually result in equivalent lung damage to smoking 16 cigarettes *a day!* These are just some of the recent findings. Many need to be tested further, but the *possible* health risks associated with heavy or regular use of marijuana may be worth considering. (Many medical authorities are not that worried about teens like Brianna who smoke marijuana only occasionally at parties. They are concerned about heavy users—and there are quite a few. The latest figures from the National Institute on Drug Abuse show that one in ten high school seniors smokes pot daily.)

Alcohol is a frequently abused drug. Alcoholism is the country's most serious health problem after heart disease and cancer. It can be a life-shortening addiction, causing damage to the brain, liver, pancreas, and central nervous system. Excessive use of alcohol can damage some organs—like the liver—in a relatively short time, and can also be a factor in malnutrition, suicide, and accidents, as well as serious birth defects in babies born to alcoholic mothers. Alcohol-abuse counselors worry about teenagers in particular because, with the physical changes and social and emotional pressures of adolescence, it may be particularly easy to proceed from being a drinker to becoming a problem drinker. The National Institute of Alcohol Abuse and Alcoholism estimates that one out of twenty teenagers has a drinking problem and of these, one of ten will become an alcoholic.

Dangerous drugs like PCP and cocaine are so unpredictable and sometimes life-threatening that even *occasional* use of them can be a medical hazard.

4. *Is your habit creating a lot of personal problems for you?*

A habit, like drinking or drug use, may cause problems in school or may cause you to have accidents. Alcohol or caffeine abuse may trigger some depression or be accompanied by poor eating habits. All substance habits may cause family hassles if you and your family disagree over your use of a substance. Most important, you may be using a substance to mask your feelings.

The later possibility is something you might think about for a moment. If you have trouble dealing with frustration, have low self-esteem, are unable to express angry feelings directly, feel shut off from your family and maybe from peers as well, or are going through a painful time (like a parental divorce, the death of someone dear to you, a major romantic breakup, or other significant loss), it can be a big temptation to reach for anything that will dull your pain. The problem is, these pains and problems are part of life, and it is in adolescence, ideally, that we learn to face problems and deal with them constructively. If you *don't* learn valuable emotional coping skills in these years, you may have a very difficult time functioning well as an adult.

In anesthetizing your painful feelings, you also anesthetize your other feelings—including joy and excitement—and you may come to feel that life has little joy or purpose.

How Can You Help Yourself If You Have a Problem with Substance Abuse?

Sometimes you may be able to help yourself if you begin to face and deal with the feelings behind your habit (see Chapter One for suggestions on coping with low self-esteem and many different kinds of growing pains).

It's important to remember that taking charge of your life takes time and effort. Take one day at a time and set realistic goals for yourself. Never say "I'll *never* drink (or smoke) again!" Tell yourself instead that *just for today,* you will not indulge. Take charge in manageable segments—and give yourself credit for trying!

It can also help to develop new interests and ways of coping. If you feel angry and frustrated, a brisk walk, jog, bike ride, or swim may be the healthful tension reliever you need. A new craft or hobby may keep your hands—which can seem so empty at first without a cigarette, for example—busy. If you're feeling upset, depressed, or under stress, try talking with someone, listening to music, or meditating. There are a lot of alternatives that can help you to deal with your feelings. The added bonus is that these alternatives might really help—rather than hurt—you.

Remember that you chose the habit you're trying to break and you have the power to change it, too. Just be patient and a compassionate friend to yourself.

If you can't quite manage alone (and this may be very

likely), a variety of help is available. You can get expert and compassionate help from your local chapter of Alcoholics Anonymous (some chapters even have special teen groups), in drug abuse programs, and at "Stop Smoking" clinics sponsored by the American Cancer Society. You can also get supportive counseling from therapists at your local mental health, youth, or free clinic. The telephone numbers of these services in your community should be listed in your phone directory or may be available if you call your local crisis hotline.

So if you have a habit that could be hurting you, if you're in *any* kind of crisis, just reach out. Caring people will be there—ready and willing to help you.

CHAPTER TWELVE

Planning Your Future

People are always asking me what I'm going to do in the future and I feel real dumb because I don't know. I'm only 15 and the future seems pretty far away. I can't decide what to do anyway. Now I'm starting to get scared because I keep thinking I should have some plans or goals, but how can I make goals for the rest of my life at this age?

Mike A.

The future scares me because what if I make the wrong choice about something and ruin my life? How can I keep from doing that?

Talia J.

I get kind of depressed sometimes because I'm so far from reaching some of my goals. I want to work with handicapped children eventually and spend a lot of time thinking about what it would be like to live on my own in an apartment. I dream about that a lot, especially when my parents are nagging me about something. The trouble is, I'm just 13, so the future is a long way off. What can I do to feel better now?

Cathy C.

At this time in your life, the future can be both exciting and intimidating.

It can be exciting to think about being on your own, having a satisfying career and the freedom to make choices about all aspects of your life—from the hours you keep to the people you see.

Thinking about the future can also be scary. You may feel overwhelmed at times thinking about the responsibility that independence requires and about the many tasks and small goals that need to be accomplished on the way to a major goal. There may be times when you think of the future and panic because you don't know what you want to do or aren't sure whether your choices will be right for a lifetime. You may cope in a number of ways: by trying to ignore the present and live with your fantasies of the future foremost in your mind (seeing all the time in between as time to be endured); by ignoring the future and hoping that it will take care

of itself; or by trying to find some sort of balance between your present and your future. The problem with living in the future is that you can miss a lot of joy along the way to a goal (and then be disappointed with your goal once you reach it). If you live entirely in the present, though, lack of foresight and planning may lead to regrets later in life. Finding a balance between present realities and your hopes for the future is the most useful alternative.

In order to find this balance, it's necessary to make goals for yourself. Some teens shy away from goals for a variety of reasons. Some may feel that setting definite goals so early in life will lock them into career or lifestyle patterns they may turn out not to like—or that early goal setting could keep them from exploring a full range of possibilities.

It's true that you may not be able to make choices that will last a lifetime when you're still in your teens. Our goals can—and often do—change as we grow and change. But having goals right now and working toward these goals can help give your life today an extra bit of excitement, joy, and purpose. Some of the *least* happy teens, in fact, are those who drift through adolescence without plans and dreams and goals for the future. Goals may change as you go along, but the satisfaction you'll get in setting and pursuing them is constant.

GUIDELINES FOR GOAL SETTING

There are many different kinds of goals and many of them are interrelated.

For example, Cheryl is interested in a business career, independence at an early age, and plenty of time for personal and social development. More immediately, she wants to do well in business math and typing this semester. In Cheryl's future plan, her goals are quite compatible. She's working hard right now to do well in secretarial classes. The skills she's developing will help her to get a good job and competitive salary when she graduates from high school, and the work she has chosen involves regular hours and fairly set duties, so is unlikely to intrude on her personal life. Cheryl seems to have a well-integrated goal plan. She is also getting a lot of satisfaction in knowing that, even at 15, she's on the way to reaching her goals.

It isn't always that simple, of course. John thinks about being a doctor and having a comfortable lifestyle at times, but he has trouble realistically seeing *intermediate* goals and requirements. He's a sophomore in high school now and although he's basically intelligent, his grades leave something to be desired. He claims that he's too bored with school to study much and would rather have fun now and get serious about his work once he gets to college. The problem is, he may have trouble being accepted into a college premed program with poor high school grades, and if he doesn't develop the discipline to apply himself to boring, sometimes tedious work now, he'll have a hard time surviving the years of study and the additional long, wearing years of internship and postgraduate training that stand between him and his ultimate goal. It might be practical for John to revise his present lifestyle and habits *or* to rethink his ultimate goal. If he were to work hard and apply himself, then discover that medicine was not for him, he still would have developed good work habits that could be helpful in other pursuits. Even if he spends more time studying now, he may find that, if he organizes his time well, he can work and still have a lot of fun.

There are educational goals, career goals, lifestyle goals, and personal goals. Since many of these can be interrelated, it's important to begin to get an idea about what you *might* want to do—educationally, professionally, and personally—while you're still in your teens. You may not know the exact career field you want, for example, but you may know that the kinds of jobs that interest you require a college education, so it would make sense to take a college preparatory course in high school. Or you may not be sure about college, but want to develop practical work skills so that you can get a job right out of high school *or* work part-time to help pay college expenses. You could start acquiring practical skills in special high school business or shop courses right now.

If you're like many young people, you may not be quite sure what you want and what your ultimate goals might be. How do you find out? Asking yourself the following questions may give you some valuable clues.

1. *When I'm free to choose my activities, what do I enjoy most?*

If you spend your free time at active pursuits—hobbies, sports, socializing, volunteer work, and the like—that tells you something about yourself. Look closely at the things you enjoy—or used to enjoy, perhaps, before you got so involved with high school or dating or both! It could be that a hobby, interest, or volunteer activity might be a first step toward a satisfying career. For example, maybe because of an interest in handiwork such as art projects, sewing, or needlepoint, you might have a future in fashion design, merchandising, textile design, interior design, electronics, or even surgery. If you socialize easily and are a good speaker, you might turn out to be a receptionist, salesperson, public relations director, market researcher, lawyer, or teacher. If you're an outdoor type and like to keep active, you might enjoy being a sports coach, civil engineer, geologist, or flight attendant. If you enjoy animals a lot, you might become a veterinarian or a vet's assistant, a manager of a pet store, an animal trainer, a race track exercise person, an animal groomer, or a zoo technician—to name only a few possibilities! If your volunteer work is hospital-related and you really enjoy it, there are many fascinating jobs in the health/science field, from doctor to recreation therapist.

If you spend your free time at very passive pursuits—like watching TV or sleeping—this could be a sign that you need to cultivate more active interests, perhaps getting around to doing some of the things you've always thought about doing—or discovering new hobbies or activities you think *might* be fun and rewarding.

2. *What am I like as a person?*

If you're independent and like to work without supervision, you might enjoy a career as a self-employed worker (anything from accounting to carpentry, art to writing), an industrial salesperson, a psychologist, photographer, physician, stockbroker, chemist, or dietician.

If you enjoy working as part of a team, you might like working in the computer field; in advertising, marketing, public relations, the restaurant or hotel business; in urban planning; or in an office management, secretarial, or clerical position.

If you're very organized and methodical, your skills could be an asset in the health sciences, engineering, banking, insurance, interior design, accounting, city or government management, or air traffic control.

If you love to help others, you may be a natural for a career in the health sciences, psychology, social work, restaurant or hotel work, sales, the travel industry, law, business management, or banking.

If you're creative, you might be able to translate your skills into a career as an actor, writer, dancer, artist, musician, photographer, or architect—if you're willing to work hard and face considerable competition and rejection. There are other, less obvious careers, too, that also require some creativity—including medicine, law, oceanography, mathematics, home economics, urban planning, and food science.

If you're not a nine-to-five type and enjoy working strange hours, you would do well in sales, the travel-hotel-restaurant industries, computer science, and all kinds of self-employment.

If you feel secure with sameness and like to live by well-defined rules and routines, self-employment would not be for you. You might be happiest in a government job or in working for a large, long-established corporation.

If you enjoy the idea of living in different areas of the country, it may be important to choose a career that has opportunities nationwide (instead of a career that is very competitive and requires you to live in one or two particular areas, whether you like those areas or not!).

If you're the kind of person whose top priority is his or her personal life and relationships, you might think twice before pursuing a career that would require a lot of overtime or weekend or evening work.

3. *How do I feel about school?*

Are you a good, average, or indifferent student? Do you see academics as exciting, challenging, as an end in itself? Or can you hardly wait to get out of school and into the real world?

Your feelings about education could influence your career and lifestyle choices. If you can hardly wait to get out of school, you might think about preparing yourself—via secretarial, word processing, technical, clerical, or trade skills—for employment right after high school.

If you're not crazy about school, but could stand an extra year or two, you could prepare for a number of medical, technical, or trade occupations.

If you're a good-to-excellent student and plan to go to college anyway, you may not have a particular career in mind yet, but by going to college you may give yourself the educational flexibility to follow any number of career paths. Some careers, of course, absolutely require college and, in some instances, postgraduate training.

4. *What's my favorite subject in school?*

If you're interested in science, you could pursue this interest while working as a health professional, science writer, engineer, scientific researcher, oceanographer, or environmentalist—among many possibilities.

If math is your thing, you might think about being an accountant, a financial analyst, an air traffic controller, a computer systems analyst, a statistician, a mathematician, or even an airline pilot!

A penchant for art or English could mean that you're suited for a career in the arts (including publishing and advertising) or for some less obvious careers like speech pathology, technical writing, or archeology.

If you love foreign languages, teaching, interpreting, and translating aren't the only possibilities. You might also find a niche in international business or law, community service, college counseling for foreign students, or the travel industry; or as a scientific researcher or a volunteer for the Peace Corps or VISTA. If you *are* interested in interpreting and translating, there will be a particular demand in the coming years for people trained in Chinese language and culture—not only for government positions, but for jobs in private industry as well.

If you hate everything about school, try to think of the subjects you dislike *least*—or about careers that have little academic tie-in!

5. *Which careers have always interested me?*

Even if some seem far-fetched now, they can give you valuable clues about your interests. Look for careers that are related to ones that interest you but may not be practical. If, for example, you've dreamed of becoming a fashion model, but are only 5'3", fashion modeling may not be a possibility, but acting in television commercials or fashion industry jobs (from fashion writing to designing, photography, styling, and merchandising) might be very satisfying alternatives.

6. *If I could see into the future, what kind of lifestyle would I like to have by the age of 25 or 30?*

Trying to envision your life ten years hence may give you some ideas about your priorities. Do you see yourself as a superachiever? Do you hope that you'll have a loving, secure home life with children and a happy marriage? Do you imagine yourself traveling a lot and/or being happily single? Or do you envision yourself still preparing for a career—like medicine—that requires years of training?

If some of your dreams collide—if, for example, you want to travel extensively, establish a satisfying career in business, AND have a family by the age of 25, this may take some rearranging or juggling of goals, especially if you're a woman. It *is* possible to have it all these days, but it may take more time than you think and will require a lot of hard work and good planning.

PREPARING FOR COLLEGE

I'm not sure if I'm going to college or what since I'm just now starting high school, but if I do, how can I prepare for it? Should I take things like typing and stuff just in case I don't go to college?

Brandi K.

If you are in your early to mid-teens and, like many people, are not quite sure of your future educational or career goals, it's important to keep your options open.

This means taking an academically-oriented high school program, including as much math and science as possible. Without extensive high school math training, a number of college majors and even future careers may be closed to you. Sociologist Lucy Sells studied entering freshmen at the University of California at Berkeley several years ago and discovered that while over half the men had taken four years of high school math, only *8 percent* of the women had. Lacking this mathematical preparation, 92 percent of the women were unable to take courses like chemistry, statistics, or economics. In turn, being unable to take such classes meant that the women were unable to pursue *half* of all majors offered by the university. Predictably, only the traditionally "feminine" areas like education, fine arts, and the humanities (where career prospects are least promising) were available to these freshman women. So, whatever your ultimate decision about college or your college major, a strong academic preparation never hurts.

Business courses like typing and shorthand can be very useful even if you *are* college-bound, and especially if you plan to work part-time or in the summer during high school and/or college. These skills can also be useful for taking fast lecture notes and for preparing class assignments.

You can prepare yourself for college early on.

In the ninth grade, you might—with the help of your adviser—plan a strong high school program and think about your special areas of interest and ability.

In the tenth grade, you might send for college catalogs and start thinking about what kind of college you might want to attend. For example, you might ask yourself whether you want to go away to school or commute from home; whether you would prefer a small or large college; what might be a reasonable choice in terms of your grades and demonstrated abilities so far; and what is financially feasible for your family (more on this a little later!). The summer between your sophomore and junior years is a good time to visit colleges that interest you if this is at all possible.

(If you're not able to visit the colleges that most interest you, ask your guidance counselor about going to a National College Fair. If you have an immediate need for specific information about places and dates of the nearest Fair, write to: National Association of College Admission Counselors, 9933 Lawler Ave., Skokie, IL 60078.)

If you're interested in taking courses for college credit, the end of your sophomore year is a good time to check with your school counselor about this possibility.

Eleventh grade can be crucial, since the grades you make this year can count heavily when college admissions officials review your transcripts. Now is the time to give more serious thought to your specific college plans, to take PSAT tests, and/or prepare for the SATs.

Your senior year is a busy one if you're college-bound, with SATs, college applications, and interviews.

What counts in getting into college? Much depends on the college and how competitive it is, of course, but your high school grades, your class standing, your extracurricular activities (which are an indication of your interests and diversity as a person), your SAT or ACT scores, your application, your recommendations, and the way you come across during the admissions interview can all be factors. If you're careful to match your abilities and interests to a particular college, you have a good chance of being accepted. At many colleges these days, the competition for admission is much less than it was a decade or two ago. However, with the very selective, high-prestige schools, it's as difficult as ever to get in, since many people apply to them, hoping that a degree from a prestigious school will provide a much-needed edge in the job market later on. At Yale, for example, only about 12 percent of those applying for admission are accepted. On the whole, though, the college admissions picture looks bright, with a number of colleges actually competing for students.

FINANCING YOUR EDUCATION

I really want to go to college, preferably a college away from home where I could be more independent. The problem is that my family isn't rich enough to pay for my college education. My parents set some money aside, but with inflation and everything, it isn't nearly enough. But my parents aren't poor either and I hear that if your family falls in the middle moneywise, it's hard to get financial aid. It's not fair! What can I do?

Still Hoping

With college costs soaring, many families—even those with higher than average incomes—are really feeling the pinch.

Fortunately, more financial aid funds are now available to students from middle-income families ($25,000 a year and over) as a result of the Middle-Income Student Assistance Act of 1979, which authorized an extra $1.2 billion for expanded student aid. The new law has almost doubled the number of students who are eligible for basic grants.

There are many different kinds of financial aid, and many of them are offered together—as a package—when you are accepted by the college of your choice if you have also applied for financial assistance.

Scholarships and Grants   These are outright gifts of money that don't have to be paid back. Scholarships—

often given on the basis of academic or athletic ability as well as financial need—can come from a wide variety of organizations, community agencies, corporations, state governments, and special competitions, as well as from your chosen college.

Don't write off the more expensive private colleges in making college plans on a moderate budget. Sometimes these schools have more financial aid—more complete financial aid packages—available than less expensive state schools. As many as 80 percent of students at some expensive private colleges are receiving financial aid.

Grants, which are usually based on financial need, come from special foundations or from the federal government. They include, for example, Basic Educational Opportunity Grants, which range from $950 to $1800 or half the cost of attending school in any given year; and Supplemental Educational Opportunity Grants, which are earmarked for students with acute financial needs and range from $200 to $1500 a year. For more information about grants, call the U.S. Office of Education toll-free at 800-492-6602 or see your school adviser.

Loans Special student loans—offered at low interest rates varying from 3 to 7 percent—often mean the difference between staying in school and dropping out. They must be paid back after graduation, but the first payment is deferred (in the case of the National Direct Student Loan Program) until nine months after graduation, and you may have up to 10 years to repay the entire loan.

You can get loan information from your college financial aid office, for the National Direct Student Loan, or from your local lending institutions—banks and savings and loans—for the Guaranteed Student Loan Program. For information on sources of loan funds, write to: The U.S. Office of Education, P.O. Box 84, Washington, DC 20044, and ask for their free booklet "Student Consumer's Guide," which includes phone numbers of state student loan agencies.

Work-Study Options These include:

• Federally funded work-study programs. These involve part-time campus jobs—usually clerical or in food service—as part of your financial aid package.

• Cooperative education programs. Here you have a chance to work part-time or even full-time part of the school year or all summer, often in a job relating to your major. This option is quite popular with students in engineering and other technical fields. For information about co-op programs, write to: National Commission for Co-Operative Education, 360 Huntington Avenue, Boston, MA 02115, for the free brochure "Un-

dergraduate Programs of Co-Operative Education in the U.S. and Canada."

• Reserve Officer Training Corps (ROTC). In exchange for five hours or so a week spent in military drills and courses plus four years of active military service after graduation, the Navy, Air Force, or Army will often pay your school expenses *and* give you a monthly allowance as well! You can get details from your local recruiting office.

• On your own. Part-time jobs of all kinds are usually available on or near campus. You might work in a bookstore or in a fast-food outlet. One classmate of mine worked part-time all through college as a supermarket checker (at good union wages) and another started his own travel agency, arranging student group flights to various destinations during Christmas, spring, and summer vacations. The possibilities are many if you keep an open mind.

You can also cut college costs in a number of ways.

You might take Advanced Placement or CLEP exams and get credit for courses and/or independent study taken while you're still in high school—thereby getting off to a head start in college. If you earn three or four Advanced Placement credits, for example, you can enter college as a sophomore, eliminating a full *year* of college expenses! One recent Indiana State University graduate estimates that by documenting her independent study with CLEP exams, she saved nearly $3,000 in college expenses. If you have a lot of stamina and are strong academically, you might take extra courses or attend school year-round in order to finish in three years.

Some other options include: taking advantage of the delayed admission policies many colleges now offer (you are accepted and your place is held for one to two years while you work to save money for school), attending a local community college for two years, working full-time and attending college in the evenings or weekends, or taking advantage of external degree programs offered by a number of colleges. (These require little or no classroom work, with your progress measured via documented independent study and special examinations.)

So, whatever your financial situation, there are many choices you can make in planning your college education.

It might be helpful to you and your parents to pinpoint your exact financial needs before you begin applying for college, even if you're still only a sophomore or junior. You could take advantage of the Early Financial Planning Service offered by the College Scholarship Service. You send for—then fill out—a financial aid form, returning it with a $3.50 fee. You will then receive a computer print-out of your estimated eligibility for financial aid and an explanatory booklet. You can get this valuable information by writing to: Financial Aid Planning, P.O. Box 1175, Radio City Station, New York, NY 10019.

Another helpful (and free) booklet—"Meeting College Costs"—can aid you in figuring out what you and your family might reasonably expect to pay. It gives information about specific kinds of financial aid and how to apply, and also includes worksheets for you and your parents to estimate costs. You can get this booklet from your school guidance counselor or by sending a large, self-addressed, stamped envelope to: College Board Publication Orders, Box 2815, Princeton, NJ 08540.

EDUCATIONAL ALTERNATIVES: JUNIOR COLLEGES/VOCATIONAL SCHOOLS

I don't think I want to go to college, but I do want to go to school and maybe train for a well-paying career after I graduate next June. Should I go to a community college or a vocational school? What are the pros and cons of each? Thanks for any help you can give me.
Joe N.

If you aren't sure whether college is the right choice for you, or if you're sure that it isn't, a year or two at a community, junior, or vocational college may be a viable alternative.

What's the difference between these options?

Community colleges are public, two-year schools offering low-cost and varied educational options for students with a myriad of needs and goals—from those planning to continue on to a four-year college to those looking for training in practical skills such as cosmetology, data processing, secretarial science, auto mechanics, and the like. Students applying to community colleges must meet only a few requirements. Generally, to attend, you must have a high school diploma and/or be over 18. SAT or ACT exams aren't usually required.

Junior colleges—also two-year institutions—may be state-sponsored or private, low-cost or expensive. Most are very similar—in terms of educational offerings—to community colleges. Some, however, have a more stringent academic orientation and require applicants to take SAT exams.

Vocational schools are oriented to career preparation rather than academics, may be public or private, and range from low-cost to expensive. They may feature a wide selection of different career training programs or intensive training in only one area.

What are some advantages and disadvantages of these short-term educational options?

If you choose to go to a community/junior college, you may cut college costs considerably and keep your options to go on to a four-year college open and, at the same time, learn marketable skills. You can also learn skills specifically in demand in your community, since these needs are taken into account when community college officials plan the career training curriculum. You also have a better chance of being taught by professors instead of young assistants. (In four-year colleges, first- and second-year students often have little contact with professors and are often taught by graduate assistants.)

On the other hand, not all academic credits you earn at a community college or junior college may be transferrable to a four-year school; the competition or level of competence may not be equal to that of four-year schools (which can be frustrating if you're a bright student); and you may not get the job training you want most if these skills are not in demand in your particular community. If you're willing to relocate, attending a community college in another area and going to a private vocational school to learn the skill of your choice are two possible alternatives.

If you're thinking of going to a vocational school, it may be helpful to keep in mind that this can be a way of getting specific, marketable skills, a quick entrance to the job market, intensive, up-to-the-minute training, and a good return on your educational dollar. Many experts point out that vocational school graduates often get better-paying jobs right out of school than many college graduates do.

On the other hand, very specific training and a narrow educational focus can limit your options. If, for example, you enroll in a school that offers training in only one career area—and you find that you dislike the career—you face the choice of dropping out entirely or continuing with something you hate. If you've completed your training and *then* decide the career is not for you, you may have to start all over again, depending on your skills, in order to change careers. It's also possible to get ripped off. Some vocational schools, unfortunately, take your money, make many promises, then train you for jobs that don't exist or poorly for jobs that *do* exist. In order to avoid such rip-offs, ask professionals in the field you hope to enter for their training recommendations. Also, go to your library and consult the Occupational Outlook Handbook, which is published by the U.S. Department of Labor and which will give you an idea of jobs offering a promising future. Listen carefully to any sales pitches and read school catalogs carefully. Beware if you are guaranteed a fantastic job. No reputable school will make such promises, though many *do* offer active placement services. Be wary, too, if there are no screening devices (such as aptitude tests) or entrance requirements. Without these, you may get into a training course for a job you can't or won't enjoy doing, *or* even if you do well, you may find many of your classmates dropping out and this can affect you adversely.

If a school won't give you names of recent graduates as references, will not divulge its dropout rate or its policy on tuition refunds, and is not accredited, or if officials try to pressure you into signing up for classes on the spot via high-pressure tactics, explore *other* schools!

Finding the right school can take time. For help, you might read "How to Choose a Career—and a Career School," which is available free by writing to: National Association of Trade Technical Schools, 2021 K Street N.W., Washington, DC 20006. You might also go to your library to look for *The Blue Book of Education,* which lists over 12,000 occupational schools—including junior colleges—plus their courses of study, length of programs, and fees. Taking your time and making a wise choice about your post–high school education can make an important difference in your future!

CAREERS WITH BRIGHT FUTURES

I have lots of interests and can do a fair number of things OK. I make "B"s (mostly) in school. What I want is a career that won't fizzle out in a few years. Do you have any ideas about what jobs will be in demand in the coming years? I guess it's unusual for someone my age to be so security-minded, but I can't help it. Maybe it's because my dad lost his job to automation and I don't want to go through what he did!

Scott R.

According to recent projections by the U.S. Bureau of Labor Statistics, having an in-demand skill and a willingness to relocate are the crucial elements of career success and security in the years to come.

The most job opportunities in the coming years are expected to be in the Sunbelt (the South, Southeast, and Southwest) and the West (including Alaska). Opportunities in areas like New York and New Jersey, on the other hand, will have only a tiny increase—if any.

What careers will be in demand in years to come?

Careers in computer science, the health sciences (from doctor to health service administrator, nurse, or technician), engineering, mathematics-related positions (including mathematician, statistician, finance executive, auditor, and accountant), sales work, and legal and medical secretarial positions are expected to be readily available to qualified workers, with many growth opportunities available.

Among the careers experiencing significant declines in growth opportunities are such overcrowded fields as high school and college teaching and journalism, as well as trades like typesetting, shoe repair, soldering, bus driving, farming, and newspaper vending. Some career opportunities will have definite geographic links. For example, young lawyers may have to relocate away from overcrowded areas like New York and California and get their professional start in places like Texas and Idaho instead. New architects will have the best job-growth opportunities if they head south.

If you have your heart set on a career like law or journalism or secondary school teaching, the gloomy statistics need not dissuade you. If you are extremely competent, talented, and skilled, willing to work hard and flexible about relocating, you may make it anyway. If you are less determined to follow a particular career or unsure about what you would really like to do, it might make sense to give the high-growth jobs careful consideration.

For more information on setting and pursuing career goals, you might read one or all of the following:

- *What Color Is Your Parachute? A Practical Manual for Job-Hunters and Career-Changers* by Richard Nelson Bolles, Ten Speed Press. (This best-seller is available in most bookstores and costs $5.95.)
- *Exploring Careers* by the U.S. Department of Labor's Bureau of Statistics. This may *sound* dry, but it isn't. It's written especially for young people and gives in-depth information about many different careers, their requirements, and their future. You can order this book by sending a check or money order for $10 to your regional Bureau of Labor Statistics office or to: Bureau of Labor Statistics, Suite 3400, 1515 Broadway, New York, NY 10036.
- *I Can Be Anything* by Joyce Slayton Mitchell. Written just for teens, this excellent book may be purchased at your local bookstore or for $7.95 in paperback from College Board Publication Orders, Box 2815, Princeton NJ 08540.
- *What To Do With the Rest of Your Life: The Catalyst Career Guide for Women in the 80's* by the editors of Catalyst. Foreword by Bess Myerson, published by Simon & Schuster. This new book should be available in your local bookstore and can be a valuable resource, taking a comprehensive view of fields offering the best advancement opportunities in the eighties and beyond.

WHEN TO MOVE OUT AND ON

I need some advice: My dad is being transferred to North Carolina and I'm sick about it. We've lived in Minnesota for almost eight years. I'm 17 and will be a senior in the fall. I want to stay here to finish my senior year. I don't have anyone to stay with really and am pretty sure I could handle being on my own, but my parents say that's probably illegal and I couldn't rent an apartment or even get a phone on my own. They're not totally against my staying. They just don't think it's possible. Isn't there some way I could find to stay? This is really important to me!

Kelly O.

I'm 16 and I can't wait to leave home. My parents are always on my back about the way my room looks, getting in late, and stuff like that. I want to drop out of high school and get a job. I already have a job at McDonald's and I could work there full-time if nothing else comes up, plus my friend Jenny might do the same thing and we could share an apartment. The only problem is that Jenny isn't sure about this whole thing. How can I convince her it's the right thing to do?

Brooke D.

In a few states (check with a local hotline crisis center to see if your state is one of these), you can legally win the freedom to be on your own—if you're between the ages of 14 and 17—by initiating a court procedure known as "emancipation of minors." Requirements for the procedure vary from state to state.

For example, a California state law providing for such emancipation went into effect in January 1979 and requires that teens seeking such legal adulthood must live apart from their parents and have their consent. They must also manage their own financial affairs. This doesn't mean that parents can't contribute to their son's or daughter's support. It *does* mean, however, that parents are no longer financially responsible for the teenager, that any financial help they offer would be strictly voluntary. With emancipation, you lose your protected legal status as a minor (which means, for example, that you could be tried in court as an adult) and gain certain adult privileges and responsibilities such as the right to sign leases, enroll in school without a parental signature, apply for credit, and arrange for phone and electric services.

Sudden emancipation can be a mixed blessing.

You are, theoretically, free to party all night, have friends over all the time, and live your own lifestyle. However, once you are responsible for paying for your own food, rent, and utilities—among many other necessities—realistic limitations become apparent. You can't party all night every night and hold a job. With no steady job, you can't get credit. And your standard of living—from the food you eat and the clothes you wear to where you live—may drop drastically once you're paying all the bills.

One 16-year-old California girl who filed for emancipation quickly found that she wasn't able to afford the new clothes, movies, and other recreational activities that she and her friends had always taken for granted. "It's all I can do to get by and I couldn't even do that without *some* help from my parents," she said recently. "It isn't quite what I thought it would be. I always thought I made plenty of money from my waitressing to pay my way. Wrong! It costs a lot to live on your own. It's nice not to be hassling with my parents all the time, but it's tough trying to make it on my own."

Whether you plan to strike out on your own at 14, 16, 22, or even later, it's important to ask yourself some questions—and try to answer them as realistically as you can.

1. *Can I be truly independent—responsible for myself financially, legally, and socially?*

If you move away from home, but continue to depend on your parents for financial support, it could place an incredible burden on them and curtail your true decision-making powers as well. In case you're not ready to assume full responsibility for yourself, it might—in some instances—be better to wait a while longer and build your resources (financial and otherwise) before moving out. "The ideal candidate for early emancipation is a *responsible* kid who is capable of stability, maturity, and who can *hold* a job," says Laurel Moore, an emancipation counselor with Interface, a Ventura County, California, counseling organization.

2. *Will moving out now limit my education or other life options?*

Early independence can be a good choice for some, but for other young people, it can tragically limit options. If you would have to drop out of high school, college, or vocational school to support yourself or if you might end up locked into an unsatisfying, low-paying dead-end job as a result of your premature move away from home, you might think about trying to tough it out at home until you have your education, some marketable skills, and a better chance for true—and enjoyable—independence!

3. *Do I have a realistic idea of what it takes to live independently? What it costs? How to cope with emergencies?*

You need a fair amount of money; the ability to budget, pay bills on time, and meet other obligations (like getting to work on time and doing a good job); and the means to cope with all kinds of situations—including the loneliness, anxiety, and fear you may feel when you realize that you're really on your own.

Before you move out, it might help to sit down with your parents or an older sibling or friend who has been through all this and make a plan. Draw up a sample budget, based on your present earnings and the current cost of living in your area, and see if you can *afford* to move out right now. It's unlikely that you can have it all—a nice apartment, a reasonably reliable car, clothes, fun money, and a savings account for emergencies—right away. So you may have to make some trade-off decisions.

Karen, for example, who needed a car to commute to work, decided that she couldn't afford a place of her own (even with a roommate) for at least a year. In the meantime, she paid off her car and put some money aside for moving expenses. (The initial cost of moving, which includes paying the first and last months' rent, a security deposit, and fees for phone and other utility installations, can really add up!)

It's important, too, to take a realistic look at the people in your life. Is your roommate-to-be a reliable person who will meet his or her responsibilities? What will you do if your roommate moves out or loses his or her job unexpectedly? What if *you* lose your job? Can you count on your parents or other family members for help in an emergency? While it's easy to cling to the illusion that disaster will never strike you, it's best to be prepared with a realistic plan for action in case the worst happens.

4. *How do I feel about leaving home? How does my family feel?*

Do your parents agree that now is the time? Or are they very much opposed to your move? Parental opposition does not automatically mean that you're making an unwise decision. Some parents find it very difficult to let go of their children. One father we know reacted with hurt, anger, shock, and amazement when his *25-year-old* daughter finally left home! Particularly if you're the youngest in your family, your parents may be reluctant to see you leave the nest. Listen to your parents' arguments for or against your move—and decide if any of these arguments might make sense considering your unique situation.

Some young people are reluctant to leave home these days—even after college graduation and beyond. A major reason for this is money. It's true that inflation coupled with rental shortages in many areas can make it more difficult to get started on your own. Independence,

in some cases, may have to be deferred for a while until you can build up your financial resources.

On the other hand, some young people get very comfortable relying on Mom and Dad, getting free cleaning, laundry, meal service, and lodging, as well as constant companionship. Some choose to remain home until they marry. This can be a fine choice for some, but it's important to keep in mind that leaving home to live independently—even if it means struggling with a limited budget, loneliness, stacks of laundry, dirty dishes, and moments of uncertainty about your ability to cope—is a vital learning and growing experience.

It is in such moments, in the daily struggle and challenge and job of creating your own adult life, that you begin to make new and exciting discoveries about who you are and what you're capable of accomplishing. It's always reassuring to know that, whatever your eventual lifestyle, whether you marry or remain single, you *can* make it on your own!

CREATING YOUR OWN LIFE GOAL PLAN

How can I keep from getting depressed when I have lots of dreams for the future, but am still just 14? (Well, I'll be 14 in three months!) What can I do now?
                                                    Mary S.

Making a Life Goal Plan might be the answer to some of the frustration you may be feeling as you see all the living, learning, and working that lie between you and a distant goal. In making a Plan, ask yourself the following questions:

1. *What are my goals?*

What do you want in terms of your education? Your career? Your lifestyle? What seems right for *you*? List both short-term goals (like getting through Spanish this semester without either failing the course or losing your mind) and long-term ones (like marriage and family, a career in the field of your choice, and achieving a sense of peace with your world, your family, and yourself).

2. *What obstacles might I face? How can I overcome them?*

Many people have a lot of reasons for not realizing their dreams and their goals. You may be busy already making excuses for what you envision as future failures:

"I'm too shy to leave home."

"I'm scared to try for what I really want because it will be too terrible if I fail."

"I want a career, but I want a family most."

"I don't have any money for college."

"I want to get married, but I'm too ugly and no one likes me anyway."

"I'm just not lucky like most people!"

There are almost no obstacles that can't be overcome. It may be *difficult* to overcome shyness, risk failure, or mix a demanding career with family responsibilities, but if you're willing to work hard and actively pursue your goals, you can usually overcome these conflicts and obstacles. For example, as we've just seen, there are a number of ways that you can find money for college. There are many ways that you can start right now to love and appreciate yourself more—which is the first step toward being loved by others.

3. *What's a reasonable timetable—for ME?*

What goals can you reasonably expect to achieve in one year? In five years? Ten years? What can you do *today* to make life more fun and interesting—and to build toward your future?

What you do now can be very important to your future. While your specific goals may change a great deal in the years to come and while your timetable may fluctuate considerably, you can start *today* to become the person you want to be. There is no age limit and no time limit for personal growth. Your journey toward a responsible, fulfilling, giving, challenging, and joyous future can begin today!